Praise for
THE PRESSURE'S OFF

"If, like me, you see blessing-centeredness rather than God-centeredness as a great weakness of American evangelicalism, you will hail this exploration of the freedom and joy of grace as timely therapy, a word in season that we all needed. May it be widely read and thoroughly digested."

—J. I. PACKER, theologian and author of *Knowing God*

"The evangelical church, choking under a pervasive legalism/moralism that suffocates the human spirit, finds a powerful voice for freedom in Larry Crabb. Writing from the inside out, he presents a vibrant way of living with passion and without pressure."

—BRENNAN MANNING, author of *Ruthless Trust*

"C. S. Lewis wrote about prosperity knitting us to this world, and while we are seeking our place in the world, the world is actually finding its place in us. Dr. Larry Crabb has constructed a compelling narrative that shows how we have imprisoned ourselves by using the world's ways to 'get something from God,' instead of appropriating God's way to receive something from Him."

—CAL THOMAS, syndicated columnist and author

"Dr. Crabb not only gives us a clear mandate to celebrate Christian freedom, he also is our accompanist and exemplar on the Way of Freedom. You know he has walked that way with you. A remarkably personal message."

—JAMES M. HOUSTON, Chancellor Emeritus and professor
of Spiritual Theology, Regent College, Vancouver, B.C.

"This book makes a very important statement about how to live the Christian life. It takes the Christian beyond the obstacles and disappointments and, above all, beyond the age-old enemy of self straight into the arms of grace. Once there, the pressure is off. A real worthwhile read."

—FRANK RETIEF, Presiding Bishop, Church of England in South Africa

"At last we have a book that confronts contemporary Christian culture with its increasing tendency to be taken up with blessings more than the Blesser. I doubt whether anything Larry has ever written, or may write in the future, will contribute more powerfully to the needs of modern-day Christians than *The Pressure's Off*."

—SELWYN HUGHES, director of the Center for World Revival and author of *Every Day with Jesus* devotional

The
Pressure's
Off

Breaking Free from Rules and Performance

LARRY
CRABB

Eight-Week Workbook Included

WATERBROOK
PRESS

THE PRESSURE'S OFF
PUBLISHED BY WATERBROOK PRESS
12265 Oracle Boulevard, Suite 200
Colorado Springs, Colorado 80921

All Scripture quotations, unless otherwise indicated, are taken from the Holy Bible, New International Version®, NIV®. Copyright © 1973, 1978, 1984 by Biblica Inc.™ Used by permission of Zondervan. All rights reserved worldwide. www.zondervan.com. Scripture quotations marked (KJV) are taken from the King James Version. Scripture quotations marked (NASB) are taken from the New American Standard Bible®. © Copyright The Lockman Foundation 1960, 1962, 1963, 1968, 1971, 1972, 1973, 1975, 1977, 1995. Used by permission. (www.Lockman.org). Scripture quotations marked (NKJV) are taken from the New King James Version®. Copyright © 1982 by Thomas Nelson Inc. Used by permission. All rights reserved.

Italics in Scripture quotations indicate the author's added emphasis.

Trade Paperback ISBN 978-0-307-73053-4
eBook ISBN 978-0-307-82267-3

The Pressure's Off and *The Pressure's Off Workbook* copyright © 2002, 2012 by Lawrence J. Crabb Jr., Ph.D., P.C.

Cover design by Mark D. Ford; cover photography by Shelly Harrison/Index Stock

Published in association with Yates & Yates, LLP, Attorneys and Counselors, Orange, California.

Published in the United States by WaterBrook Multnomah, an imprint of the Crown Publishing Group, a division of Random House LLC, New York, a Penguin Random House Company.

WATERBROOK and its deer colophon are registered trademarks of Random House LLC.

The Library of Congress has cataloged the earlier edition of *The Pressure's Off* as follows:
Crabb, Lawrence J.
    The pressure's off : there's a new way to live / Larry Crabb — 1st ed.
    p. cm.
Includes bibliographical references (p. 227–231).
ISBN 1-57856-453-0
BV4501.3 .C725 2002
248.4
                                    2002007254

Printed in the United States of America
2015

10 9 8 7 6 5 4

SPECIAL SALES
Most WaterBrook Multnomah books are available at special quantity discounts when purchased in bulk by corporations, organizations, and special-interest groups. Custom imprinting or excerpting can also be done to fit special needs. For information, please e-mail SpecialMarkets@ WaterBrookMultnomah.com or call 1-800-603-7051.

To my father
Larry Crabb Sr.

August 16, 1912
Life began, the fruit of Charles and Laura's love
for their Lord and for each other.

August 31, 2001
Real life began, the fruit of the Father, Son,
and Spirit's love for each other and for my dad.

CONTENTS

More is available to us in Jesus Christ than we dare imagine.

In 1654 Blaise Pascal encountered Jesus Christ in a new way. He recorded the ecstasy of the moment in a series of sentence fragments, including these:

> "certitude, heartfelt joy, peace"
>
> "joy, joy, joy, tears of joy"
>
> "complete and sweet renunciation"
>
> "total surrender to Jesus Christ my director"

Fellow seeker, will you dare to imagine what for so long you've feared may not be available? Will you join me, a trembling pilgrim, in putting aside the cynicism that skillfully avoids the risk of hoping? Will you embrace your desire for the *one thing* you would give all else to gain—an actual encounter with Jesus Christ, now, before heaven?

- Perhaps, like me, you've been working hard to figure life out, to get it right so things go well. The Bible calls that approach the *old way* of the *written code*. No matter how dressed up in Christian language, the old way will not form you spiritually. It leads to inward emptiness, churning, unbearable pressure. Perhaps that's becoming clear to you as it is to me.

- There's another way to live. The Bible calls it the *new way* of the *Spirit*. Those who take this route through life find themselves flowing toward the Father in rhythm with the Spirit as He opens their eyes to see the beauty of Christ. This new way leads through a life that doesn't work very well into a mysterious certitude that anchors us in storms of doubt, into moments of ecstasy that keep bigger hopes alive when good dreams die, into the terrifying experience of death to self that allows our true selves to walk out of the tomb into the light of day.

- Can you feel the Spirit's rhythm inviting you to the Sacred Dance? Perhaps He's releasing our imaginations to soar, like children the night before Christmas.
- There's a *new way* to live. It's the way of the Spirit. Let's dare to dream our greatest dream. It will not shatter!

NIGHT QUESTION

"What am I doing wrong?" The question was never far from the woman's mind. Tonight it screamed from deep places within her, demanding the answer that never came.

"Look at my life. Things aren't turning out as I'd hoped. Why don't I feel better about myself? Why is life sometimes so difficult? I must be doing something terribly wrong."

The woman did not believe she was being punished for wrongdoing by a vengeful deity, though that thought was sometimes hard to resist. She did, however, believe there was a right way to live that would make her life work. Of course there was. But she could not find the way.

Here at home, at night, she couldn't pretend as easily as she did in her busy days that she was content, that God had blessed her enough for her to call Him good. In the aloneness that pressed against her soul, memories came back—of times when she'd felt alive and happy and good, and of times when she'd felt very bad.

Those memories often came to her, especially after evening descended, and they had shaped her vision of the better life she wanted, of the blessings she was willing to work for and therefore expected to come her way. The woman longed to feel again the joy she'd known earlier and to avoid the pain she could not forget. She knew what she wanted…but she couldn't find the way. Her life wasn't working.

"Thank You, God," the woman made herself pray as she crawled into bed. "I know You will take me to heaven when this life is over. Thank You for the gift of eternal life I could never work hard enough to earn. And I know You have a plan for me now, before I go home. I will continue to trust You to bring it about."

Before sleep came, she could hear herself add, "But what am I doing that's getting in the way? *What am I doing wrong?*"

In the bedroom's quiet darkness, the woman waited. Surely God would answer her question and show her what she must do to receive the blessings of a better life now, the blessings she was sure God intended His people to enjoy. "I'd do whatever it takes…if only I could know what it is." That was her last thought before sleep rescued her from the pressure to figure it out.

How much later it happened she never knew. The woman sat bolt upright in bed, wide awake, but in a different way than when her alarm clock sounded. This wide awake was wider. Had she looked now at that clock by her bed, she would have seen the digital display of four blinking zeros. She had entered a world beyond time.

The Voice had not awakened her, but she heard it clearly: "I've come to show you the New Way."

Who was there? Who had spoken? She could see no one. Had there been a body behind the Voice, she couldn't have seen it. The darkness was too thick.

"It's a dream," she said to herself. She would lie down again and let it pass.

The Voice spoke again in the same clear tone. "It's your time. I've come to show you the New Way. It's dark enough now for you to see."

This is no dream, the woman thought. "I'm glad you've come," she said aloud. "I desperately need to discover a new way. For a long time I've prayed to know how to make my life go better. Nothing I've tried so far has worked. I need to find the New Way you speak of."

"You're looking for another version of the Old Way. I've come to show you the New Way."

The woman was puzzled but not silenced. "I quite agree there are many ways that don't work. My life is proof enough of that. I've tried everything I can think of to change how I feel and to make my life go better. Please, if you have any mercy at all, show me what I'm doing wrong that's keeping me from what I so badly want. I'm eager to learn a new way. You'll find me a willing pupil."

"You're looking for a method to make life work. That's the Old Way." The Voice was filled with patience, like the voice of a grandfather teaching his grandchild as the two walk together. "Whatever method you choose becomes your master. You've served many masters in your lifetime, but your goal has remained constant. You want nothing more than the Better Life that your experience has taught you is desirable. That goal is your idol. It must be abandoned."

"I-I see your point," the woman replied, though she saw nothing. "Yes, I do believe you're right. Quite right, actually. Your point is revolutionary. I need to find a *spiritual* way. My goal must be God and my method obedience. And prayer. Yes, I must do what's right and trust God with the outcome. You're saying exactly what I've just heard from a wise, elderly woman in my church. She was most interesting."

"She spoke truth to you. But you didn't hear. That's why I've come."

"Well, I think I *did* hear what she had to say." The woman was more indignant than unnerved. "But thank you for coming to reinforce her message. Let's see. Yes, I remember. She told me I was working hard to understand and live by the Principle of Sequence. You know, the idea that *B* follows *A* so that if I want *B*, I must discover the *A* that will bring it about. She was, of course, quite right. I want to know what I must do that will change my life for the better and keep me out of more trouble in the future. She said, too, that I must give up trying so hard and learn instead to pray.

Again she was quite right. Of course I must still obey, but since my talk with her, I've been praying far more."

"Why do you pray?" A chill suddenly swept into the room. The woman braced herself against it.

"Why do I pray? What a strange question. I'm certain you know the teachings: Ask and you shall receive; cling to God and don't let go till He blesses you; pester Him, if you must, to get a response; settle for no less than every blessing He has reserved for you."

"That's the Old Way."

The woman frowned. Did the Voice not know the Teachings of the Sacred Book? Then a frightening thought crossed her mind. Perhaps the person behind the Voice knew the Teachings but didn't believe them. Was she speaking with a demon? A false prophet? Was a serpent in the room with her?

"How can that be?" she retorted with strengthened indignation. "My life is difficult. It's right to pray. Why, I run to God with everything. Surely you aren't telling me that prayer is the Old Way."

"Prayer is not the Old Way. *Your* prayer is."

The woman began to cry. "Why do you mock me? I'm desperate. I thought you were going to show me a new way to live. All you've done so far is to make me lose what little hope I had left."

"Your desires are too weak. Small affections create idols, unworthy gods to whom you sacrifice your life. Your prayers are idol worship. You've been bound to your desire for the Better Life, which you define by your experience of pleasure and pain. I've come to show you the New Way that leads to the Better Hope."

The woman's tears intensified into sobs. The sobs turned into wailing. "I only want to do what's right so I can enjoy God's blessings. Is that so wrong? Why won't you tell me what I must do?" If this Voice was from God, she was sure her wailing would cause Him to take pity on her and tell her what to do.

The Voice said, "You want to know what's *effective*. You aren't asking to know what is *holy*."

The woman's wailing quieted. "Are they two different things?"

"Your search for an effective way to the Better Life will lead you to follow the basic principles of this world and not the paths of holiness. Following those principles can sometimes make your life more pleasant, but it can never fill your soul. It will never bring you into the Better Hope.

"Moreover, your determination to do what's effective is futile because you are sovereign over nothing. You control nothing. The Principle of Sequence guarantees nothing."

"Are you saying *nothing* I do affects what happens in my life? That I have no influence at all?"

"*Influence* is real. It brings the joy of responsibility and impact. *Control* over what matters most is an illusion. Be grateful you have none."

The woman began to feel different, like a grandchild who just realized her grandfather was wise. To this point her dialogue with the Voice had been a debate. Now she began listening to learn.

The Voice continued. "The illusion of control brings requirement, requirement creates pressure, and pressure leads to slavery, the slavery of having to figure out life to make it work. Those who hold on to the illusion of control lose the enjoyment of freedom."

"I'm not sure I understand. Don't good parents raise good children? Don't faithful tithers enjoy the promise of financial security? Aren't the prayers of God's children always answered by their loving Father?"

"As the Master wills. He is sovereign over all. Be careful never to claim promises He hasn't made. Those who make that mistake think that by doing right they obligate the Master to bless them according to their understanding of the Better Life."

Now the Voice became infinitely gentle. "My child, you're in bondage to the Law of Linearity, what the wise, elderly woman called the Principle of Sequence. It obligates you to do what's right to win the blessings you desire. That law is no longer the guiding rule for God's children. It has served its purpose. The conclusion is clear. By right doing, no one can gain the Perfect Life later nor the Better Life now. By the Master's grace, that law has been replaced by the Law of Liberty. Under the Law of Liberty, you're free to live in the mystery of trust.

"But you haven't accepted the authority of this new law because it requires you to give up the illusion of control. You've cheapened the requirements of holiness by assuming you can do enough right things to bring about the Better Life. Sometimes that works. Sometimes it doesn't. You therefore live with uncertainty and pressure, and you demand to know the way to live that will make your life work as you want. You maneuver; you do not trust. You negotiate; you do not worship. You analyze and interpret to gain control over what happens; you do not depend. You seek the Better Life of God's blessings over the Better Hope of God's presence."

The woman felt as if waters were about to rise above her head. "But I *do* want my life to work. I've been so miserable. I have to know what I'm doing wrong! Won't you please tell me what to do?"

"Seek only the blessing of His presence, and you'll know what to do. It will fill your soul with joy."

"But...only God's blessings bring me true joy. I need to know how to get them!"

"It's not so. You need only God."

"But I thought I needed God because only He could make my life better."

"When the Master walked this earth, He withdrew from people who wanted to use His power to arrange for the Better Life. He will not be used in the service of weak affections. There's a Better Hope than what you believe is the Better Life. The New Way will take you there."

Those were the last words spoken by the Voice. As soon as they were said, the woman lost consciousness. She reentered time.

The clock's digital display showed 6:30. Morning had come. The woman rubbed her eyes. The question she'd gone to sleep with was still present as she faced the new day, but it no longer seemed urgent. She still didn't know what to do to make her life better, but it didn't seem to matter as much. She was aware of a desire for something, something more than the blessings of the Better Life. *But nothing I can do,* she told herself, *will bring it about.*

A pressure that had long been sitting heavily on her soul was lifting. She felt lighter, more at rest. *Is this what I've been after all along?*

She turned her head toward the window to see the morning sun. As she did, she heard a familiar voice whispering, "You're about to discover the New Way to live." Strange, she thought. It was the voice of a wise, elderly woman.

Two Paths

Right now, at this very moment, you're walking one of two paths through life.

Either

> you've decided that what you most want out of life is within your reach, and you're doing whatever you believe it takes to get it

or

> you've realized that what you most want is beyond your reach, and you're trusting God for the satisfaction you seek. You want Him. Nothing less, not even His blessings, will do.

If you're walking the first path, your life is filled with pressure. Inside, where no one sees, your soul is weary. You see no way to step off the treadmill. Or life is going well, and you're satisfied. But you sense something's wrong, something's missing. The pressure is still there.

If you're walking the second path, you have hope. Your soul may be weary, your interior world may be filled with struggles no one sees, but you have hope. At times you rest. Something is alive in you; the desire of your heart is not smothered. You can taste freedom. And the taste brings joy.

The first path is the Old Way. It involves a quid-pro-quo arrangement with God or, if not with God, then with the order in the universe, with the rules that make life work. If you do what you should, then you get what you want, either from a moral God who rewards good behavior or from an orderly world that you effectively use. It leaves you in control of how things turn out in your life. The Old Way promises a better life filled with good things that make you happy.

But it never delivers, though it may seem to for a long time. The Old Way doesn't work for one reason: You never keep your end of the bargain, not completely. No one does.

The second path is the New Way. In this arrangement, God first plants a desire in your heart, a longing that actually values His presence over His blessings; then He invites you to live out that desire, to abandon yourself to what you most want. It takes you out of control, but it sets you free. The New Way promises a *better hope* than the good things of life. It promises nearness to God, and it delivers, though not right away and often through suffering.

Most people live the Old Way all of their lives; most people who go to church live a religious version of the Old Way. It goes something like this:

If you want good kids, raise them according to Christian principles.

If you want a good marriage, understand a biblical model for marriage and live up to it as closely as you can.

If you want God to bless your ministry, follow godly principles of leadership.

If you want to be emotionally healthy, practice spiritual disciplines and trust Jesus for your needs.

If you want close friends, learn to accept yourself and to be vulnerable, authentic, and forgiving.

People who live the Old Way believe the *Law of Linearity,* a law that states there is an *A* that leads to the *B* you want. Figure out what *A* is, do it, and you'll have the life you most desire. The pressure's on.

People who live the New Way believe the *Law of Liberty.* They come as they are. They do not bathe before they approach God. They come to God for the bath. They feel no pressure to change either their inner life or their outer life, but they *desire* change in both spheres. And they are eager to do whatever will create the opportunity for change, even if it means dipping themselves seven times in a muddy river or marching around an enemy's wall for seven days and blowing trumpets. They live for the truest desire of their hearts: to know God and to enjoy Him. They do not live for a better life in this world. And when their life here is hard, when things fall apart, they most clearly reveal who they are. They're citizens of another world who most want what this world can never provide. So they wisely indulge their deepest desire and trust God to reveal Himself to them. That's the Law of Liberty.

Most of us are living the Old Way. Some of us can feel the emptiness it never fills. We're working hard to make life work so we can feel good. The pressure's on.

There's a new way to live that takes the pressure off. Join me as together we search for it.

PART I

THERE'S A
NEW WAY TO LIVE

I Think We're Missing It

CHAPTER ONE

RULES TO LIVE BY

As I write, a new self-help book is high on the charts. The title is *The Rules for Marriage,* and its two authors are making the talk show rounds.

I've not read the book. I just caught a few minutes of the authors' latest interview. One rule, I think it was number twelve, reads like this: "Don't compare your mate to someone else's."

Good advice. Mention to your husband, no matter how sweetly, that Sally's husband cooks dinner several times a week, and you can expect a tough evening. That's true. That's how things work.

But tell him you appreciate how hard he works to support his family, even though it means he drags himself home late, slumps on the kitchen stool, and in five minutes wolfs down a dinner it took you three hours to create, and there will be less conflict. You might actually feel good about yourself for encouraging your weary husband rather than complaining, and—who knows?—he might aim a smile your way and help clear the table. At least for that evening and perhaps longer. If you consistently follow the rules for marriage, you'll likely enjoy a better life.

(But you'll be farther from God.) Not because you were kind, but because your kindness was directed toward a goal that you valued more than intimacy with God. You wrongly defined life.

Your kindness was a power play. You decided what you wanted and you went after it. You neither depended on resources the Spirit provides nor placed top priority on glorifying God. He was not the center of your affections, neither the source nor goal of your movement.

HE WANTS SOMETHING MORE

Some would critique your kind affirmation of your husband differently. The problem, they would say, is cowardice, weakness, a fearful refusal to risk conflict for the sake of something even better than a tension-free evening. According to that thinking, a better rule to follow might be "Air your feelings honestly but not antagonistically. And do it to help your husband become a more sensitive person."

Those familiar with their Bibles might claim divine support for such advice: "Speak the truth in love," an inspired author once wrote. This rule, it could be argued, has a chance of generating a closer relationship, a real meeting of souls. Notice, however, that the formula remains the same: Decide what you want, then figure out how to get it.

My concern with *The Rules for Marriage* is not whether the rules are good or bad, whether they're effective in reaching a truly better life or effective only in reducing conflict. It isn't even whether the rules are Christian or unchristian. And my intention is not to suggest a better plan to secure a better life. I have no strategies in mind to give you a better marriage, better kids, a more complete recovery from sexual abuse, or quicker healing after your divorce. Nor, I believe, does God.

I want all these things for you. So does God. And I want a better life for myself. So does God. *But He wants something more for both of us.* And only when we pursue the more will He grant the less. Or He might not, until the next life.

I'm troubled by how unquestioningly we live out our determination to make this life work. All our hopes for happiness are bound up in it. It's as if we believe this is the only world we ever plan to inhabit.

And I'm troubled most by the often unstated and unrecognized

18

assumption that lies beneath our resolve to experience a better life. The assumption might be called the Law of Linearity. It goes like this:

Choose what you want out of life, figure out what you have to do to get it, then follow the rules. Select the *B* you desire, then perform the *A* that leads to it. There's an *A*—a strategy—that leads to every *B*—a goal.

That's the Law of Linearity. Let me offer a few examples.

- Do you want to be spiritual? Then practice spiritual disciplines, not to create space for a merciful and sovereign God to work in the depths of your hungry, humble soul, but rather to generate the level of spirituality you want. There's a line between the practice of spiritual disciplines and the experience of spirituality, an arrow pointing from the practice *(A)* to the experience *(B)*. You are in control. *B* follows *A*.

- Do you want this crisis with your daughter to resolve itself well? Consult with a seasoned counselor who specializes in adolescence, not to discern where the Spirit is moving through this trial in both of your lives, but rather to build a bridge between you and your daughter that will allow the two of you to soon meet in a healing and warm embrace. There's an *A* that will lead to the *B* you desire. Don't be concerned that reconciliation with your daughter has become a priority higher than drawing near to God. Go after the better life you want.

- Do you want to overcome your sexual addiction? Join a recovery group of men who are serious about moral purity, not to revel in God's grace and to discover how badly you long to know Him, but rather to find the help you need to keep you away from pornography. The point is getting your life together, not getting closer to God. And there's a way to do it. The Law of Linearity says so. Be practical. Figure out what it takes to solve your problem.

Let me put it more generally. We all want our lives to work well, to become better than they are or to remain as good as they are. When that desire becomes our goal, the objective we most value, then we like to believe the Law of Linearity is operative. We want to believe there's an *A* we can do that will lead to the *B* we want. Our lives then become a sustained effort to discover and follow whatever principles will provide a life that lets us feel pretty good.

And it sometimes works. Stay calm rather than ranting when your teenage daughter tells you she's pregnant, and you may preserve a good enough relationship to weather the crisis. Be honest with a group of men about your sexual struggles, and you may find yourself better able to resist temptation. Spend time in contemplative prayer and *lectio divina* (a special way of listening to the Spirit as you read the Bible), and you may feel closer to God.

But you might end up farther from God. And you *will* end up farther from God if you think of these principles as methods to produce the better life you want.

Isn't That the Way Things Work?

The Rules for Marriage is a new bestseller. The Bible, the best-selling book of all time, is thought by many to offer the Rules for Life. We think it teaches us how to depend on the Law of Linearity to get the life we want. It offers principles to follow to get what we want out of life. That's what we think. No wonder it's so popular. And no wonder it changes so few lives of those who read it.

When we live to make this life work, whether we follow natural wisdom or biblical principles, we become either proud or discouraged, self-congratulating or self-hating.

Christians are no exception. When a Christian parent consistently practices a godly approach to raising children in order to see them turn out well, and when it works, that parent becomes more proud than grateful. But the pride is disguised.

"Yes, my children have turned out as I'd hoped. But I'm not surprised. I spent quality time with them. I prayed for each by name every day. And God is a prayer-answering God. I know we must do our part. By His grace, I think I did, not perfectly, of course, but pretty well. I set clear boundaries. I was involved and fun-loving, but they always knew who was in charge. I was their parent, not their buddy.

"And kids want that. They feel more secure when they play in a fenced yard. God is so faithful. He's so good. I trained my kids according to His wisdom, and He saw to it that they became fine young people. That's how it works."

The worst sermon I ever heard was delivered by a middle-aged man who made me think of a strutting peacock when he spoke. For thirty-five minutes, he explained how he'd driven foolishness out of his children with the rod of correction and had planted wisdom in them through regular family devotions. The message was clear: I did what I was supposed to do. God blessed my efforts. I now enjoy the better life of having godly children.

When the law works, we become proud, though we disguise it as gratitude. And we profoundly discourage the parents who tried just as hard to "do it right" and now ache over a drug-abusing son and a rebellious, sexually active daughter.

When the law doesn't work, we assume we simply didn't follow it well enough. We believe someone failed, usually us. We become more defeated than trusting. It doesn't occur to us that the law might no longer be in effect.

Marie's husband left her ten years ago, after twenty-two years of marriage. She was devastated. She never thought it would happen. After hearing me lecture on the Law of Linearity, she wanted to speak with me. Here's what she said:

"I never realized it before, but my thinking is governed by that law. Ever since the divorce, I wake up every day wondering what I did wrong that resulted in my sleeping alone. I've been so puzzled. I've never been able to believe I was that bad a wife. I wasn't. I really think I was a darn good wife. Lots of women I know aren't half the wife I was—and they're still married, some of them happily. I've been so confused.

"I try to convince myself it was all him. And he really was a stinker. But now I can see that whether I blame him or me, I'm looking for an explanation. And that's linear thinking. What *A* wasn't followed that would have resulted in *B?* And that question creates such pressure. I've blown it once. Now I've got to get it right."

Then she added, "But isn't that the way things work? Are you saying there's no linearity, no cause and effect? If the Law of Linearity isn't the basis for how we live, what is? Is there another way to think?"

There is. As we'll see, the Rules for Life have been replaced by the Opportunity to Live.

The pressure's off!

CHAPTER TWO

OUR SET PATTERNS

At the time of this writing, I'm pushing toward the sixth decade of my life. My hair is white, two little kids call me Pop-Pop, twenty-five minutes on the treadmill is my equivalent to climbing Mount Everest, and I can look back on nearly half a century of living life as a Christian.

I decided to become a follower of Jesus as an eight-year-old when late one evening a counselor at camp instructed all his charges to stare into the roaring bonfire around which we were gathered. "Boys," he said, "you have a choice to make. Trust Jesus as your Savior or burn in the fires of hell forever."

Put that way, the choice seemed a no-brainer. I knew what I had to do to escape hell and go to heaven, so I did it. I wanted to. I knew the *A* that led to *B,* so I put that *A* into place.

The pattern was set. Whatever else I wanted that God could provide I assumed I could secure by making the right choice. My part was to figure out the required *A* and do it; His was to provide the *B* I wanted.

I had it wrong. I didn't *do* anything of merit to win heaven. I simply presented myself to God. I came, just as I was. And I can't *do* anything good to arrange for the life I want, certainly not to guarantee it.

I remember the pressure I felt as a young father. Get it right—warmly engage, spend time, be firm, model well, affirm often, discipline with holy love not out-of-control anger—and your boys will become men of character.

For a long time, although I wouldn't have expressed it this way, I viewed Christianity as the best system available for making life work. We *enter* the Christian life by "getting saved," by trusting Jesus to pay for our sins; we *live* the Christian life by "getting it right" so God will "bless us big." We're saved by coming as we are. That guarantees heaven later. We live by doing what we should. That guarantees blessings now. That's what I thought.

If we get it right, we'll enjoy deep peace. Our kids will love us, our souls will be refreshed and rested, our ministries will provide fulfillment, we'll feel really good about who we are and excited about living till we die.

I lead a linear life. I want this life to work, and I'm willing to do whatever it takes to make it happen. No wonder I feel so much pressure and struggle with so much disillusionment and doubt. When things work well, I publicly say, "Praise God," and privately whisper, "Of course. I did what I was told. I got it right." When things go poorly, I publicly declare, "God is working for my good. I will trust Him"; (privately I wonder, "What did I do wrong?")

ALL OVER THE PLACE

Without passing the blame, I believe I've absorbed the assumption of linearity from the Christian culture. I'm naturally drawn to linearity—it puts me in control—but the idea has been communicated to me in a thousand ways as the proper basis of Christian living. Most sermons I've heard and most Christian books I've read and most counsel I've been given have taught linearity, if not explicitly, then (and this has more power) implicitly.

The idea is all over the place. It's the way we think. Listen to just a few sentences I remember that made an impact. I have thousands from which to choose.

A noted Christian leader, a man I admire and respect, once said in my hearing to a group of other leaders:

"We must convince the world that Christianity is true by showing that it works. One way is through the family. We need Christian parents to demonstrate that raising kids according to God's plan produces the kind of kids every parent wants."

Another man, this one an elder in a church we attended when our boys were preschool age, was telling us about his adult son. Beaming with pleasure, he shared:

"He just received a wonderful promotion at work. His salary nearly doubled. God is so faithful. I remember when our boy turned his career over to God. Look what's happening now!"

A missionary woman couldn't hold back the tears as she told me her sixteen-year-old daughter was pregnant by a native from the neighboring village:

"I should have spent more time with her. I was so busy with my translation work for the mission. I thought I was doing the right thing."

A lonely single man shook his head in confusion:

"All I've ever wanted was a family. I've followed God all my life. My most consistent prayer has been for a wife and children. I don't get it."

A businessman facing a lawsuit that could devastate him financially declared:

"If there's any justice in this world, we'll win this suit. I've done nothing wrong. I committed my company to God from the day I started it, and I've conducted myself with integrity ever since."

A retired professional lamented:

"God has seen fit to let me go through many trials. I've remained faithful to Him through them all. Why, at my age, do I still feel like such a hypocrite? Why am I still so troubled and discouraged, so full of doubts and self-hatred?"

Let me propose a radical thought: *Maybe we have it all wrong!* Maybe the Christian life is not about "doing right" to "get blessed." Maybe the

Christian life is not about the blessings of life we so badly want and doggedly pursue. Maybe our obedience and faithfulness are to be energized by a very different motive than receiving the good and legitimate blessings we long to experience in this life. Maybe parents ought not be so surprised when, after years of faithfully nurturing their children, an adult son comes out of the closet to announce his homosexual lifestyle.

Perhaps a loving husband, one who has failed as all husbands have but who has never broken his commitment to marriage and has honored it as best he knew, should not be stunned when his wife leaves him for another man.

The spiritual journey is *not* about living as we should so life works as we want. It's *not* a linear path.

 (It's *not* about growing up into the maturity of a good self-image and developing the energy to do good things; it *is* about growing down into the brokenness of self-despair and deepening our awareness of how poorly we love compared to Trinitarian standards. It's *not* about working hard to get it right so we can present ourselves before God to receive the blessings we desire; it *is* about coming before Him as we are, honestly, pretending about nothing, becoming increasingly convinced that we can't get it right though we try as hard as we can, then listening for the whisper of the Spirit, "Welcome! You're home. You're loved. You'll be empowered to speak with your unique voice as you hear the Voice of God singing over you with great love.")

The secular journey is rooted in linearity, the bondage of control: do this, and that will happen. That's how things work. You can have the life you want if you live wisely and well.

(The spiritual journey is rooted in liberty, the freedom of grace: Come as you are, trembling, and learn to rest. Then go out into life doing what's right because you're privileged to do so, because you want to be holy, not because doing right is the way to a pleasant life. Life may provide rich blessings. Or it may not. Either way you can know God.)

SERIOUSLY FLAWED

Three passages (representative, I believe, of the entire message of Scripture) have persuaded me that a linear understanding of the Christian life is seriously flawed. Let me list each one with a brief comment, before I discuss their meaning more fully in the next chapter.

The first passage establishes the Law of Linearity as the basis of the Better Life of Blessings from God, as it summarizes the conditions of an arrangement God put into effect with His Old Testament children:

> "Carefully follow the terms of this covenant,
> so that you may prosper in everything you do."
> (Deuteronomy 29:9)

1.

In the second passage, the writer tells us that God has annulled that Law of Linearity.

> "The former regulation is set aside
> because it was weak and useless
> (for the law made nothing perfect),
> and a *better hope* is introduced,
> by which we draw near to God."
> (Hebrews 7:18-19)

2.

X

The former arrangement of doing good to secure God's blessings has been replaced by a new arrangement. The Law of Liberty has been established as the way to a better hope rather than a better life. That better hope is intimacy with God. In any circumstance, in any condition, we can draw near to God, and from Him draw our identity, find the strength to persevere, and experience the joy of anticipation, with an occasional taste of what's coming.

X

Now the third passage:

"We were in slavery
under the basic principles of the world....
But now that you know God—
or rather are known by God—
how is it that you are turning back
to those weak and miserable principles?
Do you wish to be enslaved by them all over again?"
(Galatians 4:3,9)

The apostle Paul expresses bewildered amazement that people who had the chance to draw near to God would value the Better Life of Blessings over the Better Hope of Intimacy and would again put themselves under pressure to "get it right" to "make life work."

Millions of Christians are following Jesus to gain a better life of blessings now. We think it's our birthright. And we're doing it in a thousand ways, each one a variation of the Old Way of the written code.

The Spirit is inviting each one of us to walk a very different path, to embark on a radically different journey. We're bidden to come as we are, boldly, without fear, even though our souls still sometimes seem a cesspool of foul muck with no living waters in sight, abandoning ourselves to God for whatever He chooses to allow, waiting for Him to reveal how near we are to Him already in every circumstance of life, and to then draw us nearer. That's the new way of the Spirit.

Remember Paul's words: "We have been released from the law so that we serve in the *new way* of the Spirit, and not in the *old way* of the written code."[1]

The pressure's off!

Now, let's consider those three key passages a little further.

THREE PASSAGES TELL THE STORY

Think how you would feel, how you would think, if God appeared to you and said, "Here's the deal. You follow My principles, and I'll see to it your life works exactly as you want."

You first might respond with excitement. "Tell me what Your rules are, and I'll keep them."

Then you'd go to work. You would likely do your best to behave as you were instructed. If things went well, you would be inclined to credit your good fortune to your right doing, your righteousness. If things went poorly, you might feel either resentful or discouraged: "What more did He want from me? I did nearly everything He told me to do!" Or, "I just can't get it right. I must have done something really wrong for life to turn out this bad."

IT ISN'T GOOD NEWS

Most evangelicals properly reject the teachings commonly known as the prosperity gospel or the health-and-wealth gospel. We know those teachings are wrong. Suffering happens whether people pray or not. Godly people grow old and weak. Faithful servants of Christ fail in ministry. Some die young. Sincere followers of Jesus feel depressed and unsettled and hate the pride and lust and insecurity that remain within them after years of living for Christ as best they knew.

God is not a vending machine. We don't insert the proper change and reach into the tray to lay hold of the sweet blessing we want. Life doesn't work that way. We know that.

But sometimes we smuggle our own version of that idea into our understanding of the Christian life. Though we deplore the notion that health and wealth are available on demand, we like the idea that legitimate blessings are given to those who meet the requirements. The Bible says so, right there in the first of those three representative passages:

> "Carefully follow the terms of this covenant,
> so that you may prosper in everything you do."
> (Deuteronomy 29:9)

We find the same thought in a host of other places, such as:

"In all your ways acknowledge Him, and He shall direct your paths."[2]

"Train a child in the way he should go, and when he is old he will not turn from it."[3]

We want the good life. We may define it more spiritually than do the flagrant name-it-and-claim-it preachers. We may take into account the psalmist's lament that darkness was his only friend and his worry that he'd washed his hands in vain. But we still maintain that the good life of legitimate blessings is a worthy goal and one that may be reached by living a faithful life of obedience to biblical principles. Good family relationships, good community experiences, good ministry that provides meaning and personal fulfillment, good experiences of God—we can arrange for these blessings to come our way. All we have to do is live godly lives, pray hard, and expect great things from our great God.

But notice something easily overlooked. Once we accept this linear arrangement—*A* then *B;* you do this, God will do that—not only is the pressure on, but failure is guaranteed. We find ourselves in the same pickle as Israel: We can't keep our part of the bargain. When God instructed His people to "carefully follow the terms of the covenant," He was not setting a *fairly* high standard. He was not prepared to provide blessings to people who followed His rules *reasonably* well. The standard was perfection— perfect love for God and for others at every moment, in every interchange.

They couldn't get it right. They couldn't do it. Neither can we.

And in verses that closely follow our first passage, God made it frighteningly clear what would happen if people slipped up: "If…you are not obedient,…I declare to you this day that you will certainly be destroyed."[4]

The Law of Linearity wasn't good news then—"If you will not…carry out all these commands,…then…I will bring upon you sudden terror, wasting diseases and fever that will destroy your sight and drain away your life.… I will send wild animals against you, and they will rob you of your children.… I will make their hearts so fearful in the lands of their enemies that the sound of a windblown leaf will put them to flight."[5]

And it isn't good news now.

THE REASON FOR RIGHT LIVING HAS CHANGED

Imagine living under a powerful ruler who could prosper your life or blow you out of the water. Suppose he gave a series of commands that, if followed, would be rewarded with extravagant luxuries, but if disobeyed in any detail whatsoever, would result in agonizing torture.

Further imagine that his laws included the requirements to never complain, to never irritably snap at anyone, to always put others' needs ahead of yours. Keep the law perfectly and enjoy unlimited blessings. Break one, just once, and you spend the rest of your life on the rack. And be aware, your ruler has eyes everywhere. No misstep will go unnoticed.

If you managed to measure up to his standards for a time, you couldn't rest in the blessings he gave. You'd be too worried about making a mistake.

And when you did fail, you would likely shout "Unfair!" as you were hauled off to prison. "You knew I couldn't perform to your standards. I never had a chance."

Life under the harsh Law of Linearity would be unlivable. But if someone delivered you from that arrangement (not because the law was unfair but because you weren't good enough to keep it), if someone found a way to let you live as a beloved son or daughter of the king with a royal position established not by performance but by relationship, you would be profoundly grateful. Your one thought would be to get to know that person, to draw near to him.

That story is true. It isn't a fairy tale. It happened. The Deliverer has come. And this is the result:

> "The former regulation is set aside
> because it was weak and useless
> (for the law made nothing perfect),
> and a better hope is introduced,
> by which we draw near to God."
> (Hebrews 7:18-19)

We've been released from bondage to a previous system that was fair but unlivable. The former regulation has been set aside. Although order remains in both the physical and moral spheres, the moral Law of Linearity has been abolished as the basis upon which blessings and curses are distributed.

Now consider what that means. Our arrangement with God has changed. No longer do prosperity and trial depend on our performance. Bad parents sometimes have good kids. Good parents sometimes have bad kids or kids who do terrible things.

The Principle of Influence, of course, remains. A hundred parents who love God and train their children well will rear a greater number of responsible children than will a hundred selfish, uninvolved parents. It makes practical sense to live wisely and well as parents, spouses, friends, and workers. The book of Proverbs makes that clear.

But now, under the new arrangement, the reason for right living has changed. We no longer depend on a linear relationship between performance and blessing to arrange for the life we want. That arrangement has mercifully been declared obsolete and has been replaced by something new, something better.[6]

The arrangement under which the Better Life of Blessings is promised to those who perfectly follow God's principles has been replaced by a new arrangement. Now the Better Hope of Intimacy with a God who sovereignly assigns or withholds blessings according to an unseen plan is available. And it's available at every moment and in every circumstance to those who come to God on Jesus' coattails.

A good friend recently poured out his heart in a letter to me:

"I'm so self-absorbed it's disgusting. I struggle to live well in the midst of overwhelming demands on my life and time. Something feels bankrupt. Something is missing that I can't explain or describe. Something about me feels unanchored and untethered—and it frightens me."

My friend is broken, though not fully. I doubt if any of us will be fully broken until we see holiness. But he is meaningfully broken, more by his wretchedness than by his misery. He feels terrible. God seems absent.

When things go badly, he's tempted to blame his misfortunes on his failures. "If I could be kinder, just a little less self-absorbed, my marriage would be better. Maybe then God would arrange for a few more blessings."

But that's Old Way thinking. The blood of Jesus has opened a New and Living Way, a different direction to take, whether life is working well or falling apart, whether we're more aware of our kindness or our self-centeredness. In the New Way, the pressure's off. Living better might or might not improve our life circumstances. But now our appetite is different. We want something more than the Better Life of Blessings.

If my friend could see into the depths of his own heart (and like me, occasionally he can), he would discover a desire for nearness to Christ that's actually stronger than his desire for either becoming a better person or enjoying a better life. And he's invited to come, just as he is, to walk through the thick door that now remains open into the literal presence of God.

His broken heart is now free to do what he most wants to do: to rest, to relax in an acceptance he did not earn and cannot lose, to plead a guaranteed mercy, and to collapse into extravagant grace. And as he does so, his heart will stir with a passion to please the One who pulled him out from under the crushing Law of Linearity. He'll now be free to live better, not to make his life run more smoothly, not to arrange for additional blessings, but centrally to please the One who set him free from pressure.

DO YOU WISH TO BE ENSLAVED?

But there are two difficulties with this new arrangement.

1. One, it requires us to yield control over what happens in our lives and to trust God to do whatever He thinks best. Regular quiet times and fervent prayer do not guarantee the cancer won't come back; neither do they ensure expanded and effective ministry. We prefer to claim influence, if not control, over which blessings come our way.

2. Two, it's harder to enjoy God than His blessings. Offer a young child the choice of having Daddy present Christmas morning with no gifts *or* having Daddy absent and a stack of gifts piled high beneath the tree, and the child might choose the gifts. Only the mature value the blessing of *presence* over the blessing of *presents*.

Until we develop a taste for God, we prefer a better life of blessings from God over a better hope of intimacy with Him. And because we prefer control over trust, we return to a more acceptable kind of linearity, a version of our own making—one that we can handle—to see to it life works as we want.

It's the situation reflected in our third representative passage:

> "We were in slavery
> under the basic principles of the world....
> But now that you know God—
> or rather are known by God—
> how is it that you are turning back
> to those weak and miserable principles?
> Do you wish to be enslaved by them all over again?"
> (Galatians 4:3,9)

And we respond, "You bet we do!"

The word translated "principles" literally means "sequence." It's a word used by the Greeks to refer to elements in sequence like letters in the alphabet. The basic sequence that could be observed by watching how things work was not the rigid sequence of holy linearity established by God. By "basic principles of the world," Paul meant the natural order by which life could be managed, principles for effective living common to all religions and ethical systems. And their aim was always the same—to make life better.

Work hard and you'll likely earn enough money to enjoy life.

Keep at it and failure could become success.

Save for a rainy day and you won't drown when the storms come.

Be a parent, not a buddy, and your kids will probably be more secure.

These pithy principles appeal to Christians and non-Christians alike. A commencement speaker tells the graduating seniors that hard work and patience pay off. And they do. Not always, but often.

I hear Paul observing the Galatian believers and wondering, "How could you live for blessings from God when the ultimate blessing of His presence is available? And how could you cheapen His holy standards into general ethical principles that you then follow in order to arrange for the blessings you want to come your way?

"How foolish can you be? You received life from God by admitting your failure and weakness and trusting in Christ. Do you think you'll now live that life by doing enough things right to persuade God to give you what you want? You were saved by grace, and you'll grow by grace. The Law of Linearity is ended. Be grateful. That law imposed the intolerable pressure to live perfectly in order to live well. You now stand in the Law of Liberty. Stand tall. Live as free men and women."

It takes only a few minutes of browsing in a Christian bookstore to see how strongly we prefer cheapened linearity over pure freedom. We lower the bar of God's unlowerable standards to a level we can successfully hurdle. Then we follow God's principles, never perfectly, but closely enough to expect blessings to come our way. When they do, we feel smug. "Of course I make good money. I've tithed regularly from the day I got my first paycheck."

When blessings don't come, we're confused. "I wasn't that bad a wife. Why did he leave me?"

So these are our difficulties with the New Way. We insist on retaining some control over how things turn out. We say, "I trust the Lord," when we really mean, "I trust Him to honor my efforts to live well by giving me the blessings I want." And enjoying God doesn't come easily. We say, "I love the Lord," but we really mean, "I love the blessings He provides in this life now."

Let me sketch what I've presented so far.

As never before, the modern church is living as if there's nothing better ahead. And we live as if there's no greater joy now than to experience blessings available in this life.

Two Paths, Two Choices, Two Ways to Live

The Old Way of Moses	The New Way of Christ
Our pursuit: The Better Life of Blessings from God	Our pursuit: The Better Hope of Nearness to God
• Follow principles	• Plead mercy
• Expect blessings	• Discover grace
• Keep at it	• Experience rest
THE PRESSURE'S ON	THE PRESSURE'S OFF
You're under the Law of Linearity	You're under the Law of Liberty

---

We're living the Old Way of a corrupted and cheapened code; we reduce God's holy law to effective principles and think that, by following them reasonably well, life will work out as we wish. Then we feel proud when it does and defeated when it doesn't. Either way, the pressure's on. We insist on blessings and accept responsibility to perform in order to secure them.

There's a new way to live. The pressure to perform is relieved. And a greater joy than "a good life," however we define it, is made available. The New Way is a better arrangement.

But to millions of Christians across the world, it holds little appeal. I devote the rest of this book to presenting the New Way of the Spirit in a manner that I pray will arouse an appetite for the Better Hope of drawing near to God. But I have no power to make that happen. *Holy Spirit, reveal to our hearts that, because of Christ,*

> *the pressure's off,*
> > *there's a new way to live,*
> > > *and it's better than the old way.*

PART II

THE WEARY
GENERATION

The New Way: What It Isn't

CHAPTER FOUR

A WORM IN
THE APPLE

Ever since Eden, people have had the unique capacity to believe they're heading north while their feet take them south. Our moral compass, the internal sense that approves or disapproves of what we're doing and where we're going, is seriously out of whack.

As I observe the church and reflect on my own pilgrimage of fifty years, I wonder: Have we created a religious version of the Old Way to live? Have sincere followers of Christ been traveling along the old path thinking they were walking the new?

BENEATH THE SURFACE

Spiritual direction is an idea whose time has come. Its practice, of course, is as ancient as man. And since our Lord visited earth then returned home, the presence of His Spirit in every believer's life has only heightened both the opportunity and the importance of spiritual direction. For two thousand years, tagging along in response to God's initiative in people's lives—discerning the ongoing movement of the Holy Spirit in the inner depths of the soul and opening the path to the interior world where the Spirit speaks most clearly—has been the valued work of a spiritual director, seen as essential among serious Christians.

Only now, however, is the evangelical church beginning to realize that without spiritual direction, without one-on-one or small-group conversations where our lives are laid open in the presence of a person gifted to discern the workings of our inner life, the disease of deception will not be cured. Without spiritual direction, millions of Christians will continue to walk the Old Way, thinking they're on the path to knowing God well.

James Houston somewhere commented that a spiritual friend is necessary on our journey because of our tendency toward self-deception. Sometimes only another can see that we're heading south when we sincerely believe the road we're on leads north.

Listen to Thomas Merton assess the importance of spiritual direction.

> The whole purpose of spiritual direction is to penetrate
> beneath the surface of a man's life to get behind the conven-
> tional gestures and attitudes which he presents to the world,
> and to bring out his inner spiritual freedom, his inmost
> truth, which is what we call the likeness of Christ in his
> soul.[7]

The great tragedy in modern Christianity is that pools of living water are bubbling in the burning sand of our souls and we don't know it. We haven't dug deep enough through the debris of our self-deception, through the strategies we carefully follow to make life work, to drink from the divine stream within. We're drinking polluted water and thinking it's pure. Worse, we're feeling refreshed.

But it's false refreshment. It's both contrived and counterfeit. It has no power to turn us into people who persevere through shattered dreams for the sake of God's pleasure and others' faith. The Old Way generates sentimental refreshment, the kind of temporary and shallow good feelings that never dislodge our natural narcissism.

In this part of the book, I want to provide what spiritual direction is possible through the written page to help us enter our interior worlds and see which path we're taking. Remember the Lord's parable of the two house builders. One built on sand, the other on rock. Until the storms came, each house could be enjoyed. Until dreams were shattered, until life turned hard (as it will for all of us), both men were comfortable in the enjoyment of blessings.

I presume had we spoken to each one, had we known them as members of our church, perhaps as close friends who had been with us for years in our small group, we might have seen both as godly men, men who loved the Lord and were following Him. But one was living the Old Way; he was not building his life on the truth of Jesus. He wanted something more than drawing near to God.

But this wasn't visible for a long time, not until hurricane season. When things happened that his approach to living could not survive, his life fell apart.

With our almost limitless capacity to deceive ourselves, it's possible (and the possibility has been realized to epidemic proportions) for people to sincerely believe that they're living the Christian life when in fact they're following a highly Christianized version of the Old Way. It's for that reason these next several chapters discuss what the New Way isn't.

Come a Little Closer

It isn't possible to expose counterfeits of the New Way without getting both deep and personal. For years I've held to an image of myself that made me want to go deep, but not too deep, and to be personally vulnerable, but only to a point. Let me tell you the image.

Since graduate school days, and probably before, I've viewed myself as a shiny red apple sitting in a fruit bowl positioned on the center of a dining-room table. Look at me from a distance and you'll be drawn. The apple is big, there are no visible bruises, and it's well shaped.

Come a little closer—read a book I've written, attend a seminar I'm leading, listen to me teach the Bible—and your impression that the apple is good fruit might be strengthened. You may want to pick it up and take a bite.

If you do, you'll likely enjoy the taste. Have a conversation with me, come to me for spiritual direction, join a small group with me, combine your gifts with mine to develop a ministry—and you might conclude that indeed I'm the juicy, substantial, sweet-tasting apple I appear to be.

But I know. I know what you don't know and what I'm determined to never let you discover. There's a worm in the center. A few more bites, and you'll spit me out. I must keep you from moving too close. To know me much is to like me. To know me fully will reveal how disgusting I really am.

I've been speaking publicly for thirty years. I'm a good speaker. God has gifted me and used me to bless many from behind a pulpit or podium. After I speak, I often hear, "You're so vulnerable, so honest. You let me see that you struggle too, that you don't have it all together."

Those words are said admiringly. I chuckle with a wry inward smile. When I let you see a little of the worm, you're even more drawn to me. But if I let you see it all, you'd never listen to me again. I choose my level of vulnerability. I know what I'm doing. I'm no fool. I know how to survive in the Christian world.

Some reading this self-description would suggest I suffer from a psychological disorder. I'm sure there are a dozen diagnostic labels that could be pinned on me. Others would think more simply, "This guy sure has a self-esteem problem. Sounds like he hates himself."

Counseling, even Christian counseling, too often tries to relieve self-hatred and to promote self-love. To do that is to work at making the Old Way more comfortable. It involves neither brokenness, the realization that my self-hatred is too weak, nor repentance, a change in my thinking that shifts the focus from how I feel about myself to how I feel about Christ—or, more to the point, how He feels about me.

You see, there really is a worm in the apple. It's foolish to try to convince me it's a nice worm. There's no such thing. God sees it and hates it. So I should too. I know myself well enough to know I'm often self-absorbed. I hold grudges against people who harm me. I'm capable of hating others. My insecurities have less to do with a lack of needed affirmation, whether during childhood or now, and more to do with a demand that I be honored above another.

Of course I have intrinsic value as a bearer of God's image. Of course I can revel in the wonder and fullness of God's love for me. Of course I'm privileged to live as someone unique, as a masterpiece-in-the-making of God's creative genius who has something of eternal significance to give to this world.

But my self-hatred doesn't come from a failure to appreciate these truths. It comes from a God-denying demand that I be more special than you, that my efforts be recognized and effective, that I never be slighted or demeaned, that I have the resources to get what I want from life.

My self-hatred is rooted in pride. I insist that someone see value in me, that I see value in myself. And when one or the other doesn't happen, I spin down into the abyss of wailing about life and loathing everything in it, including myself.

When I'm there, sinking in the muck of despair, no amount of affirmation can pull me up. Until I realize that I belong there, until I see that there isn't an ounce of love for anyone else in me (at least none that's being expressed), until I'm broken by my own unworthiness to join a community of perfect love, I will think someone *should* rescue me. If someone tries, I won't be grateful. I will wonder why they took so long in coming.

Like you, I'm capable of walking out of a movie theater when the reason it was rated R becomes apparent, or extending kindness, including money, to hurting friends, or preaching a sermon on holiness—and doing it all with a cesspool of pride and self-absorption providing the energy. I can build an attractive house on sand. I can buff the apple till it shines and convince you that no worm could possibly live in such a good-looking piece of fruit.

But sometimes, like you, I stand on rock. Goodness actually comes out of me. I give for the right reasons. I love another with no preoccupying concern for myself.

Who am I? Am I the moral weakling I so often know myself to be, full of pride and fear? Or am I the man of God I long to be, centered in the Person of Christ and empowered by the Spirit to reveal His glory through my life?

I'm a mystery to myself. Sometimes the Spirit flows freely within me, and I'm full of joy and spiritual power. Other times, another source of energy takes over, and I'm out of sorts, occasionally to the point of absurd pouting and faithless despair. It's then I'm more easily tempted to find pleasure wherever I can.

Let me illustrate.

OUT OF CONTROL

Recently I came home after a full and difficult day. After I greeted my wife with a perfunctory kiss, I grabbed the most recent issue of *Christianity Today* and stretched out on the couch, looking for a few minutes of spiritual nourishment. I did what I always do when I open a new issue of that excellent magazine, I turned to the inside back cover to read a brief article by either Chuck Colson or Philip Yancey. It was Philip's turn.

Philip Yancey is a personal friend. I know him not only as one of the most gifted writers of our day, but also as a kind, humble, and genuinely tender friend. I glanced at his picture in the upper-left-hand corner of the page, recognized the thoughtful half-smile and the unmistakable hair, and began to read.

Within the space of two short columns, he quoted Henry David Thoreau, a philosopher I've heard of but never read; Walter Wink, a theologian I've never heard of; and a Dutch novelist with a name I've never heard of and have no idea how to pronounce.

As I finished his article, I could feel the worm slithering through my heart. Had you listened in on my private conversation with myself, you would have heard something like this:

"I never read the right books. I've read snatches from lots of people but I don't know any one of them well. Most I've never read at all. If I had read Thoreau and other philosophers, I'd think so much more clearly. But I haven't got time. Philip is a writer who reads widely so he can write well. His job provides the time he needs to read all those books.

"My life is so out of control. I never do what I want to do. So many people want me to join their ministry, meet them for coffee, chat with them about spiritual direction; when do I have time to follow God's call on *my* life? When will I ever get the chance to develop the school I want to start for spiritual direction? And when do I get a chance to just have fun?

"I have read Irvin Yalom; I'll have to ask Philip if he knows who that is. Someone—who was it?—told me last week they like my books better than Philip's. Am I really that petty? That comment felt good.

"Well, this is getting me nowhere. I'm weary of thinking. Can't figure it out anyhow. I've been thinking like this for thirty years. And I'm still stuck. What a waste. I'm just tired of it all. Good. It's 6:30. *Wheel of Fortune's* on."

There! Now you've bitten into the worm. Do you have hope for me? Can you see the Spirit working in me? Do you believe my core identity is saint, not sinner? Will you envision who I could become, who I already am because of Christ, even though that remains hidden? Do you know how to move me toward the maturity I long to experience? Are you in the pains of labor, loving me though you see the worm, knowing Christ is in me and wanting to see Him formed more visibly in my life?

What's my problem? Am I simply a jealous sinner in need of rebuke? Am I an insecure neurotic who has yet to believe in myself enough to say no to others who would use me, an unassertive, troubled man who needs to accept who I am and live out my calling, a candidate for some good counseling?

Or am I a Christian living the Old Way, dreaming no greater dream than seeing my life come together and working hard to make it happen, then frustrated and angry when it doesn't? *That* is who I am. Or seem to be. Sometimes.

But the resources to live the New Way lie within me. Bear with another story, a better one.

THE WORM NOWHERE IN SIGHT

My wife and I both drove to the mountains in different cars on a Friday afternoon to two retreat centers, perhaps fifty miles apart. She led a weekend with eighty women from a Denver church. I spoke to two hundred college students from Colorado Christian University, the already-up-and-still-coming school where I work.

We agreed to meet back in Denver at a soup-and-salad restaurant for lunch on Sunday a little past noon. As soon as I saw my wife, I knew her weekend had gone well. She was glowing. I said something like, "You look pretty excited. How did your retreat go?"

For more than an hour, she recounted story after story of what the Spirit had done. Many of the stories were truly marvelous, clear evidence of the Spirit's presence and unleashed power. Apparently, He was too busy blessing her retreat to show up at mine. The students were great. I later heard a few scattered reports that several were challenged by what I had said.

But I felt empty. Something in me didn't click. It was an ordinary weekend for me, nothing remarkably supernatural.

And yet, though sensing that the Spirit had anointed my wife's retreat in a way He hadn't blessed mine, I listened to her with joy. I felt not only thrilled with what had happened through Rachael's teaching, I also felt drawn to the deepest part of my wife.

I was overwhelmed with how wonderful she is, how available she is to the Spirit to lift up Christ. Later that evening, with warm sincerity I said to her, "You know, the Spirit uses you in my life like He uses no other person. I want to learn from you all I can about God. Will you describe what it means to you to listen to the Spirit?"

She said, "Really?" I said, "Yes!" She said, "That's really nice." It was a good moment. The worm was nowhere in sight. I was living the New Way.

Sometimes it's obvious which way we're taking. Sometimes I can feel the rock beneath my feet, and I stand tall in the storm. Other times I know I'm losing my balance as the sand beneath me begins to shift.

Too often I don't think about it. I'm too busy packing for the next trip, enjoying my grandkids, wondering why my titanium driver hits the golf ball so far off the fairway, worried about my elderly parents and wanting so badly to improve their quality of life, answering stacks of correspondence, calling the plumber to replace the plug in our bathtub that lets the water slowly disappear. Sometimes I'm just too weary to worry which path I'm walking.

But then I feel the pressure. I realize God has become a distant relative and I'm handling life on my own. Christ is my ticket to heaven but not my best friend. What I think represents the Spirit's nudgings only increases the pressure—"Why aren't you reading your Bible more?" "Why did you refuse to meet your friend for coffee?" "Do you think you're too important for him?"

And then I long to live the New Way. I want to know the pressure's off.

But I'm not certain which way is the Old Way and which is the New Way. I need to go deeper into my soul.

CHAPTER FIVE

WHAT DARK FORCES?

Revival in the church must begin with revolution in the soul. It does no good, and actually does great harm, to fuss about church until first we fuss at ourselves. We won't develop the power to help release the church to become a community until we wrestle long and hard with what it means for us personally to live the New Way.

(And meaningful change in our culture, enduring change rooted in improved character rather than legislated cosmetic change, can come only after revival hits the church.) We tilt at windmills when we thrust our swords at pornography, abortion, fatherlessness, and teen violence without first weeping over shallow community in our churches.(When the Holy Spirit moves, He draws us together before He sends us into battle.)

The order is important:

first, *spiritual revolution* in our interior worlds, a shift from the Old Way to the New;

second, *true revival* in our church worlds, where the Spirit works through self-effacing leadership to release congregations to become safe communities, communities that exalt the Father, not the pastor; that center on Christ, not visible success; that listen to the Spirit, not people's expectations;

third, *cultural reformation* in our everyday worlds that lifts the satisfaction of virtue and humility above the thrill of achievement

and power, and values right relationship with God over   𝒳
improved self-esteem.

Let's be clear. Our greatest need is *not* better community in our small groups or better preaching from our pulpits. Our greatest challenge is *not* to Christianize secular culture into accepting family values and biblical morals.

Our greatest need is for a fresh encounter with God that exposes sin as repulsive and reveals as repulsive sin our determination to make this life work, no matter how spiritually we may go about it.

Our greatest challenge is to recognize the Old Way of the written code, to realize how often we live it, to see the New Way of the Spirit open before us, and to discover our consuming desire to follow that path into the presence of God.

As we pray, "Thy kingdom come, Thy will be done, on earth as it is in heaven," we must not too quickly rise from our knees to get busy with kingdom work. We must for a season remain on our knees, humbled and dependent, begging the Spirit's help to realize which way we're taking.

Are we determined, beneath our moral living, generous giving, and faithful relating, to achieve the Better Life of God's Blessings? Are we strategizing how to get it, depending on the Law of Linearity to generate the results we're after?

Or are we longing with relentless passion to draw near to God, are we desperately hungry to know Christ, are we listening intently for the Spirit's voice in our noise-filled lives? Are we embracing the Law of Liberty by coming boldly, exactly as we are, into the divine community?

First, *spiritual revolution* that moves us from Old Way living to the New Way; then *true revival* of safe community in our churches; and finally, a much-prayed-for *cultural reformation* where salty believers make unbelievers thirsty for Christ. That's the order.

DESIRES BECOME DEMANDS

I want to continue the spiritual revolution that's just beginning in my own journey. A good place to go might be reflection on my own interior world when I read Yancey's article. As long as my soul is ruled by a spirit that allows jealousy, judgmentalism, and general jerkiness to so easily be aroused and then to dominate, I won't be capable of worshiping God, of relating well to my brothers and sisters, or of attracting unbelievers to Christ. I will soil the Name of God by the way I live.

But at the cost of Jesus' blood, God has provided me with a way to live that empowers me to bring honor to the Name, to reveal His character through my manner of relating. I thought I was walking that way the day I reacted so poorly to an excellent article written by a good friend who's at least as busy as I am. What was I not seeing?

Let me ask the question more generally. What dark forces sometimes rule in my interior world? What allows ugly emotions that I don't like and don't choose to develop so easily and rule so completely?

Paul selected his wording carefully when he wrote about the *fruit* of the flesh. I don't think he would say to me, "Larry, your flesh-filled emotions were a choice. You chose to feel them. Now get rid of them. You must choose to smother their expression till they disappear."

The problem, I think, is that I made a passionate, reasonable-appearing choice to live the Old Way long before I climbed onto my couch to read the magazine. It was that earlier *choice* that allowed bad *fruit* to appear. What was the choice? How had I chosen the Old Way?

I don't like having a worm in me. I don't much enjoy life when it's visible. People don't like me and I don't like myself. And I don't care for the folks who judge me, even though I agree with their judgment. So I go after a better life.

God has blessed me with a discerning mind and verbal skills. When I counsel people, I love to see them grow in their faith. And I love the favorable impressions they develop of me. When I lead seminars, I often wonder if anything supernatural is taking place. Sometimes it does, and sometimes I see it. It brings great joy.

When I write a book, as I'm doing this moment, I sense excitement when ideas flow and a rhythm develops. It gives me hope that God might use my words to advance His kingdom. The prospect of strong sales also crosses my mind.

Listen to how I'm defining the Better Life. I don't lust after an impressive office, additional luxuries, and enhanced status. I envision richer ministry, some appreciation for my efforts, and evidence that I'm part of God's larger story. And I move toward that goal by studying hard, preparing well, and praying regularly.

The choice to live the Old Way often seems innocent, even righteous. Like Israel, we're capable of calling evil good and good evil. Isaiah spoke for God when he said, "Woe to those who call evil good and good evil, who put darkness for light and light for darkness, who put bitter for sweet and sweet for bitter."[8]

It's a hard pill to swallow, but we must get the medicine into our souls. *When any ambition other than drawing near to God assumes first-place significance in our hearts, whether the ambition is blatantly self-serving or clearly kingdom-advancing, we're living the Old Way.*

Drawing near to God will purify our desires and energize godly ambitions to counsel well, preach powerfully, and write helpful books, and that's good. When our first-place privilege of nearness to God remains in first place, we abide in the vine; second-place desires become sought-after blessings. Then fruit grows on the branch. That's New Way living.

But the moment we let our desires for blessings become demands, the moment we expect blessings to come because we've met the requirements for God to grant them, the moment we think any blessing other than nearness to God is essential to life and is therefore promised now, we've chosen to live the Old Way. And that means we've forfeited the opportunity to experience supernatural reality and must now depend on our own resources to arrange for the blessings we want. We end up leading natural lives, lives energized by the flesh no matter how religiously disguised.

Preaching good sermons, raising good kids, building good friendships, developing good ministries, running good businesses—they all become activities of the flesh. The pressure's on. We have to get it right to get what we most want.

At conversion, the Spirit placed four distinct resources within us that make supernatural living possible:

> a *New Purity* that makes us clean in God's sight even when we roll in mud;
>
> a *New Identity* that permits no labels other than ones like saint, child of God, beloved, and heaven-bound pilgrim to be accurately pinned on us;
>
> a *New Disposition* that actually prefers holiness to sin;
>
> a *New Power* to draw near to God as a forgiven heir who longs to behold the beauty of the Lord.[9]

When we choose to pursue the Better Life of Blessings over the Better Hope of Intimacy, these resources become useless. Listen to Paul speak strongly to Christians who were being influenced to measure up to certain standards in order to gain full favor with God: "Mark my words! I, Paul, tell you that if you let yourselves be circumcised, Christ will be of no value to you at all.… You…have been alienated from Christ; you have fallen away from grace."[10]

Paul's point is this: *Christ promises no help when you make it your ultimate goal to secure certain blessings by doing good things.* You can pray and fast and attend seminars and buy books and double-tithe and refuse cable service on your television and practice contemplative prayer and never miss an anniversary or your son's ball games—the resources of the Spirit will have no value to you at all. God will not help us live the Old Way.

I wonder how often sincere Christian parents pray for their kids and work hard to train them well only to be frustrated by unanswered prayer. I wonder how often believing spouses pray that their troubled marriage will heal and give only nodding attention to whether they're drawing nearer to God in the midst of their heartache. I wonder how many godly business-men observe the highest level of integrity and expect that God will there-fore bless their bottom line.

MODERN JUDAIZERS

The modern church has been infiltrated by an updated version of Judaizers. In Paul's time, particularly in the Galatian church, certain teachers were acknowledging that Jesus was indeed the Messiah, but then they added the idea that Christians had to conform to the law to gain full standing with God. They were encouraging Old Way living. Because the modern church is plagued by a kind of refined Judaizing doctrine, it will be helpful to understand the form it assumed back then.

Faith versus merit was the core issue. At no time, not even when Sinai thundered, was merit the basis for God's favor. Abraham was justified by faith. So were Moses and David and Jonah and Lot. No Old Testament saint was ever good enough to merit God's blessings. Abraham lied, Moses lost his temper, David committed adultery, Jonah resisted God's call. And Lot—he committed the vilest of sins. Yet Peter called him a righteous man.[11] On what basis? He, like the others, believed in God. None of them earned God's favor by performing up to God's standards.[12]

Paul called the Judaizers "dogs, those men who do evil."[13] The phrase "who do evil" literally means workers of evil, implying that they actively fought against the true gospel. They put "confidence in the flesh";[14] they taught from a settled persuasion that merit brought blessing in this life.

One noted authority put it this way:

> The Judaizers did not attempt to introduce the economy of
> the Old Testament into the church, but a false view of that
> economy. Sinners were saved in Old Testament times by
> pure grace, just as they are today. Here was an attempt on
> the part of Satan…to ruin the Christian church, not by
> introducing Old Testament Judaism, but a false conception
> of the same.[15]

Their message was straightforward: "Do you want to enjoy full acceptance with God and the blessings that come with it? Then you must conform to certain standards of the Mosaic law, including circumcision!" The
Galatian Christians were drawn to this teaching. It returned control into
their hands and restored pride in their own value.

Paul was furious. "I am astonished that you are so quickly deserting the
one who called you by the grace of Christ and are turning to a different
gospel—which is really no gospel at all."[16] Rather than depending on New
Covenant resources that were gifted to them so they could draw near to
God in perfect liberty, the Galatians were thinking it might be a good idea
to get "religious" so they could enjoy superior blessings.

Hear again the Law of Linearity: Get it right to get what you want. Put
the *A* of following biblical principles into place and expect the *B* of desired
blessings to follow.

Modern Judaizers assume the same law but give it a different spin in their
message to today's Christian: Now that we know God by faith in Christ's
atoning work (justification), *He's now available to bless us,* to give us what we
so badly want and what we think will give us a sense of personal wholeness.

But this is a "different" sanctification, an understanding that spiritual
growth comes through the healing provided by enjoyed blessings. It's not

what the Bible teaches. Listen to Paul scold the Galatians for buying into this different view of spiritual growth:

> You foolish Galatians! Who has bewitched you? Before your
> very eyes Jesus Christ was clearly portrayed as crucified. I
> would like to learn just one thing from you: Did you receive
> the Spirit by observing the law, or by believing what you
> heard? Are you so foolish? After beginning with the Spirit,
> are you now trying to attain your goal by human effort?
> Have you suffered so much for nothing—if it really was for
> nothing? Does God give you his Spirit and work miracles
> among you because you observe the law, or because you
> believe what you heard?[17]

God is the *means* of blessing, the modern Judaizers say. Implied, but never stated, is that God Himself is not the blessing we seek. It's therefore right, and actually His plan, that we use Him to get a better life. But "using God" sounds harsh, manipulative, so modern Judaizers speak of trusting God for good things, of claiming His promises, of meeting His terms to win the blessings we want.

They assume that the Bible, from Genesis to Revelation, reveals Jesus Christ as the Savior from sin and the Provider of blessings, and makes known the faith we must have to know Him as Savior and the principles we must follow to experience Him as Blesser—principles like bold faith and right living.

Do you want a good marriage?

Communicate like this.

Do you want godly children?

Raise them by these principles.

Do you want significant ministry?

Become this kind of leader.

Do you want spiritual maturity?

Practice these disciplines.

Do you want financial stability, maybe wealth?

Follow biblical principles of stewardship.

Life will work! That's the promise. *Get it right!* That's the method.

The error is subtle and terribly appealing. God once said, "If you pay attention to the commands of the LORD your God…and carefully follow them, you will always be at the top, never at the bottom."[18]

Read that to a person in trouble. Tell him it's a word from God. But as he responds with excitement, read him another word from God: "Cursed is everyone who does not continue to do everything written in the Book of the Law."[19]

Modern Judaizers cheapen God's eternal word by twisting it, like the serpent did in Eden. Rather than insisting that the blessings of life were indeed made available to any who kept God's law perfectly from the heart, and then teaching that Christ kept the law as a man and then was cursed in our place because we broke the law, they teach that it's possible to keep the law well enough to win the blessings we desire.

And their teaching seems so practical and effective. *Follow the rules for marriage, and yours will likely work well.* That's true. *Be a firm disciplinarian with your children and love them deeply, and they'll probably bring you great joy.* That's true too.

Modern Judaizers appeal to our lower nature, to our wrongheaded idea (first suggested by Satan) that blessings are to be valued above relationship with the Blesser. They implicitly deny that we bear the image of the Eternal Community and therefore can find our deepest satisfaction only through an intimate relationship with a perfect Lover. Nothing less will do.

They disguise their deception well. "God is good," they say. "He's faithful. He longs to bless you. Now that you know Him, go for the blessings

He's eager to pour into your life. Follow His rules, fulfill the conditions, persuade Him to look with favor on you, and you'll have what you want—the abundant life of abundant blessings from our abundantly generous God."

They call it living by biblical principles. Paul called it returning to the weak and miserable principles of this world.

It's a surprising thought, and not a little disturbing, that obedience to biblical principles can be wrong. But when doing right is a strategy to get what we want, our energy is pride and our focus is self.

Biblical principles are reduced to the basic principles of the world when they're followed in order to gain the Better Life we demand. Biblical principles remain biblical principles when they become guided opportunities for Christians who draw near to God to express to others the character of Christ. They've always been commands to be obeyed, but when we're in touch with our new hearts, they're also seen as privileges we long to seize.

PASSIONATE BUT FOOLISH

My background experiences have taught me the lie that life can be found in the demonstration of personal competence and in participation in a larger story. That, for me, is the good life, the Better Life I desire.

I'm a Christian. God has gifted me to do a few things well and to join Him in telling His story. If I pray and keep my nose clean, staying within my range of competence, I can live the Christian life well enough to receive the blessings I believe I need.

So I go to work. I try to get it right, to pray enough, to not sin too much, to seize every opportunity for ministry. The pressure's on.

I *must* gain the blessings I need. I must think well, teach well, write well. Any evidence that I'm falling short unnerves me to the core.

I read a friend's article and I'm forced to admit I could do so much better if only I had the time to read more. I know so little.

I'm so weary of trying to get it right. Performance is such a treadmill. The blessings I now enjoy may not continue, and the ones I still long to enjoy may never come. *I must do better!* But I'm so tired.

And then I come to a point where an internal switch is flipped. All I want is relief. I can perform no more. I need a break. Less pressure. Even if for just a moment. Mindless entertainment helps. I turn on the television.

I understand our addiction epidemic. Deep passions stir within each of us. We're passionate people. But we're foolish. With single-minded energy, we live the Old Way, consumed by our felt need to feel alive, to escape boredom, to find ourselves in a passionate experience. When we tire of the effort, we live for relief.

That describes what was happening in my interior world when I read Philip's article. The fatal choice had already been made. I was after the Better Life that I wanted. The energy of the flesh, ruling within me, bore the fruit of the flesh. Ugly emotions corrupted my heart toward a friend. It's happened before. It happens when we live the Old Way.

Do I clearly recognize the Old Way? Can I identify the teaching of modern Judaizers and realize they'll take me away from the greatest blessing and put the pressure back on?

I need to see how I do this. More discussion is in order about what the New Way isn't.

CHAPTER SIX

THE LEFT-OUT DRAGON

The Old Way refuses to be honest, either about the unpredictability of good things or the inevitability of bad things. When Bilbo Baggins, J. R. R. Tolkien's hobbit, found the riches he and his companions were looking for, they talked "delightedly of the recovery of their treasure."

Then they heard a vast rumbling that awoke in the mountain "as if it was an old volcano that had made up its mind to start erupting again." Smaug, the evil dragon, had been provoked. Tolkien comments, "It does not do to leave a dragon out of your calculations, if you live near him."[20]

We live near a three-headed dragon. The *world* is around us, the *devil* prowls toward us, and the *flesh* lies within us. When this dragon roars, it doesn't always sound like a volcano erupting. It can seem more like a friend dropping in for supper.

Our enemy chats amiably about the good things that could happen in our lives and what we might do to up the odds that they will. He seems friendly, well-meaning, and concerned for our interests. And he isn't in the least hesitant to introduce religion into the discussion. Far from it. What Christ can do for us, what we're told He wants to do, is a regular part of the conversation.

It's difficult to recognize when it happens, but at some point a shift occurs in our thinking. Somewhere during the conversation, we stop thinking of Christ as Sovereign Lord (if we ever did) and regard Him more as a Useful Friend. The point of knowing Him becomes a good life for us now, in this world.

SHUTTING THE DRAGON'S MOUTH

Paul didn't make the mistake of leaving the dragon out of his calculations. One of his methods for resisting the appeal of the dragon's message is important to notice: *Paul spoke openly about his pain,* not in complaint, but as a reminder that the abundant life of following Jesus means abundant opportunities to draw near to Him in hard times, not an abundance of pleasant circumstances and good feelings.

Listen to his words to the Corinthians, Christians who were more intent on feeling now what God promised they would feel only in heaven. "We are hard pressed on every side, but not crushed; perplexed, but not in despair; persecuted, but not abandoned; struck down, but not destroyed."[21]

Paul's life was not a pleasant experience. By *admitting* it and by abandoning all hope that it ever would be pleasant, the pressure was off to figure out some way to make life work. Paul lived to know God, not to use Him. He lived to draw near to God, to become like Jesus, to follow the Spirit, not to live a certain way that would please God enough to get Him to pour out the blessings of a better life.

His admitted anguish became an effective retort to the dragon's invitation to live the Old Way. "If the only hope Christianity offers is a better life down here," I hear Paul say, "then the whole thing is a sham. Christians who follow Jesus with the intent of a pleasant life, even the pleasant life of exciting adventure and meaning, have their heads in the sand. If they'd lift them for a minute and look around, of all people they would be the most miserable."[22]

But Paul is no harbinger of doom and gloom. Quite the opposite. He took the dragon into his calculations, but he also reckoned on God. For him, it was a two-step sequence. Look further in this Corinthian passage.

"I believed," Paul said, "therefore I have spoken." If we don't read the whole thought, we easily miss what's in Paul's mind here and think he was expressing confidence that God would bless his life, then giving a word of testimony. But Paul was quoting a psalmist, a man whose life wasn't going well, a man whose faith in God released him to speak honestly *about how awful his life was.*

The psalmist whom Paul quotes said this: "I believed; therefore I said, 'I am greatly afflicted.' And in my dismay I said, 'All men are liars.'"

Paul then adds, "With *that same spirit of faith* we also believe and therefore speak."[23] Speak about what? About how well the Old Way is working? About how he prays, then sees everything come together in his relationships and ministry and sense of personal wholeness? No! About his affliction! Paul was making known to his community how discouraged with circumstances and beaten down he felt. But he wasn't complaining. He was acknowledging that the Old Way was a lie. He was shutting the dragon's mouth.

Listen to the psalmist continue. After openly sharing that he was torn up and miserable and that his community could not be trusted, he exclaims, "How can I repay the LORD for all his goodness to me?"[24] God's *goodness?* The man's life wasn't going well. Clearly, he wasn't living the Old Way. He wasn't assuming that God's goodness consistently translated into a Better Life of Blessings in this world.

Then he adds, "Precious in the sight of the LORD is the death of his saints. O LORD, truly I am your servant;…you have freed me from my chains."[25] When the psalmist thought about God's goodness, he didn't think of God's blessings in this life. He knew his journey was a long struggle. But he continued in a long obedience—"I am your servant"—and he enjoyed the freedom provided by the hope of God's presence now and blessings later. The chains were off. The pressure was off. He wasn't trying to live right in order to make his life more comfortable and rewarding.

Paul echoes the thought. After claiming the same spirit of faith that allowed the psalmist to admit his life was tough, Paul tells us we can face a life that doesn't work "because we know that the one who raised the Lord Jesus from the dead will also raise us with Jesus and present us with you in his presence."[26]

Climb inside Paul's mind. Move into his heart. See what he constantly thinks about and feel the passions that inflame him. Paul isn't preoccupied with making this life work. Like Baggins the hobbit, Paul left the tunnel of a comfortable life and set out to find the treasure. Baggins left his well-stocked and spacious hole in the ground where he enjoyed the whistling pot announcing it was time for tea. Paul abandoned his powerful, respected position as a religious leader among the Jews where he could enjoy the prestige of his calling.

They both walked away from the Better Life of Blessings and entered on a journey full of hardship and trouble that promised a Better Treasure. For Paul, it was nearness to God—now in measure, then face to face.

But he was no pie-in-the-sky Christian. You couldn't accuse Paul of becoming a retreating monastic, someone so preoccupied with drawing near to God that he forgot the battle around him. All his trials, he said, were endured "for *your benefit,* so that the grace that is reaching more and more people may cause thanksgiving to overflow to *the glory of God.*"[27]

A REFUSAL TO REALLY LIVE

A friend invited me to breakfast, asking me for most of my morning. "I'd like to be the focus of your curiosity for a couple hours," he said. "My life is falling apart in every way. I've lost all hope that things will get better."

By noon, after joining together in a search for where the Spirit was at work in his soul, he said, "I'm deeply confident God is blessing me with the chance to know Him as I never have before. And it's happening. I've never felt so confident in His goodness, and somehow that confidence and my trials have made me not care as much what people think or even whether things turn around, though I wish they would. I'm miserable but I'm content. As I lose hope for things ever getting good, I'm gaining hope in God's doing a good work in me."

I replied, "I want you to know how profoundly that encourages me. Your life, as few others, nourishes my commitment to chase after God as my greatest treasure."

"I'm glad," he said. It wasn't trite. He was truly glad his trials were of benefit to me and brought glory to God.

The Old Way is a refusal to really live. It involves a demand that something less than my truest self come alive. The Old Way identifies real desires in the human heart, desires for meaning and love and fulfillment and freedom, then goes no deeper. It fails to discover our pure, consuming, relentless desire to be in the presence of a perfect person, to gaze at the beauty of absolute holiness the way a beginning artist stares at a Rembrandt masterpiece. The Old Way sees only desires that point inward, to the self, and assumes that Christianity is centrally concerned to satisfy these desires through whatever does the job.

"Find a way to get on top of life," the dragon whispers encouragingly. "You don't have to feel hard pressed, perplexed, persecuted, struck down. Have you been to the latest conference on the spiritual life? Perhaps you should read the best-selling book that promises to unveil the secret of a happy family. There's a new therapist in town who seems to be helping a lot of people move beyond their depression into a much more satisfying life. And prayer. There are some intriguing new approaches you might want to consider. They seem to work."

The dragon sounds like a preacher, like a Bible teacher who knows his audience and knows how to make the Bible relevant. He begins with religious talk that not only could but often does come from a pulpit. But it's only a small step to encouraging divorce or pornography or ethical compromise, because if we live for the satisfactions of a better life, the pleasures of sin will seem quite reasonable when that life falls apart.

The Old Way is all about me. It's all about my emotional health, my spiritual maturity, my soul's satisfaction, my circumstantial happiness, my meaningful ministry, my business or family success. It teaches me to be savvy, to know how to navigate through life so things work pretty well. The savvy required to be effective replaces the wisdom needed to honor God. If we raise our child *this* way, *that* will never happen. If it does, we'll determine what went wrong and fix it. Drawing near to God is reinterpreted to mean little more than a frantic drive to the emergency room to relieve kidney stone pain. "Thank you, Doctor," we say, and we leave without ever knowing the physician who helped us. But we do feel better.

I am fifty-six years old as I write, a week away from turning fifty-seven. I've been a Christian for nearly fifty years. Two things are becoming clearer to me than ever before. First, I'm drawn to the Old Way to live, the way of a written code, a plan to get the blessings I want in this life. I've been living it, not completely but fairly consistently, most of my Christian life.

The second thing becoming clear is that the New Way to live is the way of the Spirit. The Spirit is the Third Person in the Trinity. He knows the Father. He issues forth from Him. He knows the Son. He's the literal Spirit of Christ. The Spirit is God. He is therefore holy and He is love. Every time He speaks, it's to point to the Holy Path, to the way into God's presence. Every feeling He feels, as He searches my heart and sees so much that wants God's blessings more than God, is saturated with kindness. And hope. His passions stir Him to stir my passion for Christ, to turn my heart toward home, to position my feet on the road into God's presence, to let me see the sparkle of the diamond that is Christ.

But His Voice isn't the only one I hear. I hear a sweet-sounding voice, a kind-sounding voice, a persuasive voice, that reminds me how lonely and disappointed I am and how deeply I long to feel good about myself, to be honored, to fit somewhere, to feel significant and secure. That voice encourages me to believe that those longings can be satisfied and that they should be; that the only thing separating the spiritual path from the secular is how I go about arranging for their satisfaction. When I listen to that voice, I can see no higher value than my fullness, felt and enjoyed now or, if not right now, then soon.

It's the voice of the dragon.

It's time to hear another voice. I have recently heard it, and my interior world is being turned on its head. What I thought was good I now see as bad. What I thought was spiritually elitist and suspiciously mystical, I now see as available to everyone and intensely practical. Let me tell you what happened.

COME OUT OF THE CAVE

A few months ago I was brushing my teeth at three in the afternoon. Why then, I'm not sure. That's not my habit.

Without warning, I entered a different world. The sink, the counter, the toothbrush became less real, part of a world that wasn't home. It's the closest I've come to stepping through the back of a wardrobe into Narnia.

In my deepest heart, where the inaudible is clear, I heard the Spirit say—and these are the exact words—"I want to tell you something. I want to tell you what you've been wanting to know."

My "other world" experience lasted ten seconds, perhaps fifteen. I quickly went downstairs to my favorite chair by the fireplace. I knelt, I opened my Bible, and I listened.

Nothing. I heard nothing. After a few minutes I sensed a powerful urge to move to the family room and watch television. I was tempted to dismiss the toothbrushing moment as a bit of silly nonsense, a psychological aberration of self-induced wish fulfillment.

I called several friends. I told them what had happened, and I asked them to pray, to plead with God that the Spirit would draw me to listen, that I would hear whatever the Voice wanted to tell me, that I would humble myself enough to actually hear from God.

Nothing. I sat for three hours, reading Scripture, listening prayerfully, waiting. Nothing.

Several weeks passed. I woke one morning at 5:30 A.M. and felt a desire to get up and sit in the chair by the fireplace. I did. I turned in my Bible to Romans 7:6, the verse that has inspired my new vocational direction, what I call New Way Ministries. I listened as Paul told me again that I had been released from bondage so I could live a new way, what Paul called "the new way of the Spirit." I wondered again what he was talking about when he announced the great news that I no longer had to live "the old way of the written code."

Then I flipped to Hebrews 7:18-19. There I read familiar words that this time nearly lifted me out of my seat. "The former regulation"—the Old Way of getting it right so God would bless—"is *set aside.*" My heart leaped. And I read that we've been given "a better hope" than the promise of blessings for obedience; we've been invited to *"draw near to God";* people like me can now get chummy with God. Amazing! My heart leaped higher.

I began declaring aloud, "It's in the text! It's in the text! It's in the text!" I knew to distrust impressions I felt in my stomach, but I also knew to fully trust sentences I read in the Bible. I cried for joy. I cried with hope. "The pressure's off," I finally shouted. "I don't have to find a way to feel good before I love. I don't have to make my life work before I can glorify God or benefit others." And I realized that's what I wanted. Yes, I long to feel complete and whole and loved and valued. But I long to know God more.

Then I sensed a stirring in my deepest soul. I closed my eyes and listened. I felt like Lazarus, hearing a Voice from heaven reaching into my cave. I can only attempt to attach words to what I heard. They flowed from the text.

"Larry, there's a new way to live. You've been alive with My divine Life for five decades. For most of those years, you've been living a cheapened version of the Old Covenant; you've been living the Old Way of following the basic principles of the world[28] to make this life work better. You've been decorating the dark space you've chosen to inhabit and trying to pretend it's home. My Spirit is now speaking to you through your disillusionment with this life—your brother's death, your cancer, your mother's Alzheimer's, the relationships that have turned sour, family heartaches, so little reality in your interior world. He's telling you, on My behalf, that real joy in this present evil age never depends on the Better Life of Blessings and that it's both foolish and futile to value your satisfaction above knowing Me. Realize this: Pursue the latter and you'll find the former.

"You're becoming aware of the life you possess and of the unique privilege it affords. You can now draw near to God, you can come as you are into His presence, and when you learn what that means and the obedience it brings in its wake, then my Father and I will draw near to you. There's no higher blessing! You'll be full of a joy that won't always feel good, but you'll be aware of a deep longing to know Me and reveal me to others, no matter what's happening in your life or how you're feeling. You'll be solid, no longer a vaporous ghost pretending you're real.

"It's time! It's time to leave the Old Way that's causing you so much pressure—having to keep people happy with you, having to succeed in your relationships and ministry, having to feel at least a little good—and to live the New Way, the way My blood has opened to you.

"Larry, come out of the cave. It's time!"

TIME TO LIVE

A few months later I shared a rich evening with a close friend. We spent three hours in my hotel room, with my friend slouched in a chair with his feet propped on one of the twin beds, and me stretched out on the other.

He invited me into his personal cave. His dark space had a few lamps, providing enough light to see considerable blessings in his life. But disillusionment had done its work. He'd lost all hope that life would ever consist of enough blessings to give him true joy. He had discovered his desire for God.

But like Lazarus, graveclothes still bound him. He feared his father's disapproval, he struggled with feelings of low value, his ministry felt futile. His spiritual journey was taking him on a roller-coaster ride of incredible highs and devastating lows.

As he spoke, I saw myself drawing near to God, more stumbling than gracefully walking—I kept tripping over *my* graveclothes. But I was coming to Him. It's what I wanted most to do.

I could see my friend's heart bursting. The life within him was pressing for release. I sat up on the bed. I leaned forward. With tears of hope flooding my eyes, I said, "It's time! It's time for both of us, and many others around the world thirsty to know God, to live the life we've been given. It's time to live the New Way!"

I say it again today. It's time to live the New Way of the Spirit, to leave behind the Old Way of the written code.

But there's a problem: I still like the Old Way. I want my life to work. And I can make it work, not always and never perfectly, but I have the resources to arrange for some satisfactions, to avoid some difficulties. And when I can't, there are things I can do that bring relief. I may kid myself that it's otherwise, but too often that's my priority.

And none of it seems wrong. The Old Way looks reasonable, normal, even good. Flames from the dragon's mouth are reducing my soul to cinders, and I cozy up to them like a weary man sits before his fireplace on a cold winter morning.

I don't see the danger. I don't recognize the evil of the Old Way. But I must. It doesn't do to leave a live dragon out of our calculations if he lives nearby.

CHAPTER SEVEN

WHAT'S SO WRONG
WITH WHAT
WE WANT?

What makes the Old Way wrong? Is it really *evil* to live for blessings available in this world? Or, for some unfortunate people, is it merely frustrating?

How can anyone seriously maintain that trying hard to make this world a better place for us to live is immoral, especially if we do so "Christianly," if we take no unfair advantage of others and resist the lure of illegitimate pleasures? And suppose we aim for spiritual meaning, and fill our days with ministry activities, and carefully and seriously follow biblical principles as best we can. We might corrupt the search for satisfaction into a selfish pursuit—and that would be wrong—but if we trust Christ to fill our lives with adventure and fulfillment and community, are we not walking a good path? Are we not then His disciples?

A SAVIOR FROM PAIN, NOT FROM SIN

The dragon can look like a dove. He can encourage us to hate adult movies and abortion and rape, to never miss church, and to be there for hurting friends, when all the while our commitment to a better life, however we define it, occupies first place in our hearts. The only consistent message

71

coming from the world, the flesh, and the devil is this: *Seek your deepest enjoyment somewhere else than in God.*

Jesus came to earth to tell us He is the way, the truth, and the life. His death opened the *way* into God's presence, the greatest blessing of all. His teaching made clear the *truth* that life does not consist in a return to Eden's comforts; it doesn't even consist in graduation to heaven's bliss. True life is knowing God. Jesus said so.[29] And the *life* is Christ Himself, not the bread He could multiply or the corpse He could resurrect, but Him. Being in Him, having Him in us, living with His energy, chasing after His purposes, loving what He loves, seeing Him form in us until we're actually like Him—that's life. And it can be enjoyed in bankruptcy or affluence, from a hospital bed or a deck chair on a cruise ship, or when you walk out of a divorce court you never thought you'd see or into a surprise party celebrating fifty years of your wonderful marriage.

When we live the Old Way, we don't believe what Jesus said. Anne Graham Lotz isn't making that mistake. I listened to her on a tape where she recounted some hardships in her life, then said, "Don't give me sympathy. Don't give me advice. Don't even give me a miracle. *Just give me Jesus!*"

The Old Way sees things differently. The dragon thoughtfully suggests, "Yes, you do want Jesus. He's the one who can restore your marriage, provide great ideas on raising kids that really work, and prosper your ministry. Jesus teaches principles to live by, He offers methods to follow that will give you the life you want. What must you do to be saved from an unfulfilling life and strained relationships? What must you do to be saved from persecution and trouble? He'll tell you. Go to Him to find out what you must do to make life work!"

I'm learning to distinguish between the dragon's voice and the Spirit's. The dragon directs my attention from the person of Christ as the source of the deepest joy toward the blessings of life as what I really need to be happy. If those blessings can be gained only by obvious sin, fine; if living a good

Christian life keeps life working well, that's fine too. The dragon doesn't care, as long as I chase after the Better Life of Blessings. After listening to the three-headed dragon for a while, I tend to see Christ as a savior from pain, not from sin; as a responsive benefactor rather than Holy Lord.

The Spirit always points to the Christ of the Bible, the One who offers no guarantees that my marriage will survive, that the biopsy will yield good news, or that I won't lose my job. The Spirit exposes a problem in my soul worse than my suffering, then reveals the God of grace. He tells me I can know this God; I can know His heart, rest in His power, and hope in His purposes. And I can see it all in Christ. He keeps stirring my heart to say, "Just give me Jesus!"

But I like what the dragon is saying. I want my life to work. I enjoy it when it does. I hate it when it doesn't.

Only when my dreams shatter, and then only for a moment, do I sometimes feel a desire to draw near to God that I know is stronger than my desire for restored blessings. Only during specially intense times with God—rare in frequency and short in duration—do I pant after Him more than His blessings.

I've written six chapters in this book. My deadline is fast approaching. Do I really want to know Him more than I want Him to empower me to write the remaining chapters on time?

I say that the pressure's off. Do I have any idea what I'm talking about? Does anyone? Am I describing a way of living that nobody lives, that nobody *can* live? Am I stepping out of my tenement into the dirty slum we all call home and speaking of a resort we'll never enjoy? Maybe it would be better to drag out a hose and clean the street, to talk about making our marriages better, our kids more responsible, our friendships closer, our ministries more effective, and our bodies slimmer and healthier.

Instead, I'm writing a book on living for the Better Hope of drawing near to God, on living not to make our lives better but rather to bring Him pleasure and to reveal Him to others. Do I have any idea what that means? Maybe I really do value what Christ can do for me in this life more than I value the opportunity to get better acquainted with Him. Have I ever actually derived more pleasure from spending time with Him than from vacationing with my wife or watching my sons do well or holding my grandchildren? Is there really more joy in knowing Christ than in standing before large crowds and watching good things happen and making good money to boot?

And yet that's what I'm writing about. I'm in deep water. I'm not certain I can swim.

This chapter is proving difficult to write. It's my fifth time through. I've thrown away more than fifty pages of scribble that seemed important when I wrote it. And now I'm rewriting what I thought was the final version.

I began this book by declaring that more is available to us in Jesus Christ than we dare imagine. Leaving everything behind to know Him better is really a good deal for us. Do I believe that? When I wrote that introductory sentence, passion was flowing through me. Is it gone?

I must not try to get it back. That would be the Old Way. I must rather seek Jesus. I must draw near to God.

It helps to know it *can* be done, that the way to God has been cleared, that the resources needed for the trip have been provided, and that the Spirit can stir up the waters that will carry us, like a fountain carries a leaf, into the presence of God. It also helps to be convinced that any other priority is evil. Let me talk more about both points—that the New Way can be and has been traveled and that the Old Way is evil.

MORE IS AVAILABLE THAN WE DARE IMAGINE

First, a few reminders that the New Way has been traveled. Pascal, whose sentence fragments of ecstasy are in this book's opening lines, is only one of a great cloud of witnesses to the truth that supernatural reality can break into our lives and gush out of our souls, and that it sometimes does! John is another.

It was a Sunday, about two thousand years ago. As John wrote about what happened, he tells us he was "in the Spirit"[30]—indicating, I think, that a sense of expectancy seized him, likely after many desperate days of waiting on God to meet him on the rock he called home. The apostle was an old man, living in the prison of a barren island, exiled there for the crime of preaching Jesus, eating poorly, sleeping uncomfortably, performing hard labor that not even a twenty-year-old should be forced to do, aware that the band of disciples was gone (most of them martyred), and discouraged by the spiritual condition of several local churches.

If he had followed Christ in hopes of enjoying a better life, he would by now have been sorely disillusioned. But then Christ appeared to him. Notice, however, what *didn't* happen when He appeared. Christ did not bring John a mattress. He did not spread a table with good food. He did not magically lift John off Patmos and set him on the mainland to hold seminars in Sardis and Laodicea.

What did happen was far better. The Spirit revealed Jesus Christ. I can hear John saying, "My life is miserable, but I ask not for sympathy, not for help, and not for a miracle. Just give me Jesus!" And that's what the Spirit did. It's a prayer God always, eventually, answers.

The Jesus whom John met that day did not appear as the gentle carpenter, the loving teacher, the good friend who had once invited John to lean on His chest after dinner.

Listen to John describe the Jesus he saw that day:

> His head and hair were white like wool, as white as snow,
> and his eyes were like blazing fire. His feet were like bronze
> glowing in a furnace, and his voice was like the sound of
> rushing waters. In his right hand he held seven stars, and out

of his mouth came a sharp double-edged sword. His face was like the sun shining in all its brilliance.[31]

Small wonder that when John saw Him, he fell at His feet as dead. Not even for a moment did it occur to him to say, "Could you get me off this rock? And I would really like a cup of hot coffee. It's cold in this miserable place."

More is available to us in Jesus Christ than we dare imagine. There's more to Jesus Christ than we've ever dreamed. We experience so little of Him when we approach Him only with requests. We taste so little of the mouth-stopping, complaint-ending, desire-deepening awe that His presence creates when we think more about our problems and how to solve them than about *meeting Him.* We experience so little of the joy that sustains us in suffering and the hope that anchors us amid shattered dreams when we come to Him looking for the pathway out of hardships instead of the pathway *into His presence.*

In his unpredictable expressions of mercy, the Spirit gives us glimpses of Christ that fill us with supernatural reality and shine a spotlight on the entrance to the New Way. I recently dropped my younger son at the airport. As we said good-bye, he handed me a Father's Day card. Before I drove off, I read the personal words he'd written. They came from God's Spirit working in my son to my arid soul, to a heart more aware of God's absence than His presence. They're too personal to share. I felt stirrings in deep places that I gratefully indulged as I wheeled my way home. Within minutes I was weeping, for some reason envisioning my last moments on earth before I see Jesus. My family was gathered around me. I felt indescribable love as I looked at them, grateful beyond words for each one. Then I said to them, "God gave me you, and now I'm about to see Him. I'm going to see Jesus. *I'm going to see Him.* Soon you'll be with me, looking at HIM! Joy beyond joy. Fullness of joy. I die a happy man."

And then the moment passed. My eyes dried and I drove on home. I paid some bills, watered some plants, and answered some calls. But the moment was real!

More is available to us in Jesus Christ than we dare imagine. We settle for so much less. We taste Him so little. Why?

Is it because we don't live as we should? If our failure to measure up to holy standards is the cause of our impoverished experience of Jesus, there's no hope. We never measure up, not for a minute, and we never will until we're home.

AN INSULT TO GOD

But that's not the central problem. And now I approach my second point. The central obstacle to His life flowing in us and pouring from us is this: *We want something else more.* And that's evil. We want the blessings of a better life more than we desire to draw near to Jesus. We approach Him the way a child approaches a weary Santa Claus in the mall, who for the hundredth time asks, "What do you want for Christmas?" I wager no child has ever pressed close to Santa's chest, looked up into his eyes, and said, "You! I want only you." No child believes having Santa join him for dinner could bring more joy than watching Santa stack presents beneath the tree. Our problem is unbelief in what can be called His "Immanuel Agenda," the relentless obsession He has for forming a family to gather at His dinner table, with Himself at the head and each of us thrilled to be there.

God is committed to building a community where He is our God and we are His people. That's been His agenda since Eden. When we move in a different direction, we're like the prodigal son telling his father, "I could care less about being with you. I just want your wealth. You can die as far as I'm concerned. *Just give me my inheritance.*"

That's the Old Way. It's not only foolish, it's evil.

It's foolish because life will never work well enough to create the joy we desire. God sees to that. When Adam and Eve were expelled from paradise,

God rigged the world to make sure we would never have a reasonable basis for settling down in the satisfactions that life on this planet affords. Weeds grow in every garden. Every time we try to remove them, a thorn pricks our finger. Relationships never achieve the full joy of complete intimacy. Self-centered competition gets in the way. Our every effort to reach pure harmony is spoiled by our attitude of "I hurt; you failed," and our focus on what the other can do to satisfy our needs.

We can't get it right. We can't get life to work; it never will until heaven. And yet, like well diggers walking by an already dug well and forcing our shovels into dry dirt, we try to figure out what we can do to find the water we want. Most of our prayers consist of a request for God to guide our shovels to where springs hide beneath the baked dirt.

One day Jesus addressed a group of religious well diggers. "You're thirsty. You know that. But you don't know you're thirsty for *Me!* Come to Me. Put down your shovels. The well is already dug. Come, drink the water I supply. Come to My table. Eat what is good. Let your souls delight in the richest of fare. And there's no richer fare than relationship with Me. I am available. Come!"[32]

And yet we continue in the Old Way, valuing the Better Life Jesus could give us above the Better Hope of knowing Him well. That is both futile and wicked. We treat Him with contempt, spurning His invitation to draw near to Him, and instead try hard to follow whatever principles we think will bring us the blessings we want.

We can meet Jesus. It's happened before. And the hope of that encounter far surpasses the hope of a better life in this world. That's the first thing we must know.

And living for a better life in this world with more energy than we pursue a deeper relationship with Christ is evil. That's the second thing we must know. It's an insult to God. He gives us the best heaven can offer, and we ask for something else.

A Different Kind of Peace

Each of us is walking either the Old Way or the New.

One of Christ's choice followers, Augustine, said the same thing. Augustine knew what it was to live for a better life. He also knew the emptiness of a soul that could be satisfied with nothing and no one other than God. That emptiness carried him into sexual activity he could not control. Only when he had an encounter with Jesus and began pursuing the Better Hope of Intimacy with God did he discover a joy he preferred to sexual pleasure. There's no other real cure for any addiction.

Later in life, he wrote about two cities that together claim every living person as citizens, either in one or the other: "One city is that of men who live according to the flesh. The other is of men who live according to the Spirit. Each of them chooses its own kind of peace and, when they attain what they desire, each lives in the peace of its own choosing."[33]

There's a peace the world gives. It's the tranquillity of a life that works reasonably well—decent relationships, adequate health, enough resources to enjoy life, meaningful work. Citizens of the City of Man follow the basic principles of this world to gain their goal, and in gaining it they enjoy a certain kind of peace for a while. *That* kind of peace, however, never survives death.

Jesus offers a different kind of peace. "*My* peace I give you. I do not give to you as the world gives."[34] The peace Jesus gives isn't dependent on deserved blessings. It depends entirely on the one supreme blessing He guarantees to all His followers: the opportunity to draw near to Him, to put every egg in the basket of His presence with us even when His absence is all we feel, to depend on Him to be doing a good work in us even when everything that happens seems bad.

A friend just yesterday described the hell he and his wife have endured over their rebellious son. "It about destroyed us. We couldn't figure out what was going on in him, or in us for that matter; we had no idea what to do." He lacked the peace the world gives.

He went looking for it. "We read so many books, talked to the wisest people we knew, and we prayed. Boy, did we pray. We begged God to tell us what to do, to give us wisdom, to show us how we could reach our son. We couldn't figure it out. Nothing we tried worked."

That's the Old Way—discern which principles to follow that will bring about the blessings we want, then put them into practice as best we can, then pray, trusting God to honor our obedience by making our lives work better. With all our heart, soul, mind, and strength, get it right so life works. Desire the peace available in this world.

"It didn't work," my friend confessed. "We got more and more confused. We didn't know what to do. We couldn't understand our son's rebellion. The pressure and the guilt and the frustration were unbearable. They about destroyed our relationship. Then we gave up."

God has rigged the world so that our best gardening efforts can never get rid of all the weeds. The angel with the flaming sword kept these parents from returning to Eden. He keeps all of us out.

"Eventually we stopped trying to be good parents who could straighten out our kids." Shattered dreams created an unsolvable pain that helped them abandon the Old Way.

"We decided that all we could do was cling to God, get to know Him better, see what was keeping us from real worship, and rest in His sovereignty. Only the Spirit can reach our son, and we're not in control of Him. Our son still breaks our hearts in some ways, but we're less caught up with changing either our heartbreak or his rebellion. The pressure's off. At least it's less. And the power struggle to make our son better is much less intense. I think we're actually wiser parents. We're certainly more relaxed. And our son is showing some good movement. We're really grateful. We *love* it. But his straightening out isn't our goal anymore. It certainly is a desire, and a strong one, but it isn't our goal."

My friend is discovering the New Way. He has found his desire for God and is living for the Better Hope of coming to Jesus rather than the Better Life of effectively parenting his son toward responsible maturity.

The Old Way is evil, as Augustine reminds us: "When a man lives 'according to men' and not 'according to God,' he is like the devil."[35]

But the pressure's off; the New Way is available. "Come to me, all you who are weary and burdened, and I will give you rest."[36]

CHAPTER EIGHT

BLINDING DECEPTION

We're never more deceived than when we think we're living for God but in fact are living for His blessings. When we persuade ourselves that our job is to pray properly, live morally, and love meaningfully, and that God's job is to reward us with whatever blessings we most want, we're deceived. We have a fleshly view of the Christian life. We live apart from grace.

C. H. Spurgeon, the great English preacher, suffered all his adult life from excruciatingly painful arthritis and gout and from depression, often severe. And he pastored the largest church in his time, his books were bestsellers, and he was acclaimed as a powerful speaker. How do we account for the mixture of trial and blessing in his life?

How do we account for the bewildering blend of trial and blessing in ours? Did Spurgeon get certain things right that won him great ministry but missed a few other requirements that left him in poor health?

Does God provide ministry blessings if we pray properly but allow health trials if we harbor a grudge toward someone? Exactly how does it all work? The question matters a great deal if we're determined to arrange for the blessings we most want and to avoid the trials we most dread.

No Other Blessing Is Guaranteed

There is order in the world. In many areas of life, what we do determines or at least influences what happens next. Look up when you're walking and you may trip over a curb. The proper response is not to keep looking up and pray for protection. It's to look where you're going while you pray. Put gas in your car if you want it to run. Only religious fanatics turn the key in a car with an empty tank and, because they're heading for church, expect it to start. God could make the car run, but He rarely does.

But how about the blessings and trials over which we have no obvious control, no clear influence? Do husbands stay faithful to wonderful wives? The answer is often yes, but not always. The relationship between wonderful wifing and faithful husbanding is not linear.

Are ministries blessed if we pray and dried up if we don't? Often, yes. Always, no. When things go wrong, should we assume we didn't pray properly or enough? Does a certain prayer *always* work? That's the assumption of the Old Way.

Although it brings me to deeper levels of brokenness to say it, it must be said: *Whenever we focus on the blessings we want, even if they're worthy blessings, and study Christianity to understand how to get those blessings, we're sowing to the flesh.* We're living the Old Way.

We speak often of God's favor. And we should. It's a wonderful blessing. A pastor friend recently told me how God had given his church favor in the community. They had been diligent in treating their neighbors well. God had blessed. And I rejoiced.

But I would not rejoice if that pastor now writes a book entitled *How Your Church Can Win Favor from God!* Perhaps it would sell. We're so easily drawn away from Christ to a blessing we more highly value and to a formula for bringing it into our lives.

Understand this: *The flesh always values something more than Christ.* It doesn't have to be pornography; it could be a successful family or a growing church. But the Spirit points to richer treasure. *He always holds up Christ.* The battle between competing affections defines the war between the flesh and the Spirit. Which treasure will be our first-place passion? What do we value most?

Perhaps the greatest mistake in the modern church is its unrecognized tendency to encourage Old Way living. Books, sermons, and seminars present an appealing blessing, then tell us how to get it. "God longs to bless you," we hear. "Live in such a way that His blessings are released into your lives."

We're living under deception. The supreme blessing He longs to give us is Himself. No other blessing is guaranteed until heaven. The blessings we now claim are so often something less than an empowering, enlivening, pride-destroying, self-effacing, joy-giving encounter with God.

This widespread deception has consequences. Let me list four:

1. *It breeds confusion and pressure.* Wasn't I a good enough husband? Is that why she left me? I tried so hard to be a good parent. What did I do wrong? Was I too firm? Not firm enough? What do I do to make things better? God, why won't You tell me what I can do that will work? I promise I'll do it! Anything! JUST TELL ME!

2. *It weakens our view of God.* If the Christian life is all about blessings, then when trials come instead, we conclude either that we aren't living right or that God isn't really in control. In *this* situation, at least, Satan must enjoy the upper hand.

When I developed cancer, I was told it was from the devil and that I should engage in spiritual warfare against Satan on behalf of my health. The front line of spiritual warfare, in that view, is not to abandon myself to God in the middle of trial, but to align myself with God to defeat the devil. And the measure of victory is restored health.

That, I believe, is the Old Way. In the New Way, we resist the fleshly demand that blessing replace trial and instead follow the Spirit, through *whatever* comes, into a deeper encounter with God. In the New Way we fight against the demand for blessings on behalf of knowing God.

In the Old Way we fight against trials on behalf of blessings. Our deepest affections lie in this life. And in the process, God and I join forces to defeat a common enemy. My righteous living releases God to do what He otherwise couldn't do, to destroy the works of the devil and to give us back the blessings Satan has taken away. Our view of God's sovereignty drops a notch.

3. In the Old Way, *humility becomes a technique.* We humble ourselves and draw near to God in hopes that He'll draw near to us, not to let us *encounter* Him, but with *blessings* in hand. Humility becomes a maneuver. We come with empty hands but with a finger pointing: Give us that! Dependence gives way to methodology.

And when the method works, we become rather satisfied with our humility. We share in the glory. We got something right, in this instance humility, and God blessed. What a team!

When we live under the Old Way's deception, the destructive consequences come in many forms. I've just mentioned three of them:

Confusion and pressure

A small God

Pride

There's one more consequence I want to mention: *We develop a wrong view of psychological problems.* The therapeutic culture, I believe, is built on a flawed foundation. Let me spend the rest of this chapter suggesting what I mean. I think it's important.

BENEATH PSYCHOLOGICAL DISORDER

Apparently I went through graduate school in the dark ages. During my five years of doctoral training in clinical psychology, I was never required to take a course in eating disorders. I don't think one was offered. A couple of lectures in a second-year course on basic psychopathology familiarized me with terms like anorexia and bulimia, but that was it. I read Hilde Bruche's classic *The Golden Cage* and, when I graduated, knew little more about anorexia than one woman's theory.

In my second year of private practice, a physician friend referred to me a young woman, seventeen I think, who was suffering from unhealthy weight loss. I pulled my copy of *The Golden Cage* off the shelf and skimmed it again to get ready. I began the interview by feigning confidence. I didn't have a clue.

In the first few minutes, I learned she was thirty pounds below normal weight, that she ran forty miles every week and crunched her already tiny waist with five hundred sit-ups every day, and that she ate like a bird. Then she said, with eyes staring at the floor and a voice of steel, "I know you're going to try to get me to put on weight. But I'm still fat. I won't do it."

I was twenty-nine at the time. This was my first direct encounter with the dangerous puzzle called anorexia, with a starkly thin woman who insisted she was overweight and was determined, against all pressure, to shed a few more pounds.

After forty-five minutes of getting nowhere, still without a clue about the cause or cure for her disorder, I muttered, "I really think you ought to put on some weight."

I had no idea what I was up against. I might just as well have told my four-year-old son, "Try not to sin anymore."

What *was* I up against?

Since Sigmund Freud, psychological thinkers have generally agreed that something has gone wrong in the development of an innocent self. Every child longs to feel loved and valuable and has some intuitive sense of what blessing is needed to satisfy those longings. Experience sharpens the focus. Painful traumas teach us what to avoid, and pleasurable encounters shape our understanding of what to hope for and, if possible, to arrange for.

Two problems may develop. If serious enough, we label them pathological. Because of especially dysfunctional relationships, we either go after unrealistic goals—such as no rejection, total perfection, or constantly pleasant feelings—or we depend on ineffective strategies to get us where we want to go. Or both. (Understanding ineffective methods to reach unrealistic goals is now a field of study in itself. We call it psychodynamics.)

When a therapist uncovers a person's goal that is unreasonable in the real world, and when the therapist recognizes that person's attempts to gain internal relief that are too costly, the process of healing can begin. The process, most often, involves an effort to help someone behave more effectively in order to experience greater satisfaction through some blessing available in this life. It's the Old Way.

I've been wondering: Could Old Way living have more to do with our troubles than we suspect? Does our insistence that this life provide more satisfaction than it can, and our determination to figure out some way to get it, lie beneath what we call psychological disorder?

"Although they knew God," Paul said, people "neither glorified him as God nor gave thanks to him, but their thinking became futile.… Although they claimed to be wise, they became fools and exchanged the glory of the immortal God" for something else. "Therefore God *gave them over* in the sinful desires of their hearts to sexual impurity…to shameful lusts…to a depraved mind, to do what ought not to be done. They have become filled with every kind of wickedness, evil, greed and depravity."[37]

People pursue a source of primary satisfaction other than God. They do not value Him above all other treasures. That's the Old Way. Their thinking becomes futile. Their lives revolve around the false gods of better kids, good health, fulfilling relationships, effective ministries—anything other than God. And that devotion to a lesser god turns loose all manner of trouble. Selfishness rules. The springs of human nature are polluted. Vile water gushes out.

Like a shopper who mistakenly purchases the wrong size garment, we've exchanged the glory of God for an outfit we think might fit our soul a little better. We turn away from God and chase after other blessings.

What we've done can be simply sketched:

Three outcomes are possible:

1. *We may experience enough blessings to persuade us we're on the right track.* Old Way thinking is confirmed as good. We're getting it right, and life is working. We become successful law keepers, modern Judaizers, happy Pharisees.

2. *A mixture of blessings and trials may keep us in the game and open us to any method to make life better.* We become pragmatists. Biblical principles are bent if we see personal advantage in compromise. Or we become legalists, more rigidly resolved than ever to do it right so life will work. We may decline into neuroticism, getting caught up in strange behaviors that protect us from internal pain.

3. *Life may become so hard, and our efforts to improve things may seem so futile, that we give up.* Now we slide into major depression, conscienceless living, or insanity—serious neurosis, character disorder, or psychosis.

THE LIGHT WE CANNOT SEE

With these thoughts in mind, I read another verse from Paul—and I tremble:

"The god of this world has blinded the minds of the unbelieving so that they might not see the light of the gospel of the glory of Christ, who is the image of God."[38]

Unbelievers do not see Christ as their greatest treasure. *Neither do most believers.* We live as blind people, chasing after the light we can see—the satisfaction that blessings bring—and not valuing the light we cannot see—the glory of Christ.

It could be different. We could live a new way. "For God, who said, 'Let light shine out of darkness,' made his light shine in our hearts to give us the light of the knowledge of the glory of God in the face of Christ."[39]

God is not only capable of removing the scales from our eyes so we can see the beauty of Christ. He has already done so! Christians are now able to see Christ as their greatest treasure. We can live the New Way. "And when we are satisfied in Him," John Piper says, "we are crucified to the world,"[40] and to the flesh. The devil loses his foothold in our lives. We can learn to exult, not in the prospect of a better life of blessings, but in the better hope "of the glory of God."[41]

Perhaps trauma is not the real culprit. Maybe a traumatized self is not the real disease. Listen to Piper again:

> We were made to know and treasure the glory of God above
> all things; and when we trade that treasure for images, every-
> thing is disordered. The sun of God's glory was made to
> shine at the center of the solar system of our soul. And

when it does, all the planets of life are held in their proper
orbit. But when the sun is displaced, everything flies
apart.[42]

At last count there were more than four hundred Web sites and chat
rooms available to help anorexics stay thin, to help them resist pressure
from parents, counselors, and friends to gain back healthy weight. The sites
have names like My Friend Ana, Pro-Ana Sanctuary, aNOreXiC Wanna B,
and Stick Thin Pixies. One site declared, "Anorexia is a lifestyle or a friend,
not a disease." Another said, "Pro-Ana: Join us and become PERFECT!"

What is happening? Why are girls by the thousands embracing destructive eating habits and clinging to them as if to a piece of wood in a stormy
ocean?

Listen to Katybelle on one Web site:

"I always felt that I was alone and that no one understood me, so one
day I went surfing the net, looking for someone out there who was like me
and thought the same way I did."[43]

Another wrote:

"To me, my anorexia is EVERYTHING, it's my life and everything I
want and need…yes, I NEED this. It has become such a big part of my
life…but certainly not something I just decided I wanted…it gives me the
control I need, it gives me the sense of achievement that I can't get from
anything else, it makes me feel happy when nothing else can."

When I worked with my first anorexic client years ago, what was I up
against? Certainly I had to do battle with controlling parents, with my
client's deep resentment over being stripped of any sense of separate identity, and with her profound terror that she would disappear into the quick-
sand of a smothering world.

But none of those things, as terrible and stubborn and painful as they
were, lay at the root of this young girl's troubles. *She was blinded by the god
of this world.* She could not see the glory of God in the face of Christ. In her

mind, there was nothing to live for but the control her anorexia provided. *That* was what I was up against.

The anorexic shouts, "To me, anorexia is everything." And we shout with her, "To us, a better life is everything." It may not be the experience of power that anorexia brings. It may not be the instant pleasure that pornography brings. It may be the rush of achievement that seeing our kids do well provides, or the quiet joy of climbing into a nice car we can afford, or the deep pleasure of spending an evening with a much-loved spouse, or the excitement of a growing ministry.

If something other than Christ is the reason for which we live, if we depend for our deepest joy on anything other than seeing Christ, if the Better Life of Blessing is everything to us, then we're living the Old Way.

Then the pressure's on. And we're vulnerable to troubles of every description.

But if we live the New Way, the pressure's off. We may still experience a variety of trials, but our souls will be in line with the Immanuel Agenda—God will be our God, and we will be His people.

It's time to feel the wind of Immanuel's Spirit.

PART III

CAN YOU FEEL THE WIND?

The New Way: What It Is

CHAPTER NINE

BEHIND A DOOR MARKED PRIVATE

A quiet revolution is underway, and those carrying it out are not at all like many churchgoers. They're decidedly irreligious. They don't live to make their lives better, whether by doing good deeds or praying harder or volunteering to serve on the missions committee.

They don't do all they can to remove themselves from pain. They live in its midst. And they live there with joy.

They aren't driven by their desire for success, however they define it. They want success, but it isn't their idol, and they're self-aware enough to know when it is.

New Way revolutionaries understand what Old Way conformists do not. They know that falling short of God's glory does not consist merely in their impatience or gossip or jealousy or sexual compromises. With a brokenness that sweeps away all confidence in their resources to make good things happen, they realize that to fall short of God's glory means "that none of us has trusted and treasured God the way we should. We have sought our satisfaction in other things, and treated them as more valuable than God."[44]

They recognize the Old Way for what it is, a philosophy of life and an approach to life that thinks God should make things go smoothly and cares little whether He reveals Himself to anyone.

To See and Savor Jesus

Christians come in two varieties: those who trust Jesus to get them to heaven while trusting Him now to provide a good life of blessings till they get there, and those who trust Jesus to get them to heaven and discover that what they really want even now is to "see and savor Jesus Christ."[45] They're actually willing to lose every blessing and suffer any indignity if it will bring them into deeper relationship with Jesus.

This second variety of Christians—they're the New Way revolutionaries—have been disillusioned by the Old Way approach to life. Unexpected troubles, ones that cannot be traced to a specific failure on their part, have shattered their dreams of how their Christian lives would turn out. Senseless suffering, the kind they have no guarantee of avoiding in the future, has confronted them with a choice between two responses:

1. *Abandon God.* What good is He when life falls apart? It was His job to see to it that it didn't. He failed. He's a grocery store with empty shelves,[46] holding no appeal to a starving man. If He doesn't stock what we need, or if we lack the money to meet His price for what is available, why bother with Him? To someone whose job was just lost, who cries every night from unrelieved loneliness, whose most important dreams have been shattered, a God who declares His benevolence is worth nothing.

2. *Abandon yourself to God,* humbling yourself enough to stop telling Him what He should be doing in your life, committing yourself to whatever He's doing, and believing it is good.[47]

Christians who live the New Way do not pass by the empty grocery store to find a well-stocked convenience center or a fast-food restaurant. They rather enter the barren store, stare for a moment at the empty shelves, then head down an aisle toward the door marked Private, expecting on the other side to find better food than the shelves on this side have ever carried. And they boldly open that door.

Let me introduce you to a few of these New Way revolutionaries:[48]

"This past year, my marriage of thirty-one years was destroyed by my adulterous husband. A few months later, I was diagnosed with breast cancer. Two of my three children have walked away from God. And my financial situation is grim.

"But God"—that's the slogan of these folks: *But God*—"has never been so real to me. I've found a place of complete transparent communication with Him that I wouldn't trade for all the relief the world can offer. I'm fearful of even more shattered dreams, but now I know there's a better way, a better relationship than any flawed one in this world, a higher dream, a more perfect love than I can ask for or imagine, in the person of my Lord Jesus."

A second revolutionary says, "So many dreams have been shattered in the last six years it's hard to count. Yet there's something *new—better*—taking place in my heart."

Listen to a third, this one wanting to join the revolution but not sure how to sign up:

"I have been divorced twice and have struggled terribly for years. I seek the spiritual community you speak of in your books,[49] and I want the intimacy with Jesus you describe. I've been depressed and I'm struggling to get through the pain, disappointment, and loneliness. God has been pretty silent.

"My community wants me to either get on medication, go to therapy, and/or somehow find the hope and peace in God's promises that I don't feel." I suspect the hope and peace her friends long for her to experience belong to the Old Way; they want her to *feel good* more than they want her to *know God*. She confirms my suspicions as she continues:

"They want me to feel better. I've tried most of these things, and I've also tried to find the temporary 'happiness' or at least the relief from pain that the world offers. I DON'T WANT TO DO THIS ANYMORE! I want to live the New Way you speak of, but I don't know how."

Family Only Beyond This Point

I dedicate the rest of this book to the growing number of people whose journey through life has been deeply disillusioning. Perhaps you feel as Oswald Chambers once felt when he said, "If what I've so far experienced is all there is to the Christian life, the whole thing is a sham."

Your life isn't working, and you're losing hope that it ever will. You worry that your faith is weakening, that you're losing confidence in God. Consider the possibility that your waning faith and confidence need to weaken more, to completely disappear; that your faith is in promises God never made; that the god you're losing confidence in is a god who doesn't exist, a god who could not be loving if he gave you something less than himself and expected you to be happy.

That faith needs to end. The god in whom you've placed *that* kind of confidence is not the God of the Bible.

Even when things go well, when wrongheaded faith and misplaced confidence seem validated, you sense an ache in your soul for something more. Your good marriage, good kids, good friends, good health, good church, good job, and good ministry don't satisfy. You receive whatever blessings come your way as mercies from God, and you're grateful. You do enjoy them—and you should. (Anhedonia, the loss of the capacity to enjoy what is pleasurable, is evidence of disorder, not maturity, and certainly not spiritual maturity.) But in the midst of enjoyed pleasure, you cannot suppress the question, "Is this all there is?" You're disillusioned by the emptiness of blessings.

Either way, whether through the emptiness of blessings or the anguish of trials, you're disillusioned. The ache won't go away. Something is missing. But whatever it is, it's hard to find. The ache continues and deepens. Pornographic fantasies or expensive travel or rich desserts or frenetic ministry or hardened cynicism provide more relief than prayer. Or they provide no relief, and you're just miserable.

You want a new way to live, but you're not sure what it is, and you're not sure how to live it.

I invite you to join me as I journey with you through a profoundly disillusioning life, a life filled with opportunities for shallow and temporary pleasure and fraught with unpredictable experiences of deep and lasting sorrow. Walk with me through the grocery store of existence on this planet, and notice that there are only a few stale donuts on the shelves.

But let's keep our heads up and our eyes forward. I can see that door marked Private. Beneath that forbidding word I can make out the fine print: *Family Only Beyond This Point.*

Let's remember that the blood of Jesus has opened a new way, a *living way*—not into a method for making life work, but into the presence of God.[50] Let's not forget that Christ died for sin not to make our existence here pleasant, but rather to bring us to God,[51] and that if we draw near to Him, He will draw near to us.[52]

There's a new way to live. It settles for nothing less than the richest of fare. New Way revolutionaries believe there's living water that actually slakes real thirst. They therefore contentedly pass up the chance to guzzle the sweet syrup that only leaves them more thirsty. The New Way recognizes that the best cut of steak in the butcher's freezer is food fit for dogs compared to one bite of the meat that awaits us behind the door marked Private.

CHAPTER TEN

COMING DIRTY
AND DANCING

I introduced this book by suggesting that each of us, at any given moment, is traveling one of two paths through life: Either we're under pressure to do something right so life will work, or we're living for the Better Hope of knowing Christ. A spirit of arrogance energizes the first way—we think we can do enough right things to deserve good things to happen. Humility characterizes the second—it's all about Christ; He has done what we could never do.

In the second way, the New Way, we come to Him *as we are*, with full self-disclosure. Although we feel no pressure to be better or different, we intensely desire personal holiness more than we want relief from personal pain, and we're broken by how far short we fall. Tears over our self-centeredness and arrogance burn hotter in our eyes than tears over trials.

We come humbly, gratefully, and boldly, trusting that because of the Cross, God will come near, not to destroy us, but to embrace us, change us (sometimes painfully), and use us for His purposes. We keep coming and trusting, even when we see not a shred of evidence that He's warmly moving toward us or that we're meaningfully increasing in holiness. To keep coming toward the Light when all we can see is darkness is a measure of our absolute dependence. We have no other direction to go.

ONE SUPREME PASSION

Whether we travel the Old Way or the New, there's a certain passion that fuels our movement along the path. Consider with me what that passion is. If we explore the depths of our hearts, and if we close our eyes to everything else long enough, we'll discover a core motive, a supreme desire, a compelling urge around which our entire lives revolve. Whatever we want *most* becomes the center of our lives. Like tribesmen dancing around a totem pole, our movements are all oriented around the object of our longing.

Call it our *first thing* passion. It isn't the only passion in our lives, but when a choice must be made, we dance around the thing that attracts us most. We're all loyal worshipers of something. God asks only one question: "Am I your supreme passion or is it something else?"

In the Old Way the passion that rules comes in a thousand varieties, but it consistently aims toward its central value—a *better life now!* Something must come to pass—some emotion must be felt, some increase in our sense of personal worth must be experienced, some thrill must delight us, some blessing must be granted—before life is worth living. As one woman put it to me after I preached on this subject, "Why would I come to God if He didn't give me what I wanted?" She hadn't yet realized that what her heart most deeply wanted was actually God Himself—and that's what He longs to give her.

In the New Way blessings are hoped for, healing is prayed for, happy families are worked for, a sense of wonder and excitement in serving God is humbly expected, and whatever blessings come our way are joyfully celebrated—but nothing, absolutely nothing, is demanded. The passion for a better life, though real and deep and felt without shame, is not at the center. A better life is not the point; it doesn't drive what we do; it isn't the first thing passion in the heart of a New Way revolutionary. We dance around a different God.

New Way revolutionaries are ruled by one supreme passion, the passion for God, to meet Him, know Him, enjoy Him, reveal Him, be like Him. We demand nothing, but we trust God for the best He has to give. Whether in pleasant circumstances or hard, whether a son has just announced he's leaving his wife to live with a man or anticipated bankruptcy is averted by an economic windfall, the passion for God continues to rule.

Satisfaction of that desire is another matter. We may want God, but experiencing God is not a predictable reality. We can arrange conditions favorable to encountering God, but we aren't in charge of whether He shows up.

Followers of the New Way realize they're mere beginners in the School of Divine Delights.

New Way revolutionaries accept their place in kindergarten; they realize they don't know much, but they're hungry to learn. And they're focused. They know what they're after.

Months in kindergarten, sometimes years, yield just a little knowledge of what it means to meet the triune God.

At times they're able to hear something, to see something. Recess is skipped. The chance to hear the Voice of Christ, to catch another glimpse of His beauty, keeps them in their seats. Anticipation sends tingles up their spine. That sound and that glimpse fill them with delight. For just a moment.

Distractions pull them away. The annoying kid in the adjoining desk, perhaps a member of the same small group, shoots a spitball of criticism their way. A headache develops. Life in school gets hard. Like students laboring over arithmetic, they work and work; sometimes they get it, sometimes they don't. And when they do, they move on to more difficult questions, and the cycle continues.

And they stay at their desks. *Another glimpse might come!*

On their first day in first grade, they learn to rest, not on mats brought from home and spread out on the cold classroom floor, but in the Principal's office. Word comes, "The Principal wants to see you." Panic! Heart racing terror! What did I do wrong? The follower of the New Way summons the courage to walk down the hall. He knocks on the door marked Principal's Office; a voice is heard: "Come in." With dripping nose, dirt-smudged face, and torn clothes, the first grader enters.

"You look wonderful! So good to see you." The Principal gathers the student in His arms and begins to sing, overcome with emotion that they—Principal and student—are together. The student looks in the mirror hanging on the wall of the Principal's office. His nose is dry, his face is clean, his clothes are new. He has no idea how it happened.

HOW COULD I LOVE HIM MORE?

New Way revolutionaries encounter God because that's what they value most. And they build their entire hope for meeting God on the Cross, more exactly on the One who died there. It sounds extreme, perhaps unrealistic, but followers of the New Way want to know God more than they want anything else. Delightful children who love them; close friends they can trust; honor for what they do; success in family, job, and ministry; an experience of adventure and wonder as they live their lives—all desires, but all *second thing* passions. No blessing matters more to these people than the Blessing of Encounter.

For followers of the New Way, the Spirit's nudgings become recognizable. His wind fills their sails. They discover their center; they embrace their identity as spiritual, Spirit-ruled people; they cease defining themselves by their reflection in the thousand mirrors of others' expectations.

When they speak, they hear themselves as sheep bleating. Only then can they make out the Shepherd's voice.

Over time, after embarrassingly clumsy attempts, they begin moving to the Spirit's rhythm. They feel His nudge the way a woman feels her dance partner lead. They fix their eyes on Christ just as the dancing woman adoringly looks up to the one she trusts to set the pace. And they find themselves dancing toward a throne filled by the glory of sheer love. The Spirit blows them to their knees. The Son walks up the steps and stands by the throne, on the right-hand side. The Father speaks, "Welcome into My presence. Come like a child and sit on My lap." Joy! Joy! Joy! Peace! Love! Inexpressible joy! An encounter with God! A taste of what's to come. A taste never enjoyed by followers of the Old Way.

Followers of the New Way dance with Christ to the rhythm of the Spirit into the presence of God. But they don't dance especially well. Sometimes they trip over their own feet. Sometimes they lose step with the rhythm and trounce on the Lord's toes.

A good friend was dying of cancer. His time was short. He knew it. His friends knew it. But only he could feel the agony of his physical pain and the anguish of his soul's longing to experience God in the middle of denied healing.

God could cure the cancer. If He wouldn't do that, then why at least didn't He relieve the pain? And if even that blessing were withheld, then surely He would grant a comforting sense of His presence.

It hadn't come. Nothing. The experience simply wasn't there. His first thing passion was God, but he had abandoned himself to a God he couldn't find. His frustrated hopes revealed how strong were his second thing passions. He wanted a better life, just a crumb of blessing.

What possible purpose could such intense agony serve? With loud tears, thinking he was imitating Christ, he'd often begged God for *something*. If not a cure, then relief. If not relief, then an experience of God. Something!

"What must I do? How must I pray? You say You long to bless me! What am I doing wrong? I'll meet Your terms. Just tell me what to do!"

The thought occurred to him: If God exists, He must be the devil. Maybe He doesn't exist. Maybe the whole thing is a fable, cunningly devised by religious leaders so they could enjoy power and make a buck while they're at it.

He slid back and forth between the two ways. Second thing passions sometimes ruled. He tried to figure out what he could do to get some evidence that God was with him. Nothing happened. Nothing worked. He'd done everything he knew to do, including telling God he was grateful for the cross he had to bear. He had tried to mean it. God hadn't budged. The Law of Linearity failed. Its failure brought him back to the New Way, to radical dependence on the Law of Liberty. Here's how it happened.

One day several friends came to pray. The first to pray said, "O Lord, give our brother the peace that only You can give. We ask for healing. We ask for physical comfort and rest. We believe you can perform a miracle that will baffle the doctors. Do it for Your glory! But if that isn't Your perfect will, then we ask for a spirit of thankfulness. Fill our brother with gratitude for Your goodness so that Your peace will rule in his heart. And Lord—"

My friend could endure no more. He broke in on the other's prayer. "God," he interrupted, "right now I hate You. I wish I felt a deep love for You and deep gratitude for what You're doing. But I don't. I'm really upset. And mad. I don't know any way to come to You anymore but honestly. I'm through playing games. I just can't do it. I'm coming as I am. I know it's awful." Nose dripping, face smudged, clothes torn, he entered the Principal's office.

He then stood up from his chair, painfully, with help, and said to his friends, "I'm going to bed now. I'm tired."

A few weeks later, as he lay within minutes of death, he asked his spiritual director, "Will I love Jesus more when I see Him than I do now?"

The older man replied, "Well, yes, I would think so."

Blinking back tears, the dying man, still in pain, said, "I don't see how that's possible."

He had learned to dance. He'd been led by his Partner into the presence of God. His first thing passion was satisfied, perhaps for just that moment. That's the New Way.

If the blood of Christ lacked power, the angel of death would strike us dead for saying we hate God. How dare we speak like that to almighty God. Aaron couldn't even come into God's presence without first bathing and putting on special clothes. And then he had to generate a cloud of smoke to obscure the covering of the ark. That was where God revealed Himself. Aaron wasn't allowed to see God's glory. The sight would have killed him.

And now my friend tells God that he hates Him—and God pours love into his heart. The New Way has been opened into God's presence by the blood of Christ. Without that, we do well to keep our distance.

I remember, as a nine-year-old boy, telling Mother that I hated her. She had properly refused to let me play till my homework was done. I didn't like her rules. So I expressed myself.

A whack was warranted. Instead, she looked at me. I will never forget her eyes. They were filled with deep hurt and profound tenderness. She began to cry. In that instant I saw beyond my selfishness to my mother's heart. I began to sob. "Mother, I don't hate you," I cried. "I love you. I really do! I'm so glad you're my mom!" At that moment, I don't see how I could have loved her more.

New Way revolutionaries believe in radical grace. They know there's no other way to become holy than first by being declared holy, then by wanting to be holy, and eventually by actually becoming holy.

So they come as they are—insolent, filthy, whimpering, demanding—but they come. How else can they come? That's who they know themselves to be. But they come humbly. They know they're not attractive. They want God—He is their supreme desire, their first thing passion; they depend on grace—it's their only hope. It's our only hope. It's enough. So we come.

And God draws near—in His timing, never in automatic response to our request. But He comes. The Spirit sends us to the Father's office. The Son escorts us there. As we enter, we realize that our nose is dripping, our face is dirty, and our clothes are torn. We don't yet see that Christ has already cleaned us up on the way. The Father looks at us, beaming with delight as if we were the most beautiful children in the universe.

Then we realize: We're as beautiful to the Father as Christ is because we're *in Him!* The Father sings. And we collapse with gratitude at His feet. Filled with joy. The Son touches us on the shoulder. We stand.

How could I love Him more?

FOR ONLY ONE THING

The Old Way misses out on the chief blessing of seeing God. It requires that we pretend. We wipe our own noses, wash our faces, and sew the rip in our clothes—we make ourselves presentable. Then we say to God, "Look what I've done. I got it right. My nose is clean. Now give me the blessings I want."

Another friend is making the shift from the Old Way to the New. He tried to make life work, but the Law of Linearity failed. Dreams that mattered deeply to him lay shattered. He wrote these words in his journal and has given me permission to share them with you:

> I tend to view life as prescriptive. I want to believe, I *desperately* want to believe, that if I "do the right things," all will be well. Whether in parenting, work, marriage, whatever—I hope for a cause-effect relationship in life.
>
> I see it especially during this past year. In my worst nightmares, I never expected that what has happened would ever happen in my family. So many voices have told me to see my failure as a father, as a husband, as a Christian, to *explain* what's happened by what I didn't do right. If I had just done THIS, then THAT would never have happened.
>
> I've come to realize that I made a deal with God. I've arrogantly come to Him, not to know Him, but to parade my

efforts. "God, I read the books. I followed the principles. I did family devotions, I told my kids I loved them, I went to their games, their school plays, and their recitals!"

And then I presented my checklist to God and said, "I did all this. NOW PRODUCE!" My fist was clenched in His face. I never saw it. I thought I was praying for blessings.

By many measures, I've done really well. And that has created expectations—great kids, beautiful grandkids, high school celebrations like everyone else. The list goes on. Reality rarely meets my expectations.

I did a lot of things right, but my life isn't working very well. It's so confusing. All I know to do now is to come to God, to plead with Him to let me know Him better. "God, I want to draw near to You. Whether You bless my life as I want or not, I ask for only one thing: Please, God, draw near to me."

We can't make life work—but the pressure's off. Disillusionment has changed us. We no longer want life to work as much as we want *Him*.

A way has been opened, the New Way of the Spirit, for us to come to Him—and dance.

CHAPTER ELEVEN

REAPING WHAT
WE SOW

Let me share two lessons I'm learning while I continue my lengthy stay in kindergarten. With these two lessons, my diet may be changing from milk to meat. I might be about ready to enter grade school.

The first is this:

The Spirit of Christ is always nudging us toward the New Way if we're not on it and always nudging us farther along if we are. In every circumstance, at every moment, He's stirring our affection for God until He makes it the strongest passion in our hearts.

When an ex-husband poisons the mind of a teenage son against his mother, she has every right to cry, "Foul!" She's the one who changed every diaper, worked two jobs because he wouldn't provide support, carted her boy to every game and stayed when she could to cheer him on, and spent countless evenings drilling him on spelling and math to get him ready for the next day in school.

She must not be faulted for hurting terribly. What's happened is unfair and it hurts, perhaps even more than the divorce. The second shoe dropping usually feels worse than the first. Her desire to see her relationship with her son restored deserves support. *Unless it rises to the level of a first-place passion.*

If that happens, and it almost always will, she'll find herself living the Old

Way. She may not realize it, but she'll be following a spirit other than God's. God's Spirit will be quenched. There will be no peace, no rest, until the Better Life she demands is given. And then it will be the peace and rest of the world.

When something terrible goes wrong in our lives, the first question we typically ask is, "What should I do?"

"To accomplish what?" the Spirit wonders.

"Why, to win back my son's affection, of course. I've never felt such pain. I must know what I can do to make it happen."

Counselors and friends who compassionately offer ideas for reaching that objective are working at cross-purposes with God. Spiritual directors are more on track when they encourage quiet listening for whatever the Spirit may be saying. They can hear Him whispering to the distraught mother. They want her to hear Him too.

"I know your pain. The Son felt it when His own people turned against Him. But He found His gladness in staying close to the Father. Let Me direct you into His presence. He is wonderful, and He is enough to free you to love your son."

Perhaps God's Word will penetrate the mother's heart so that she hears Him say, "You will be my treasured possession."[53] He offers us relationship in suffering so that we learn to value intimacy over blessing.

The Spirit is constantly nudging us toward the New Way and away from the Old, toward the Better Hope and away from demanding the Better Life. This first lesson I'm learning includes a radical and wonderful truth: *Pursuing my deepest pleasure and moving in rhythm with the Spirit both take me in the same direction—toward Christ!* Self-interest and worship go together if worship comes first.

MOVING TO THE RIGHT

Picture yourself walking into a large, unfamiliar shopping mall. The first thing you look for is a directory. Your eyes scan the boxes and numbers until you see a red dot with the words printed next to it: *You Are Here.*

Where is this mother? She's furious at her ex-husband, alone in her responsibilities, and devastated by her son's rejection. Now what direction will she move? She asks herself, "What do I do?"

To the left of her, there's a large department store named The Better Life. The directory indicates that this store carries "restored relationships." Her heart leaps. She looks closely at the map and memorizes the directions.

Before she sets off for the department store, for reasons she can't explain, she looks again at the directory. Her eyes drift to the right. There, tucked away in a far corner, is a little shop called The Better Hope. It advertises "the richest of fare for your soul." For some reason, she gives in to a deep stirring and moves toward The Better Hope.

The image can be sketched like this.

First the Old Way:

Then the New Way:

But there's more to the New Way than coming to God. The mother must still deal with her son:

By moving to the right, as this mother understands the distinction between first-place and second-place passions, as she realizes that her deepest desires are to know and glorify and enjoy Jesus Christ, she will hear the Spirit guide her to speak with her son in ways that reflect Christ.

The power struggle would be over. Her demand that her son love her, disguised as concern for her son, would dissolve. *She would truly love her son.*

And he would be confronted with his freedom. Released from a determination to resist control, he would more easily access the longings of his heart buried beneath his confusion and anger. The Spirit could move more deeply into his soul to do significant work.

The mother would rest. Pressure to figure out what to do would yield to freedom, the freedom to wisely express her Spirit-ruled heart to her son. She would know what to do without an expert's telling her.[54] She would still have no idea how to arrange for the Better Life of having a changed son, though she continues to long and pray for that blessing. But that would no longer be her goal. The Spirit would release her to glorify God by revealing her already changed heart in the presence of her son.

That release might take many forms, some unexpected and some, in Old Way thinking, unwise. Perhaps a rebuke: "Son, your attitude is wrong. Your spirit is ungrateful." She might open her soul to say, "I hurt deeply over the way you're treating me." I could envision truth telling that would be sinful if delivered in a wrong spirit, but not if spoken in the Spirit's wisdom and love: "Your father has misled you. I think it's time you heard more of the story behind our divorce."

The key doesn't lie in her selection of words. It lies in the energy from which they're spoken. Is she eager to get through to her son or eager to represent and please God? Is she trying to make something happen or trying to present what is in her as a gift of love, perhaps tough love, to her son?

If she's following the Spirit into the presence of God, if she hears the Principal's welcome and feels His embrace before she speaks to her son, none of her words will aim toward control, manipulation, pressure, or revenge. Each one will be carried by a spirit of forgiveness, mercy, unthreatened rest, and grace.

OUR COLD HEARTS WARMED

The Spirit always leads God's children in a good direction—first toward God in worship, then toward others in Christlike love.

That's the first lesson. The second is this:

My passion to know Christ often seems weaker than my desire for blessings. And unless this changes, I will not consistently live the New Way. I must therefore give disciplined thought to how my desire for Christ can be nourished.

I tend toward superficial living. If life presents only a few bumps, especially if they're small, I don't particularly care whether I know Christ well or not. I figure He's doing His job of blessing me and I'm doing my job of living responsibly. Rather than a thirsty deer panting after water, I'm more like a hibernating bear with paws resting on my full stomach. Would the prodigal son ever have returned had his money not run out? As someone said, repentance begins in the belly.

Blessings can be dangerous. In the days of Amos, Israel enjoyed prosperity. Because life was moving along rather nicely, they assumed that when God came, it would be to congratulate them and to judge their pagan neighbors. They were wrong.

But that's often the way we think. We assume church growth and strong book sales are proof of God's blessing. They may be only the result of good marketing and fleshly appeal.

My life is right now richly blessed. There are trials, but I have enough sources of comfort to experience some level of happiness without knowing God better than I do. I don't always see the need to stir up my first-place passions when second-place passions are pretty well satisfied.

And when they're denied satisfaction, it's easy either to react with discouragement or to strengthen my resolve to solve whatever problem has arisen. Both reactions quench the Spirit. They lead me in the Old Way.

In the middle of good times or bad, we sometimes hear God's invitation to know Him, and we respond with a yawn. We lift our hands and sing, "O Lord, You're beautiful; Your face is all I seek," while our hearts demand, "Now keep the blessings coming and give me back the ones I've lost."

What has happened to our Spirit-implanted appetite for God? It's as if we're still standing at the foot of Mount Sinai, listening to commandments that we want to obey only to keep ourselves safe from a thundering God. Our hearts remain cold, unmoved, and indifferent. The prospect of knowing God is no great thrill.

The Puritan Thomas Chalmers once spoke of the "expulsive power of a new affection." We might just as easily speak of the smothering power of our old affections. Our desire for the Better Life keeps our flame of longing for the Better Hope from becoming a bonfire.

But God has moved us from Mount Sinai and placed us before Mount Zion. Our cold hearts have been warmed. Sinai's law—all of it, every expression of God's holiness—has been stamped into the center of our being. Now when God commands, we hear an invitation.

"Love your wife!"

You mean I get to do that? How wonderful! Thank You! Thank You!

We're children whose taste buds have been altered. Now carrots taste like cookies. That's the truth. It's the heart of New Covenant theology, and New Covenant theology is the heart of New Way living.

JOY GUARANTEED

Why then don't I feel it? Why do cookies still taste like cookies and carrots like carrots? I prefer cookies. I want a sweet life now. So I choose the Old Way.

That choice has consequences. Earlier I noted the passage in Hebrews that said the former regulation has been set aside.[55] From that statement, I suggested that the Old Way formula of linearity has been abolished. No longer can we work hard to get it right and claim a guarantee that life therefore will work. The Judaizers were dead wrong. The Law of Linearity, which they depended on, is not in effect.

But another linear relationship still holds. And when we see what it is, we'll be deeply interested in nourishing the appetite that will sustain us in New Way living.

Listen to the apostle Paul: "The one who sows to please his sinful nature, from that nature will reap destruction; the one who sows to please the Spirit, from the Spirit will reap eternal life."[56]

That linearity is still in effect. We reap what we sow.

But notice it isn't the linearity assumed by the Old Way. The promise of a cause-effect relationship between *getting it right* and *a life that works* is gone. God has put into effect a new linear arrangement:

If we choose the Old Way, we'll end up miserable. We may feel quite good for a long time, but every follower of the Old Way will end up feeling miserable.

GUARANTEED!

If we choose the New Way, we'll experience joy, perhaps after a long season of suffering and searching. But we'll find ourselves and be full, alive, happy.

GUARANTEED!

Choosing the New Way matters. Once you're saved, there's no more important choice.

And we'll not be able to sustain that choice unless our passion for God becomes stronger than our passion for everything else, including a restored relationship with a rejecting child.

Let me state in a different way those two lessons I'm learning about New Way living.

First, the Spirit is always nudging me to follow His lead, and it's always toward knowing Christ better. That's His word to me when life goes sour and when it goes well. That's always what He says: Come as you are to find God.

Second, I will not follow Him unless I somehow cooperate with His work in deepening my desire for Christ. As long as I want blessings more, I will end up on the Old Way.

My conclusion is also twofold:

First, if I don't learn to hear what the Spirit is saying, I'll walk the Old Way, and the results will be disastrous. *B* follows *A.* That's where linearity still holds.

Second, if I do learn to hear more clearly the Spirit's voice, both in leading me in the New Way and in strengthening my first-place passion for Christ, I'll experience deep joy and rich meaning in the middle of any circumstance. My soul will be in line with the Immanuel Agenda. God will be our God, and we will be His people. Guaranteed!

CHAPTER TWELVE

THE IMMANUEL AGENDA

John, son of Zebedee, wrote three books that found their way into Scripture. The first, John's gospel, was written to help us believe in Jesus.

After reflecting on all the incredible things Jesus did, and realizing he had included only a few, John put it this way: "These are written that you may believe that Jesus is the Christ, the Son of God, and that by believing you may have life in his name."[57]

In Revelation, his last book, John unveils the glory of Jesus. These twenty-two chapters help us keep believing in Jesus when the evidence makes it difficult. Even John the Baptist once wondered if he ought to look for another messiah to follow. There are times, sometimes long seasons, when life simply doesn't work very well, and no matter how hard we search, Jesus seems to have disappeared. Maybe He was never there.

"He is here," John declares,[58] "and He has not disappeared. God has let me see all that's happening from heaven's point of view. It's breathtaking. The Lamb is roaring His way through history to complete the Immanuel Agenda.

"I saw the Holy City, the New Jerusalem, coming down from heaven. It's coming down to us, to you and me. And as I watched, I heard a loud voice declare: 'Now the dwelling of God is with men, and He will live with them. They will be His people, and God Himself will be with them and be their God.'"

I hear John saying, "That's why God sent Jesus. It's the Immanuel Agenda: *God will be with us!* When that happens, when the Better Hope of drawing near to God is fully realized, we'll want nothing more. And that's when the Better Life will be ours as well. No more shattered dreams. Blessings beyond our wildest imagination. No reason to cry, ever, not even to sigh. And all of that with Jesus at the center.

"Stay the course, weary pilgrims. Don't lose heart. The Immanuel Agenda is about to be completed."

We listen to John and we say:

- *But John, my husband neglects me. I'm not sure I can remain in this marriage much longer.*
- *But John, I live with unbearable pain every day. Only the blessings of an improved life now can take it away.*
- *But John, that's good for then. But for now I'm alone. I can't pay my bills. I have no real fellowship at church. I don't like my job. I need some help now.*

I hear John reply:

"My little children, if you could see the Better Hope ahead, you would not require the Better Life now. He who was seated on the throne said—with my own ears I heard Him—'I am making everything new.' Then He looked straight at me and told me: 'Write this down, for these words are trustworthy and true. My people need to hear them.' I've written Revelation so you would never, no matter how difficult your life may become, lose confidence in Jesus."[59]

Paul said much the same thing to people who thought the journey to heaven should include a few more blessings. "If only for this life we have hope in Christ, we are to be pitied more than all men."[60]

In other words, if you've signed on to Christianity in order to get a better life now, you've made a serious mistake. There is joy now, but every bit of it is rooted in future hope. Eliminate that, and Hugh Hefner will be tough to resist.

THE PRECIOUS THINGS

John's middle book, really three short letters, was written to help us draw near to Jesus now, when life isn't what we want it to be, and to taste the deep joys of communion with God until we sit down in heaven for the full meal.

Listen to the great Puritan John Owen talk about John's first epistle:

> Christians in those days were poor and despised. Christian leaders were treated as the filth of the world. So to invite people to become Christians, to join in their fellowship and to enjoy the precious things they enjoyed, seemed to be the height of foolishness. "What good thing will we get if we join up with those Christians? Are they inviting us to share in their troubles? Do they want us to be persecuted, reviled and scorned and to suffer all kinds of evils?"
>
> It is with these objections in mind that John writes. Notwithstanding all the disadvantages their fellowship lay under from a worldly point of view, yet in truth it was, and they would soon find it to be, very desirable. "For truly," says John, "our fellowship is with his Son Jesus Christ."[61]

Owen understood the apostle John to say that the appeal of Christianity doesn't lie in a better life now. "What good thing will we get if we join up with these Christians?" Those who are after fewer troubles in life might do better following another messiah.

But there *is* something available now that's "very desirable." John invites us not to a life that gets better, but to the "precious things" of fellowship with God. His epistle calls us to draw near to God, to come to Christ, not for the Better Life now, but for the Better Hope of a soul-satisfying relationship with the Trinity now, until the Best Life is ours to forever enjoy, a future that will mean God with us in full measure, Jesus before us in plain sight, and the Spirit competing with no other desire as He points us to Jesus.

To John, the "disadvantages" of following Jesus, which included the *absence* of legitimately desired blessings and no guarantee that they would be given till heaven, were nothing in comparison with the "precious things they enjoyed," the Better Hope of Intimacy with the Trinity.

If we could taste that intimacy, if we knew what it is to draw near to God and to feel Him draw near to us, if we realized how we're the ones to whom the Father and Son through the Spirit reveal themselves and in whom they make their home, we would keep the Better Life of Blessings in its place as something merely desired, never demanded, never desired as a first thing passion.

We would know that we've experienced so little of an actual encounter with Jesus because modern Christianity has devoted itself to providing a better life for its followers. We would know that because we've found no real joy in *fellowship* with God, we've lived for the *advantages* of being related to God, and we've concluded that those advantages—less suffering, more blessings, some form of a better life now—are our due.

We would know that we've sold out to linearity, that we've seen the spiritual journey variously as a wild adventure, as a fulfilling experience of impact on others and meaning for ourselves, or as a blank check on which we can write whatever good blessing we desire, sign with power of attorney for Jesus, then cash in at the drive-up window of prayer. The only requirement is obedience, not perfect, but some consistent adherence to biblical principles.

We would know that blessings have become our most precious things: Do *this* and that *will* happen, guaranteed; it's the promise of God. We would know that we've sold out to linearity, and that the result—and this *is* linear—has been the widespread failure of Christians to cherish the opportunity to come near to God. We come for blessings; He invites us to come for fellowship, for the Immanuel Agenda.

We come and we say,

"God, my marriage is so full of tension."

"God, the consequences of my divorce are so much worse, and
    lingering, than I ever anticipated."

"God, living alone in this retirement home is so hard. I cannot
    resist feeling sorry for myself."

"God, I'm so afraid of the medical report. *Please* don't let me have
    cancer."

"God, my sexual passion for lesbian relations is relentless. I know
    it's wrong, but I can't control myself."

"God, I never knew I could feel such pain. My fourteen-year-old
    daughter is pregnant."

Into each of these lives, and into ours, the wind of the Spirit is blowing. But it isn't moving our ship toward the smooth seas of a more pleasant life. It's rather carrying us into the eye of the storm, into the presence of God. And we must adjust our sails accordingly. If we aim for calm waters, we go alone. We resist the wind of the Spirit.

The Agenda Is on Track

The apostle John invites us into the enjoyment of precious things, not into the satisfaction and pleasures of improved circumstances, closer relationships, and happier feelings, but into the inexpressible joy of drawing near to God.

Listen to him speak about it:

"We have heard! We have seen! Our hands have touched! *Life has appeared!* And we proclaim it to you. We can now have fellowship with God. Our fellowship is with the Eternal Father of Endless Love and with His Magnificent Son, the One who died for us, Jesus Christ. We can draw near to God. I know the joy of coming into His presence. I want you to know that joy as well. Then my joy will be complete."[62]

In his gospel John tells us, "You can trust Christ. He is who He says He is. Life is knowing Him."

In the unveiling (our book of Revelation) he says, "You'll stay the course through any storm if you know what's coming. And right now, when everything goes against you, the Lamb of the Cross is the Lion of Heaven moving toward His sure purpose. And it's a *good* one. Hang on!"

In his epistles, John issues an invitation: "In the middle of a difficult life, draw near to Jesus. It's the source of your deepest joy."

In everything he wrote, John is presenting the Immanuel Agenda. From the beginning of time, God has determined to be with us. *He will be our God,* as we value no treasure more than knowing Him, and *we will be His people,* gladly clinging to Him in worship and absolute dependence no matter what happens in this life.

The agenda is on track. God is with us now. He's here. Not the way He'll be here when the Holy City comes down, but He's here to be enjoyed. Our highest calling, our deepest joy, is to celebrate His availability by drawing near to Him, not to use Him to make our lives better, but to enjoy Him for who He is.

It's a different understanding of the spiritual journey. John invites his readers to walk a new path, to live a new way. We're asked to experience without complaint the disadvantages of a difficult life in order to more deeply experience the "precious thing" of communion with God.

The Better Life of Blessings now to those who get it right? No! The

Better Hope of Communion now, with the Trinity, to those who value it most—*that's* the Christian life!

The pressure's off. We've been released from the obligation to do what we should to get what we want. There's a new way to live, and it lines up with the Immanuel Agenda.

CHAPTER THIRTEEN

THE BARN DOOR'S OPEN

Someone in the congregation came to me after I preached and said, "Am I hearing you right? Surely you aren't saying that we come to God only to know Him. Unless He gives me the blessings I need to be happy, I can't see why I'd come to Him at all. Your teaching makes me want to not even bother with God."

I mentioned this woman in an earlier chapter. I think she's related (as all of us are) to a man who once called out to Jesus while He was teaching.

RICH TOWARD GOD

Listen to Luke tell the story.

"Someone in the crowd said to him, 'Teacher, tell my brother to divide the inheritance with me.'"

He wanted a better life of more money. Likely it was his due. Fairness was probably on his side. Notice the Lord doesn't even enter the "who's right" debate, something I often do when I listen to one spouse tell me how wrong the other one is.

"Jesus replied, 'Man, who appointed me a judge or an arbiter between you?'"

Well, I thought Christ *was* the judge. Who could be more qualified?

Jesus would know the heart of both brothers, and He would know what was right. Apparently, He had a different agenda than making this life fair.

"Then he said to them [to the whole crowd, leaving the bitter man still indignant over his plight], 'Watch out! Be on your guard against all kinds of greed; a man's life does not consist in the abundance of his possessions.'"

He sidestepped the fairness issue completely. It wasn't His concern. It would be difficult to imagine a clearer warning against living the Old Way: *Don't make it your goal to get out of life what you want.* He called it greed. It's the foundation of Old Way living. To drive home His point, He did what He often did. He offered a story.

"And he told them this parable: 'The ground of a certain rich man produced a good crop.'"

Some people are blessed. I know godly men and women who are rich. I know godly men and women with effective, far-reaching, and much-honored ministries. Blessings are good. We're to enjoy them and use them well. But blessings are dangerous.

"'He thought to himself, "What shall I do? I have no place to store my crops."'" He doesn't even mention God. All that's on his mind is to enjoy his good fortune and to keep it coming. When your goal is a better life, you're completely selfish.

"'Then he said, "This is what I'll do. I will tear down my barns and build bigger ones, and there I will store all my grain and my goods. And I'll say to myself, 'You have plenty of good things laid up for many years. Take life easy; eat, drink, and be merry!'"'"

He had worked hard, and it paid off. *A* led to *B*. And he liked it. The Old Way is deeply satisfying—not, however, in the deepest depths and not for long.

"'But God said to him, "You fool!"'" Today, we'd expect congratulations. "Way to go" seems more appropriate. We've worked hard, we've been diligent in wealth management, and now we can enjoy the Better Life of Blessings. We honor people, including ourselves, whose priority is achievement and who have succeeded. God called this one a fool, and said, "'This very night your life will be demanded from you. Then who will get what you have prepared for yourself.' This is how it will be," Jesus promised, "with anyone who stores up things for himself but is not rich toward God."[63]

Then Jesus went on to warn us about worrying over our lives down here, what we will eat, how our bodies are doing, whether we'll be able to provide for ourselves what we need. He finished this thought by telling us that our hearts belong to what we treasure most.[64]

Either we live to store up things for ourselves, or we live to become rich toward God. We cannot do both. No one can live the Old Way and the New Way at the same time. This man hoarded possessions. We chase after fulfillment, importance, a community to belong to, security in relationships, emotional health, a good reputation, honor and appreciation, a self-protected soul, happy families—the list is endless. And so many items on it don't seem selfish. They're blessings God wants us to have. But never as our chief treasure.

When blessings, even noble ones, become our chief treasure, we hoard them. We may seem generous and giving, but we never sacrifice what matters most. Christians who store treasures other than God in the barn of their souls do not worship God. They can't. Their core worship is directed elsewhere. Living the Old Way turns us into selfish fools, no matter how we may appear to others. That's the point of the parable.

I hear Jesus telling us:

"Don't live the Old Way. If you value the blessings of life over communion with God, you'll end up miserable. Guaranteed! But if you live the New Way, if you draw near to God, not to exploit His power but to enjoy fellowship with Him, then He'll supply everything you need to participate in furthering the Immanuel Agenda. Guaranteed! And you'll know My joy, the joy I experience in the fellowship of the Trinity."

We've substituted the Rich Farmer's Agenda for the Immanuel Agenda.

It's more consistent with our natural point of view: If we work hard, keep our nose clean, and live a decent life, enough things will go our way to keep us feeling pretty good.

Jonathan Edwards once said that the spiritual journey requires an "intense concentration on God's point of view." Such concentration, he said, will "cause an intense narrowing of all our interests on earth, and an immense broadening of our interests in heaven."[65]

When we shift to the New Way, when we discard the Rich Farmer's Agenda for the Immanuel Agenda, we value encounter with God over barns full of blessings. Our earthly interests narrow.

It isn't that we *care less* about things down here—we still fervently desire close community, good children, and negative biopsies—it's that we begin to *care more* about something else. Our greatest treasure, our chief blessing, our supreme passion, becomes God Himself. His glory assumes center stage. Communion with Him becomes our deepest joy.

DRAWING NEAR

We must be clear: Following the Rich Farmer's Agenda is the Old Way. The New Way looks at life from God's point of view and experiences an "immense broadening of our interests in heaven." New Way revolutionaries fall in line gladly with the Immanuel Agenda. They understand what the old spiritual directors meant by *attending* to God (where He is going), *abandoning* ourselves to God (following wherever He leads), and *union* with God (enjoying Him on the journey).

We must realize what God is doing whenever He withholds blessings we legitimately desire: He is pursuing the Immanuel Agenda. *He will be with a people who value Him above every other blessing.* He will create that people at the cost of His Son's death and at the cost of being hurt every day by children who really don't want Him except to use Him. He is allowing good dreams to shatter to arouse the better dream of knowing Him.[66]

If we're to resist the Rich Farmer's Agenda and climb on board with the Immanuel Agenda, one article of faith above all others is required. It's the article of faith most missing in contemporary Christianity. It is this:

Experiencing God is in itself a source of greater pleasure than experiencing anything else.

A father can leave no richer legacy to his son than to live in such a way that his son can say, "Dad desired God more than anything." Are we living in such a way that the speaker at our funeral will say, "This follower of Jesus wanted God more than every other blessing"?

Recently a friend of many years called to ask, in case her next round of cancer treatment fails, if I would speak at her funeral. She wrote just yesterday to say she's getting her wigs out of storage. "Come visit," she invited Rachael and me, "if you don't mind hanging out with a bald sick lady."

If I do speak at her funeral, I may mention her sense of humor. It's wonderful. But that won't be my focus. Some unbelievers die bravely, with a quip on their lips.

Her letter ended with these words, "Isn't God wonderful? I love Him so much!!!"

Why does she love Him? Because she knows the treatment will work? Because God will keep her from losing her hair? Because she is guaranteed minimum pain? No! Those are the blessings of a better life that we desire and pray for. But there's nothing any of us can do, including praying fervently, to ensure they come; the Law of Linearity is no longer in effect. But still we pray, primarily to take our place as dependent little children. And He may grant our requests. But our first thing passion is directed elsewhere.

In the midst of a difficult life, one made more difficult by her limited opportunities to minister and by the fact that she lives alone as a divorced woman, she's drawing near to God. And He's drawing near to her. *That's* what I'll talk about at her funeral.

I can hear the apostle John, as he looks down from heaven, say to my friend, "Now my joy is complete. You're enjoying communion with God above all other joys. You know it's your greatest blessing. Oh, daughter, if that communion is so sweet there, can you imagine what it is up here?"

I can hear James chime in, "Chemotherapy must be awful. It's a terrible trial. But you're welcoming it as an opportunity to draw near to God, to become like Jesus. You're living the New Way, you're coming to God. He's coming nearer to you. Imagine when the Immanuel Agenda is complete."

Paul must speak: "When we intensely concentrate on God's point of view, and only if we do so, then even things as awful as loneliness and economic struggles and returning cancer can be seen as light and momentary afflictions that are achieving for us an eternal glory that far outweighs them all. Fight the good fight, as I did."

Of course Peter can't resist joining the conversation with his reliable wisdom: "Dear sister, though you haven't seen Him, you love Him. What a wonderful miracle of His gracious Holy Spirit. Even though you don't see Him now with your physical eyes, you believe in Him and are filled with an inexpressible joy, for you're receiving what you most want—you're being saved from distance from God into nearness to Him. You're living the New Way of the Spirit. *The pressure's off!* Hallelujah! Wait till you see what's coming! It's *Him!*"

New Way revolutionaries cling to their hope that they're indeed receiving the salvation of their souls, even as they walk through the door marked Oncology Department. They know they're redeemed *from* the futile search for soul pleasure in anything or anyone but God. Their barns may be full of blessings or they may be empty; either way, the barn door is open and their hearts are fixed elsewhere. They're redeemed *to* enjoy God.

As followers of Jesus, they can drink living water that satisfies their thirst and eat rich food that fills their souls with delight. No matter how life is treating them, no matter how discouraged, angry, or empty they may feel, no matter how badly they've failed, they can walk boldly into the Holiest Place. They actually encounter God. They meet the Principal, and He hugs them.

That is God's purpose in everything He does. It has been His purpose since Creation—and it will be His purpose until it's fully realized. It's the Immanuel Agenda.

The pressure's off.

We can abandon the Rich Farmer's Agenda. There's a new way to live.

It's all about God and His glory and our satisfaction in Him.

That's been His plan since Eden.

CHAPTER FOURTEEN

STORY OF GOD

God has made an arrangement with us. He didn't invite our input. We don't always like the terms. So we pretend they're different. If we could see the whole picture, we'd pretend nothing. We'd fall to our knees in worship.

One of Scotland's greatest but unknown preachers, Arthur J. Gossip, lost his wife suddenly. His first sermon after her death was entitled *But When Life Tumbles In, What Then?"*

In that sermon, he said, "You people in the sunshine may believe the faith, but we in the shadows *must* believe it. We have nothing else."[67]

I read those words and I'm moved. But I also ask, exactly what is it that we must believe when life tumbles in? For many, it's Old Way thinking: If we do our part, if we pray and live the way Jesus wants, then God will improve our lives. He'll turn bad things into good. We'll be safe from the shoe dropping, or at least from another one falling to the floor.

THERE IS NO OTHER STREAM

In *The Silver Chair,* the fourth book in C. S. Lewis's *The Chronicles of Narnia,* a girl named Jill is lost in a scary forest. She cries and cries and develops a terrible thirst. As she looks for water, she happens upon a stream and eagerly runs toward it. But then she notices a Lion is lying beside it.

She stops in her tracks. The Lion, knowing she is thirsty, invites her to come and drink.

"May I—could I—would you mind going away while I do?" said Jill.

The Lion answered this only by a look and a very low growl. And as Jill gazed at its motionless bulk, she realized that she might as well have asked the whole mountain to move aside for her convenience.

The delicious rippling noise of the stream was driving her nearly frantic.

"Will you promise not to—do anything to me, if I do come?" said Jill.

"I make no promise," said the Lion.

Jill was so thirsty now that, without noticing it, she had come a step nearer.

"*Do* you eat girls?" she said.

"I have swallowed up girls and boys, women and men, kings and emperors, cities and realms," said the Lion. It didn't say this as if it were boasting, nor as if it were sorry, nor as if it were angry. It just said it.

"I daren't come and drink," said Jill.

"Then you will die of thirst," said the Lion.

"Oh dear!" said Jill, coming another step nearer. "I suppose I must go and look for another stream then."

"There is no other stream," said the Lion.[68]

Lewis puts these words in the mouth of Aslan, the Christ figure, as he talks to a scared little girl: "I make no promise." Concerning what? The Lion makes no promise that Jill will not suffer. He will not promise her the Better Life.

But he does invite her to drink the water she needs.

What do we need? We've often answered, this particular set of blessings, safety from more things going wrong. God says, fellowship with Me, safety to come into My presence.

We've changed the terms of the agreement. We've wanted the Better Life *and* the Better Hope, the blessings of life *and* fellowship with God—both, now. If we had to choose one, we might be tempted to choose the blessings. "God, just get my son off drugs. I'll do whatever You say."

When the Lion won't move and when He refuses to guarantee safe passage to the stream of living water, we've looked for another stream and figured out how to get there. There is no other, but we've pretended there is.

A man diagnosed with inoperable cancer listened to his friend's reassurance: "Everything will be okay. I just put your situation on the Internet. Before this week is out, more than twenty thousand people will be praying for you." Drawing close to God is not the chief end; getting healthy is. And lots of prayer is the means; a few prayers won't do.

That's Old Way linearity.

The New Way begins with a different promise: Water is available, and you may drink it, but life may be tough as you draw near. The focus of the New Way, however, is not on the trials; it's on the availability of cool water and rich food.

"Whoever believes in me...streams of living water will flow from within him."[69]

That's New Way linearity: Believe and water flows.

"Come, all you who are thirsty, come to the waters.... Eat what is good, and your soul will delight in the richest of fare."[70]

More New Way linearity. It's a promise! Come along the path God has opened through Christ into His presence—and you'll be satisfied!

"Give ear and come to me; hear me, that your soul may live. I will make an everlasting covenant with you."[71]

That's the arrangement. It's a good one. If we hear what He offers, we'll not want to change a thing.

It's Monday morning. Rachael and I spent Sunday evening in the emergency room. About six o'clock, a familiar pain hit. Another kidney stone. My first response was, "I have so much to do. Life was finally going pretty well. The timing is awful. God, couldn't You have kept this from happening? Have I not been praying enough? Or maybe I've been griping too much about my insanely full plate."

The natural response to trial is to travel the Old Way, to tame the Lion (as if we could) and ask Him to lead us to the Pool of Siloam, where life gets better. If I thought twenty thousand prayers would make a difference, I'd spread my plight across the Internet.

Then I hear the Lion say, "I make no promise about your pain. Your stone may pass, it may not. Come to Me and drink."

The view from an emergency room bed does not inspire faith. It energizes demand. "God, do something. That poor baby is screaming. The old woman next to me behind the curtain feels terrible. And I'm not doing so hot myself. Where are You? What do I have to do to get You to do something?"

As I lay there last night for several hours, I asked what I could count on God to do. Exactly what had He promised? He said He has put in force an everlasting covenant, an arrangement that, by His choice, binds Him to do what He promised. But what's the promise? What's the arrangement? What is it that I'm to believe when a shadow falls on my life?

THE BIG PICTURE

Because we modern Christians are so conditioned to assume the old arrangement is still in force, that if we get it right life will work, we may need to take a few steps back, a few big steps, and see the big picture. When tragedy strikes, we so easily say, "I wonder what God is teaching me through this trial." Listen beneath that sentence to its motivation and you might hear something like this: "If I learn my lesson, I'll be able to get it right next time so more trials won't come." The Old Way is instinctual.

We assume that's the arrangement: We get it right and God blesses. But God has a very different arrangement with us, and it will last till heaven.

Let me outline the Story of God, the way God has moved through history guided by the Immanuel Agenda to reach the present arrangement, what the Bible calls the New Covenant.[72]

It's a seven-chapter story that begins a long time ago.

Chapter One: When There Was Only God

Everything but God is created. Our small minds can only grasp that, during infinity past, only God existed. Before He created anything, there was only God. Nothing else. No one else.

I envision a Divine Party. The Eternal Community was having a good time. Perfect joy. Perfect peace. Perfect persons in perfect relationship. God enjoys being God. Always has and always will.

But it's His nature to share. So He created angels.

Chapter Two: God and Angels

God created angelic beings and immediately put them in their place. It was a wonderful place. They were designed to experience awe in the presence of His majesty and delight in His service. But something happened, as God knew it would; it was part of the Immanuel Agenda.

Chapter Three: Evil Begins

Lucifer was the most beautiful of all the angels. For reasons we'll probably never know, it went to his head. Pride was birthed. He decided he wanted a share in the glory that belonged to God. He wanted something other than what God was giving. With that passion, evil began. Evil is treasuring something more than God; in Lucifer's case, it was the chance to feel a certain way.

He managed to persuade a sizable number of lesser angels to search for a better life apart from God. So they left the place God had assigned them. Satan and his demons were now a force to be reckoned with.

Chapter Four: People Arrive on the Scene

God created the heavens and the earth. On the earth, He designed a paradise named Eden, a word that means "delight." It was there He created the first people. His purpose from the beginning was to share the delights of Perfect Community and the blessings of a wonderful life.

Human beings were formed with the capacity not only to bow in awe before majesty and to serve the Master, but also to enjoy the depths of God's heart. In that, we're distinct from angels.

He is love, and the extent of His love reaches all the way to grace. He's willing to forgive people who hate Him and to find a way to hug filthy urchins. He actually *loves* them—and they are us.

Until Adam and Eve sinned, they had a limited appreciation of God's goodness. Grace was not yet required and so was not visible. God's first arrangement with people was straightforward: Follow the one rule I've made, and you may continue to enjoy a wonderful life in paradise. Hawaii forever. Side trips to Fiji. Never a kidney stone. And a great marriage with great sex to boot.

But there was one thing they couldn't enjoy in paradise—a relationship built on grace. So God stood by and watched as the devil persuaded them to sin.

Chapter Five: A Corrupt Race Is Sinned into Existence

That one sin released a deadly virus into the human heart, a virus till then contained among the fallen angels. From that point on, every person born of a man and woman approached life with the idea that there was something better than knowing God. We believed we could find more pleasure in God's provisions than in His Person. So we lived for pleasure without worrying whether we drew near to God or not.

If those pleasures didn't come, we felt justified in seeking relief from our pain any way we could. When God told us we were wrong, we became indignant and asked Him what He'd done for us lately. If pleasures did come, we felt smug. We thought we somehow deserved them. After all, we hadn't asked to be born; whoever put us here ought to take care of us.

It was time for God to kick the Immanuel Agenda into visible gear.

Chapter Six: God Goes to Work

The first thing God did, after watching people get worse and worse, was to destroy everybody—all except one man and his family.

After the flood, He entered into an arrangement with Noah. It was this: "Noah, look up. Do you see that rainbow? That rainbow is My pledge that, even though you and your kids and their kids after them will turn away from Me to find their joy, I will never again destroy all living creatures as I just did."[73]

What was His point? I believe it was this: Revealing only His judgment would never achieve the Immanuel Agenda. He could never punish people into treasuring Him above all other joys. So He entered into the Noahic Covenant, the first of five Special Arrangements with people.

Years passed. Things were no better than before. The next phase of the Immanuel Agenda was introduced—the Abrahamic Covenant.

God chose a man, from our perspective at random. He appeared to this man and ordered him to begin a journey. "Follow me," God said, "to a place I'll show you later. I have a plan. I want to bless people through you."

Though Abraham didn't know it when the journey began, the plan was for God to put Abraham in a terrible bind that only a miracle could solve.

"Abraham, you will father a son."

"But God, my wife and I are childless. Will it be my servant who will be my heir?"

"No! Trust Me. I know what I'm doing."

Then God cut the deal.[74] He instructed Abraham to tear some animals and birds into pieces and lay the pieces in two lines, forming a path down the middle.

The custom of the day in covenant making was that whoever walked the path was saying, "Cut me into pieces if I don't keep my word." On this occasion it's striking to observe[75] that God walked the path alone, as if to say, "The Immanuel Agenda is moving forward. I guarantee its progress, all the way to fulfillment." God envisioned a people who lived in the shadows by faith, a people who would draw near to Him no matter what happened because they believed He was their greatest treasure.

More years passed. Abraham's descendents through Isaac, born to Sarah and Abraham when they were ninety and one hundred years old respectively, were now the children of Israel. God brought them out of Egypt, then told them to sit still in front of a mountain to hear the next phase of the arrangement. Today we call it the Mosaic Covenant.

"Here's the way things will now work: I intend to be the God of a people who will want nothing else more than they want Me. If that's your heart, here's how you'll live: Do everything I say, prove to Me you love me above everything else, and I'll see to it your life works well. You do what I want, and I'll provide the blessings you want. That's the arrangement."

No one kept the terms. No one could. In their heart they wanted a better life for themselves more than they wanted to enjoy relationship with God; they wanted a good life more than they wanted to reveal to others how good God is. They remained selfish, committed to protecting their own souls and enhancing their own interests. So God cursed them. He brought troubles into their lives.

The only solution was for God to place an affection for Him in their hearts that was more powerful than the virus of sin. Before He did so, He moved the Immanuel Agenda along with one more preparatory arrangement, this one called the Davidic Covenant. He made it with David, king of Israel.

"David," He said, "I'll set up a throne in the middle of My people and see to it that My man occupies it. I intend to create a community that dances for joy around My throne, in My city, with My man in complete charge. You are a picture of that man. Your throne will last forever."

Each of those covenants advanced the Immanuel Agenda in ways that continue today.

Noah's rainbow is still over us. The earth will not be destroyed until the new race is removed.

Like Abraham, we're agents of blessing to this world. But our influence never depends on natural means: Ishmael, the son through a fertile young woman, has been cast out. Isaac, the son of two old people who were far beyond the age of childbearing, is our model. It's only when the Spirit works supernaturally through us that God's agenda is advanced.

The law that came through Moses is now in our hearts. God's arrangement with Israel—get it right and life will work—is nullified. But the law still stands. What's different is that now we have an appetite for holiness; the requirements of the law are now our hearts' delight. And we obey in order to enjoy fellowship with God, not to make our lives work. *That's* different. It's a new way.

The kingdom promised to David is now present. Christ is already on the throne, and we already reign with Him, though not yet as it one day will be.

The final stage on earth of the Immanuel Agenda is now in place. God has established a new arrangement with His people. It's the New Covenant, cut in Jesus' blood.

The centerpiece of this new arrangement is this: *We now have direct access to God at any time, in any circumstance.*

The Better Hope of access to Him leading to a joy-filled, hope-anchored encounter with each member of the Trinity is now in place.

This new arrangement is eternal. It will continue until the coming of the final chapter in this story.

Chapter Seven: Communion Forever

As the final chapter unfolds, we'll no longer *come* to God; we'll be *with* Him always. Then the Immanuel Agenda will be complete—and permanent. God will be our God, and we will be His people.

Sin will not be impossible; it will be unthinkable. Our hearts' cry, *Just give me Jesus,* will be fully satisfied. *We will see Him.* Without a moment's hesitation we'll bow at His feet and say, "My Lord and my God. You're my greatest treasure. Beside You, I want nothing."

When the Better Hope is fully realized and there's no possibility of valuing blessings over the Blesser, God will pull out all the stops. Eden's wonder will pale in comparison. Everything will go right, not because we do everything right—although we will; everything will go right because Jesus did everything right and now God gives us every blessing His infinitely generous heart can conceive. His presence and His blessings—that's heaven!

But we're still in chapter 6 of the Story of God. It's a good place to be, no matter what happens, *if* we live the New Way of the Spirit. The Old Way is gone. The pressure's off. When our kids behave poorly, we don't have to figure out what's the right thing to do that will help them behave better. Strange as it sounds, that's not only unnecessary, it's wrong. That strategy treasures our kids above God. We can draw near to God, then move toward them with the Spirit's passion and wisdom.

That's the New Way to live. And it's available to all whose supreme treasure is God, who bow before God and make no demands, who know He's always doing us good, even when a kidney stone gets stuck in a bad spot.

We can reject the Old Way and live the New. But how? I still want the stone to pass, maybe more than I want God. And if I'm brutally honest, I sometimes treasure my kids being healthy and happy more than I long to know God better. *How do we live the New Way?*

That's the question I take up next.

PART IV

LET THE
REVOLUTION BEGIN

The New Way: How to Live It

CHAPTER FIFTEEN

ENJOYING GOD

It is possible to actually *enjoy* God. It's the point of living. It's the reason we're alive. Getting started on the New Way depends on that idea finding its way into both our heads and hearts.

Listen to John Owen again:

> The knowledge that God and man can live in fellowship is
> hidden in Christ. It is too wonderful for sinful, corrupted
> human nature to discover. But we have, in Christ, the way
> into God's presence without fear.... Those who enjoy this
> communion are gloriously united to God through Christ
> and share in all the glorious and excellent fruits of such
> communion.

If I were sitting with Owen, I'd want to ask him, "What can we know of that enjoyment now, on this fallen earth, in this wearying, sometimes difficult life?"

He replies:

> This communion will be perfect and complete when we
> enter into the full enjoyment of Christ's glories. Then we
> shall totally give ourselves up to him, resting in him as the
> fulfillment of all our desires.... This communion is now only

partial because we presently only enjoy the first fruits of that future perfection.

Partial enjoyment now, *but partially enjoying God is better than fully enjoying anything else.* I think that's true. And yet we insistently long to enjoy something fully today. That's the appeal of sin. It's the appeal of control. That's why the Old Way has had such a stranglehold on us. What we fully give ourselves to, we want to fully enjoy. But Christianity calls for full surrender and promises only partial enjoyment until later.

I imagine myself telling all this to Professor Owen. I picture him sitting back in his chair, closing his eyes, and tasting a meal I don't yet see. If I could enter his thoughts, I think I'd hear him testing me silently, "You said it, but perhaps you don't believe it: The partial enjoyment of God is so surpassingly greater than the complete enjoyment of any other pleasure that it's foolish to pursue anything but the knowledge of God." And then, opening his eyes but looking through me to something higher, he speaks aloud. He is talking to God on my behalf and to me on God's behalf.

This is what he says:

> I pray that the God and Father of our Lord Jesus Christ who has, by the riches of his grace, brought us from a state of enmity into this glorious fellowship with himself, *may give you such a taste of his sweetness and excellence in this communion as to be stirred up to a greater longing for that eternal enjoyment of him in eternal glory.*[76]

Perhaps the Spirit is stirring you as He is me. I long to live the New Way. If there's a road that leads to whatever enjoyment of God is available in this life, I want to take it.

My prayer is that you do as well. I trust this book so far has aroused your desire to leave behind the pressure of arranging for your own satisfaction and to live in the freedom of knowing God. If it's possible to actually meet God in joy-producing encounter (and even partial joy in meeting God is inexpressible), then you want to walk whatever path leads into His presence. That's my prayer for you and for me as well.

A FORK IN THE ROAD

If you believe it's possible to enjoy God and if you're becoming aware of your desire to actually meet Him, then you've come to a fork in the road. The Old Way—trying hard to do things right so the good things of life come to you—is still available. The allure is powerful. The bird in your hand (control over blessings) seems worth more than two birds in the bush (the promise that if you draw near to God, He'll draw near to you).

But you see another path. The sign marking its entrance is shaped like a cross, and the words on the crossbeam read "The New Way of the Spirit." You have a choice to make. Let me look into my own heart and see if I can understand a little of what's going on in yours as you confront that choice.

You've felt the shallowness and pressure of life for a long time. The pleasures you experience don't seem to reach all the way into your soul. They leave you empty and under pressure to keep them coming. You feel a little like Atlas holding the world on your shoulders, but your shoulders aren't as broad.

Life has proved disappointing. You don't feel the disappointment while you're closing a deal, having sex, eating, or involved in fun and meaningful activities. Which, of course, explains your addiction to these things. As one successful Christian leader put it, "When your life is working as you want and the pleasures keep rolling in, it's hard to crank up much interest in a spiritual journey. This one's just fine. So we call it the Christian life, and relax. But when life gets hard, or when you realize the good life you have isn't satisfying something deep inside, your interest in a new way to live develops quickly."

Perhaps you're there. You're no longer as excited by the seminar or sermon that promises to teach "skills for getting out of life what you want" or "techniques for tapping into God's power." What you want is power to know yourself and to know God (what theologians call "double knowledge") and power to bring the two of you together. You long to enjoy God.

Your soul, the real you that you've nearly lost sight of beneath all the posturing and busyness, lies empty, alone, bored. It could be different. You know that. It's supposed to be different. You know that, too.

The phrase *image of God* begins to mean something. You realize that your identity, your joy, and your purpose are completely wrapped up in your relationship to God. He is the source, the only source, the complete source, of everything you were built to enjoy. More money, great marriage, beautiful kids, close friends, good ministry—nothing else does it. Perhaps you've tried a few out-of-bounds pleasures. They worked well, but only for a moment. Then deeper emptiness. More addictions. You began to realize you'd been sold a false bill of goods. Lies, all lies.

Something's missing. Something's wrong. The way you're living, the way most of your friends are living, isn't leading to a good place.

The abundant life Jesus provides doesn't consist in what we usually call the blessings of life, despite what you've heard from too many pulpits and read in too many books. Blessings are good, but they're not enough. Not for your soul. And now you know you have a soul. You *are* soul, created by God for God to find yourself in God and then to live your life through God.

You cannot rest until you rest in God. You cannot celebrate as you were meant to celebrate until you celebrate God more than everything else that is good—or bad.

It may never have occurred to you before that what's missing is the partial enjoyment of God,

> not more obedience,
> not more discipline,

not more blessings,

not more ministry,

not more emotional security,

not more prayer,

not more self-esteem.

What's missing from your life is a genuine, deeply felt experience of the presence of God, an experience that is enjoyable in the deepest parts of your soul.

And what's wrong is that you're living the Old Way. That explains why you're not enjoying God. You're living to use God to enjoy something else. You've never seriously considered the radical invitation to live the New Way, to put all your eggs in the one basket of God and to take a risk, to come to Him in the hope that knowing Him will make you whole, but only when you stop demanding wholeness and revel only in His glory.

TIME TO MOVE BEYOND

Have you ever realized that living for the Better Life is an insult to God? It's the same insult paid by the prodigal son to his father: "Your only value is what you can do for me. I don't have any interest in knowing you. Just give me what I need to enjoy this life." That's too close to how we think.

"Nana Marcia," a close family friend, with her husband, "Randyman," often bring presents to our four-year-old granddaughter, Josie. At her mother's birthday party, Josie wondered what Nana Marcia had brought her. "Josie, tonight we're all giving gifts to your mommy. Isn't that wonderful?"

When Josie's expression signaled that she wasn't so sure, Nana Marcia added, "But I always give you the greatest gift I can give you—my heart."

Josie smiled. I think she still wanted a new doll—what little girl doesn't? She wants blessings just like we do, but something in her developing soul enjoyed that special moment with a special friend. She understood—not everything, but a little, an important little. She experienced partial enjoyment in relationship with a person who loves her. She may be further ahead than many of us.

Something is missing from our lives. *It's the enjoyment of God as our supreme treasure.* Something is wrong with our approach to life. *It's our foolish determination to enjoy something else as much as only God can be enjoyed and to value our pleasure more than God's glory.*

Every person who enjoys any form of sexual pleasure outside of marriage makes that mistake. So too does every person who values great ministry for God over deep communion with God. Pornographers and Pharisees are not that different, and many pornographers may be nearer to finding God.

The Old Way is evil. It's driven by our passion that something other than God satisfies our soul. The pressure's on; we have to get that "something other." It's the pressure to enjoy something other than God that keeps us too busy, too religious, too committed to ministry, too involved with our family, too responsible for friends, too conscientious as parents, and too determined to live as we should.

This is the weary generation. Christians are as burnt-out as pagans, sometimes more. We're discouraged with ourselves and how life is turning out for us. We thought for years it would be different. Sometimes we wonder if there's any point to living as a Christian. Make sure the blood covers you to secure your place in heaven, then live for this life. If Christianity helps, wonderful. If not, well…

It's time to shed our cynicism, to move beyond nonsacrificial living, and to abandon everything getting in the way of a deep experience of God. I hope you're desperate for a divine encounter, a genuine, noncontrived, deeply felt meeting with God that *both* exposes sinful pleasures as cheap counterfeits of soul joy *and* reveals to us that our nervousness about whether our lives will turn out well is an insult to the God who gives us Himself and says, "Enjoy the feast!"

Of course we'll continue to hurt when bad things happen. *Hurt* over trials, like pain from a kidney stone, is human, not sinful. But *despair* is sinful. It's subhuman to feel as if your source of real joy has been taken from you when a child rebels or a loved one dies or a business fails or an immoral temptation wins.

God is still present. There's no cause to tear our robes.[77] I once heard worship defined as celebrating the availability of God.

A former mentor, now partying in heaven with full enjoyment of God, told me, "The Christian always has reason to celebrate. When we fail, celebrate His grace. When we are blessed, celebrate His mercy. When others reject us, celebrate His love."

Is It Really Possible?

As you discover your appetite for God, you may also be discovering your secondary appetite for relationship with others. You long for conversations that matter. At some point, you'll realize how strongly you want to bless others even if you're not blessed by others. If you're where I am on the journey, you're more aware of wanting to relate in ways that will lift you to a higher level of spiritual experience.

You long to be involved in a few relationships where you can be

known in loving safety,

explored with genuine interest,

discovered by hopeful wisdom, and

touched from the source of spiritual power.

The New Way of the Spirit is a path that leads to an encounter with God, community with others, and spiritual formation within yourself.

Is it really possible? Does a new way actually exist?

I look at my own life and sometimes wonder. The idea of a New Way sounds faddish, like a well-marketed overstatement. Even biblical discussion of this New Way, what you've read so far in this book, can seem like cotton-candy theology. Although the phrase "the new way of the Spirit" was inspired by the Spirit and written by the apostle Paul, it can come across as a lot of fluff and sweetness that offers nothing to sink your teeth into as you live in this world.

The phone rings. Something has gone wrong, and you must deal with it. At that moment, talk of enjoying God sounds like an annoying platitude, a pious irrelevance, something of interest only to monastics, contemplatives, people so right-brained that they're out of touch with real-life challenges, people so mystical that they're more interested in spiritually retreating than facing life.

You've got a problem on your hands, a fire to put out. You're wide open to help from God—but *enjoying* Him? Right then that seems as useless as chatting socially with your surgeon on the way into the operating room. Fellowship? No! Not now! Just *function!* Do your job! Don't show me pictures of your kids—I don't care if your son plays soccer. Wash your hands, glove them, then get out your scalpel and fix me. *For God's sake, fix me!*

What we mean, of course, is fix me for *my* sake, not God's. We say "for God's sake" because we cannot imagine a good God would have any greater interest than straightening out what's wrong in our lives. We have "instrumentalized" truth. Truth, including biblical truth, has been reduced to useful ideas, to an understanding of things that we can harness to reach our ends. We have lost truth as a person to love. Small wonder the postmoderns have introduced a false version of the New Way. Small wonder New Age ideas remain popular and influential.

Enjoy God?

When your son's been arrested?

When your marriage isn't working?

When your wife comes down with Alzheimer's?

When your loneliness reaches new depths you can no longer tolerate?

When the sexual struggle you thought was under control comes back with more uncontrollable passion than ever?

Enjoy God? *In the middle of all that?* Pipe dream! Spiritual nonsense! Pie-in-the-sky escapism! Cotton-candy theology!

Or is it?

The Bible is never wrong. In it, God says there's a new way to live. It's the way of the Spirit. The Spirit delights to reveal the beauty of Christ. Christ has no greater pleasure than revealing the love of the Father. The New Way of the Spirit invites us to participate in the pleasures of God, to happily commune with each member of the Trinity.

Enjoy God? Yes. In the middle of hard times? *Especially* then.

The same hard times and choices face both New Way revolutionaries and followers of the Old Way. They both must decide whether to post bail for their imprisoned son. They both must stop yielding to self-pity and make themselves get out of their lonely apartment. Sometimes they both must white-knuckle it in their efforts to stay sexually pure. And sometimes they both fail.

But *why* they do what they do is different. Those who still travel the Old Way feel the pressure to figure out which course of action will produce the results they want—a repentant son, new friends, weakened temptation. The Christian life for them is a technique, a formula for generating an outcome, a recipe to make life tasty. Truth is instrumentalized.

In the New Way, whatever we do comes out of a heart that has already come to God, that is anchored in that relationship, that looks to God for whatever joy and hope is needed to carry on, that demands nothing but celebrates God in everything. In the New Way, truth is personalized. For New Way revolutionaries, to live is Christ—not raising godly kids or making new friends or even living morally.

LET ISAAC BE BORN!

Is the New Way possible? Can anyone actually live the New Way of the Spirit?

Abraham wasn't so sure. When God appeared to the patriarch and said, "You, my aged friend, and your elderly wife will have a baby in one year," Abraham was not excited. "God," he replied (the story is told in Genesis 17), "I've heard that before. Years ago, You told me that Sarah and I would bear a child. Well, it hasn't happened. And now it's too late. It would take a miracle for us to conceive now. I'm not sure I want to be stretched to that level of faith. I've lived by faith in a lot of situations. I left my home on nothing more than Your word. But now You're pushing it. I'm a little tired of living by faith. Frankly, God, I've about given up hope. I think I'd prefer a manageable life, a natural one."

Then Abraham looked across the plains toward his tent. There sat his once beautiful wife, now a ninety-year-old woman, sexually uninviting, sexually inadequate, and probably sexually disinterested. Ishmael, his teenage son by another woman, was there too. A fine, healthy young man.

Abraham had an idea. "God, how about if You provide me Your promised blessings through the son I already have? Ishmael was born in the natural way, I grant that. No miracle was required, just a moment of compromise. That would make things so much easier. I already did something that worked. Couldn't you let that be enough? Oh God, *let Ishmael live!*"[78]

That's been my cry for fifty years. I want to know that I can do something that will bring about the blessings I desire. To wait for a miracle puts me out of control. I don't like that. I want to believe that if I get it right, my life will work, that God will bless me with whatever I think I need in order to feel joy. "Please, God. You didn't do it for Abraham, but You had special plans for him. In my life, please, *let Ishmael live!*"

To get started on the New Way, we must change our prayer. "God, I don't know how You can produce the fruit in my heart of a consuming love for You. I seem to find so much more enjoyment in the good things of life, and sometimes in sin, than in knowing You. I like blessings more than I love You. I experience more pleasure in other things than in You. It will take a miracle to change that.

"You tell me the miracle has already happened, that I have a new heart that wants You as my ultimate pleasure. But I don't know how to make that real. I can come to You as I am, like Abraham came to Sarah, as a tired old man. It took a miracle for them to conceive. But You did it. I will trust You for a similar miracle in my life. God, I now cast out Ishmael and his mother.[79] I want no more temptation to return to the old way of making my life work. I want to lead a supernatural life. I come to You as I am. *God, let Isaac be born!*"

May that be our prayer, as we now look together at what it means to live the New Way.

We're tired of managing life. The Old Way has worn us out. We now believe it's possible to enjoy God, though not as we will in heaven; we also believe that the *partial* enjoyment of God available to us now far surpasses the *complete* enjoyment of anything else.

We're ready to come to God, as we are—dripping noses, dirty faces, torn clothes, desperate to meet Him, claiming grace as our only hope, insisting on no timetable for our sovereign God to follow, but trusting that He'll reveal Himself to us because that's what He wants to do. It's what He has promised to do, even at the cost of His Son's ugly, beautiful death. It's the Immanuel Agenda.

So what do we do?

Now that we're willing, how do we live in the Spirit's New Way? That's the question I discuss in the remaining chapters of this book.

The pressure's off!

It's time to experience our freedom.

CHAPTER SIXTEEN

FIVE BUILDING
BLOCKS OF NEW
WAY LIVING

There is no assured linear relationship between how we choose to live as Christians and how God chooses to distribute blessings to us in this life. A general pattern, yes, but not an unvarying, cause-and-effect *linear* relationship. Nothing we do guarantees the blessings we want.

Good parents more often have good kids than bad parents. But not always. We aren't in control over how our children develop. It's wrong—it's part of the Old Way—to try hard to parent well if our *primary* motive is to raise kids we can enjoy. That is idolatry. It's loving something else more than God. It's looking to something other than God for ultimate pleasure.

And if you succeed, you'll be proud. If you fail, you'll go back and forth between contempt for yourself ("What did I do wrong?") and contempt for your children ("How could they turn out like this after all I've done for them?").

Christian leaders who serve God faithfully often enjoy His blessing in their lives and ministry. But not always. Humble servants may labor unrecognized in visibly ineffective ministries for years, then die in obscurity, while talented egoists may develop well-funded, internationally known ministries that attract followers by the thousands.

NOT QUICKLY, BUT IT HAPPENS

There is no guaranteed linearity between righteous living and visible bless-ing. The Old Way thinks there is.

But there *is* a linear relationship between the choice to live the Old Way or the New and our experience of God. Old Way living never leads to enjoying God or to becoming like Him. It is preoccupied with using God, not knowing Him. The fruit of the Old Way does not include true wor-ship, real community, or spiritual formation.

If we sow to the flesh, we reap only what the flesh produces. Ishmael lives. Isaac is stillborn. We're guaranteed a merely natural life and its inevitable fruit, a starving and contentious soul, however well disguised. Our inner emptiness then drives us to a style of living that revolves around our felt needs and longings. We live the Christian life in order to satisfy our hunger, not for God and for seeing and savoring and sharing in His glory, but for a full sense of self, a journey of adventure and meaning, a life filled with whatever blessings we enjoy. Sometimes the choices we make in pur-suit of the Better Life are visibly wrong. Other times they are recognizably wrong only if the self-serving motives beneath them are exposed.

If we sow to the Spirit, we reap what only the Spirit can produce: love, joy, peace, patience, kindness, goodness, faithfulness, gentleness, and self-control.[80] In the womb of our souls, Isaac is conceived and eventually born. If we keep on the New Way, he grows to maturity. Miraculously, we en-counter God, experience community, and become like Christ. It doesn't happen quickly, but it happens.

Living for God's glory, and not for the blessings this life may provide, guarantees God's active presence with us, sometimes felt and enjoyed, sometimes unfelt during long dark nights of neither visible blessings from Him nor experienced intimacy with Him.

But the Spirit is always at work. We believe it and have hope. Eventu-ally we experience it and know joy. Along the way, the New Way, we are liberated from the drive to fill ourselves, to keep feeling good based on good things in our lives, and we are released to live for Christ and to love both God and others. We enter into communion with the Trinity, like first graders enjoying elementary knowledge, but our joy is real; it is partial but real. It comes eventually, guaranteed. There *is* a linear relationship between living the New Way and enjoying God.

So the question comes, How do we live the New Way? We want to, but how?

The revolution I envision will be fueled by the New Way to think, live, and relate. It begins with thinking. We're transformed by renewing our minds, not our circumstances; we're changed not by rearranging blessings in our lives or strategizing to make life work a little better or overcoming our low self-esteem and troubling emotions, but by renewing the way we think about this life.

I want to propose five building blocks of New Way living, five elements that together lay a foundation and indicate a direction for all we do. These five ideas grow out of the nature of the New Covenant, the arrangement now in place between God and us. They take seriously what God has revealed to us in the Cross of Christ, both His estimate of our sin and the revelation of His holiness, wrath, and love.

In one sense, they're nonlinear ideas. How we come to God doesn't guarantee how God will come to us or when He'll let us feel His presence with us. Nothing we do *makes* anything happen.

But since the New Covenant is now in place, drawing near to God does guarantee that He'll draw near to us, in His own time and in His own way, not because of the merit of our coming, but because of His gracious promise to draw near to us if we draw near to Him.

If we follow His Spirit, if we walk the New Way, we'll experience the love of the Father and behold the beauty of Christ. Jesus promised to show Himself to those who love Him more than blessings.[81] It's a linear relationship: Sow to the Spirit and you'll reap from the Spirit.

FIVE CORE IDEAS

The New Covenant provides both the resources we need to come to God and the guarantee that He'll come to us. The New Way leads to intimacy with God.

With the cry rising from our hearts, *I'll send Ishmael away; let Isaac live!* let me now suggest the five core ideas that will guide us into New Way living and briefly describe each one. (I'll devote the rest of the book to presenting them more fully.)

If you want to live the New Way of the Spirit, then:

1. Reflect on where you are.

Not many Christians find the red dot on the mall directory that tells them where they are. Not many even look for it.

Every new journey starts from where you are. Knowing what is going on inside you matters. Double knowledge is important: You cannot know yourself without knowing God, and you cannot know God without knowing yourself.

So commit yourself before God and His Word to pretend about nothing.

Take time to reflect, sometimes with others who will give you honest feedback, about where you are, especially about what is happening in your interior world.

You'll know this reflection is doing its work when you begin to feel the painful liberation of brokenness, not over the hurts in your life that you cannot relieve, but over the pride in your life that you cannot eliminate.

Old Way energy is still in us. Until heaven, it always will be and it won't improve. But New Way energy is in us as well, if we're Christians. Reflect on the battle for ascendancy between these two sources of energy.

2. Recognize the fork in the road that is always before you.

Two ways constantly present themselves before you. Especially when something goes wrong in your life—money problems, a lost relationship, the appearance of an emotional problem—you have a choice to make between the Old Way of trying to handle it right to make things better or the New Way of drawing near to God and then engaging with your problems with new energy, wisdom, and purpose.

The Old Way may identify deep personal longings, but they're always about you, about your well-being and comfort. Old Way wisdom never reveals your deepest hunger, your desire for God, your craving for His glory above all other ends. It rather highlights how passionately you desire life to work and focuses on developing effective strategies to make that happen.

The New Way offers a very different path. It begins with identifying not your deepest longings but your deepest flaw. Out of brokenness comes repentance that surfaces your longing for God's glory, a longing that then attracts you to the New Way.

3. Refocus your goals.

Admit what your ruling passions have been, what goals you've been pursuing.

Remind yourself that our hearts were made for God and, as Augustine said, we'll find no rest until we find our rest in Him.

It never comes naturally to eagerly pursue an *encounter* with God, or spiritual *community* where people are known, explored, discovered, and touched, or *transformation* that makes us more like Christ. If we don't think about it, we'll chase after goals that come naturally—material *affluence,* personal and physical *comfort,* and socially acceptable *effectiveness* in arranging for the life we desire.

New Way revolutionaries continually refocus their goals so they pursue what they were created to enjoy: spiritual encounter, spiritual community, and spiritual formation. The New Way is the way of the Spirit.

4. Realize what God provides as the means of grace.

Only grace will birth Isaac. The grace to do so is available, in unlimited supply, in any circumstance.

We must humble ourselves to receive grace the way God chooses to give it. If that means dipping ourselves seven times in a dirty river, we must do it. Receiving grace always requires humility; it requires the death of pride and self-sufficiency.

The essential means of grace include worship, meditation on God's Word, and learning about and depending on the sevenfold work of the Holy Spirit (which I'll especially highlight later). There are others.

5. Reorient your prayer life to match New Way living.

If we live for blessings, we pray a certain way.

If we live to know God, we pray another way.

There is a way to pray that grows out of appreciation for the access the New Covenant gives us into God's presence and that moves us along on a New Way journey.

You can adjust the sails of your prayer life to the wind of God's Spirit. It's a prayer structure with spiritual rhythm. I call it the Papa Prayer, and this also is something I'll explore with you later in further detail.

The pressure's off!

We can live a new way.

Let's begin in the next chapter by reflecting on our journey and honestly admitting where we really are.

CHAPTER SEVENTEEN

WHERE AM I?
FINDING THE
RED DOT

I invite you now to join me in taking a deeper look into our interior worlds. As we do so, keep in mind one vital truth that will sustain us: *Brokenness is the path to freedom*. When we see in ourselves things we wish were not there and realize we can do absolutely nothing to clean up the dirt we find, we enter into the liberating experience of brokenness.

How long we stay there before we feel freedom is up to the Spirit. It may be days, weeks, years. Sometimes the fruit of our affliction is visible only in our legacy. We simply must trust the Spirit. Comfort is His sovereign work.

God ordains afflictions and trouble,[82] but always for the purpose of setting us free to serve Him in the New Way of the Spirit. That Spirit, on His timetable, shines the spotlight on grace and lets us feel Him pour the Father's love into our hearts no matter how we fail and struggle.

It's the taste of divine love, unlike any love we've known, that draws us to the table for more food. At times we can almost see the Spirit smile as He nudges us toward the table and pulls out our chair for us to sit.

Listen closely and you might hear Him say:

"You can come as you are, right now. No penance, just repentance. Yes,

I know—you see the mess. I've helped you see it. But the Father sees only the beauty of Christ. Come! Eat. Drink. Enter His presence under the terms of the New Covenant. You are as pure as Christ. You belong to the Father. You desire Him above all other desires. And now I'll deepen your awareness of all that is true, freeing you to come boldly into a place where many have died. Come in the merits of the Cross."

Brokenness and freedom go together, in that order; first suffering, then comfort; first trouble, then joy; first felt unworthiness, then felt love; first death to the self, then resurrection of the soul.

It's a cycle. First down, then up, then down again, farther down, then up again, this time higher. When we discover the red dot that marks where we are on our journey, we'll always experience brokenness. It's the continual starting point for every next step toward God. Brokenness helps us turn our eyes, not toward the blessings of a better life—those blessings never heal brokenness; they only cover it—but toward the intimacy promised as our better hope.

It is the failure to discover where we are at any moment that keeps us from realizing where we most want to go. Until we face an inner brokenness that no blessing in this life can mend, we'll be drawn irresistibly to the Old Way.

Now let's see how this works. The New Way journey begins with a stunning revelation, not about us, but about God. The unapproachably holy, incomparably magnificent God wants us to *enjoy* Him, to actually come close and feel really good. He made us for the pleasure *He* enjoys when *we* enjoy Him.

But He, quite properly, is a jealous God. For Him that's only reasonable. He demands we enjoy Him as our supreme good because that's what He is. But we don't see it that way, not without supernatural help.

God will never allow us to fully enjoy Him as long as we think of Him as one good among many. There's one simple reason: It can't be done. No diner fully enjoys the prime rib before him if he regularly interrupts his meal by rushing next door to sample someone else's ribs.

When God's people declare loyalty to Him but demand pleasure elsewhere—spouse, children, friends, ministry, health, success—God charges them with adultery. That's a capital offense. So, first, God kills His Son in their place. Then like Hosea with Gomer, He separates Himself from them, *but only* to win them back to enjoyed nearness. The separation is designed to arouse their appetite for what is missing, to heighten awareness that only God's presence can satisfy the depths of human desire.

Consider God's invitation to us. It is *not* "Pray this way, not that, and, like a genie in a bottle, I'll give you whatever you think will make you happy."

No, His invitation is quite different. As our Father, God welcomes His children to the family table and there spreads a magnificent feast—*Himself.* "Come, take your place secured by My Son. My Spirit has brought you here. Now, look at Christ to see Me. Drink Me. Eat Me. Satisfy yourself with My love that lets you see Me and live. Be awed by My splendor and majesty till you realize there is none brighter, none like Me, that you are fish and I am the ocean. All other water is but a puddle of mud in comparison."

Where You Are

Now we're ready to ask the question: *Where am I?* Where's the red dot?

On the authority of God's Word, I can tell you where you are. It's where I am. I can tell you what's going on inside you. And if you see it, if you recognize where you are, you'll be drawn to the New Way. You'll abandon your love affair with blessings, and you'll bow low before God, demanding nothing. So will I.

There are two distinct attitudes within us. The first is in everyone, Christian or not. Isaiah looked at the people in his day and saw that all of them, like sheep, had gone a wrong way. Everyone had turned to the way that made natural sense: *Do whatever you think is best, and expect life to work.*

Isaiah's diagnosis is severe: "From the sole of your foot to the top of your head there is no soundness—only wounds and welts and open sores."[83]

He is describing the natural energy that rules in every son and daughter of Adam until they become a child of God. That energy, still in us after conversion, can be thought of as our response to God's invitation. God offers us the chance to delight our souls in the richest of fare, to sit at His table and feast on Christ, and we don't get it. We're like children offered a one-thousand-dollar bill who choose instead a bright shiny dime.

"Well, yes, thanks very much. Yes, I do that Sunday morning for an hour. I *do* adore Christ. Why, without Him, I'd go to hell. I'm enormously grateful.

"But now that the matter of my eternity is happily settled, I was wondering. You see, I'd be so much happier, fulfilled really, even joyful, if You would grant me this one particular blessing. It would mean ever so much to me. And I would sing Your praises. I would testify loudly to Your unfailing kindness and faithful love if only You would—

"What? You tell me Your love is already on full display in Christ? Oh, I quite agree. And now that I have Him, well, I'd like the rest. Of course, I'm willing to do my part. I'll raise my kids and love my spouse and relate to my friends and pray for my ministry and tithe my money all according to Your teachings. I'll do whatever You require. Just let me know what I'm to do, and I'll try my best. You can count on me. And I know I can count on You. Why, You've already given me Christ, so I know You'll withhold no other good thing. Now bring on what I really want. Great is Your faithfulness. I thank You in advance for the blessings You're about to pour out on my life. *Thank you!*"

That is the energy of the Old Way. I feel it moving in me. And I know that it's strong. I know it's so strong that only a direct encounter with God will stir the better energy in me until it rules my life.

Let me speak very personally to you. I have tasted the better energy in me that prefers drawing close to God over using Him to bless my life. Scripture assures me that it's there whether I feel it or not. It's the new heart promised and provided in the New Covenant.

But I struggle to believe I will ever, during my journey on earth, encounter God so immediately that the better energy of the Spirit will thrill me with Christ no matter what happens. I'm just not there. My idea of life continues to be heaven later and blessings now. I still await the encounter with God that will change that. It happened for Isaiah. It happened for Paul and for Luther and Wesley and Bunyan. Will it ever happen for me? Sometimes I lose hope.

And when I do, I try to manage my life without God. He invites me to enjoy Him. In frustration, I reply, "But You must reveal Yourself to me. I can come to You, but You must draw near to me. I don't experience Your presence as the most real and enjoyable reality in my life. Until I do, please, let me use You to get what seems more available—less depression, more self-confidence, more powerful ministry, an even richer marriage, children who continue on with the Lord."

The list is long. But it seems reasonable and possible. The items in the list define what I mean by a better life. So I try to live well, hoping blessings will come. It's the Old Way.

What did Jesus have in mind when He said there's a way to the abundant life of knowing and enjoying God, but "small is the gate and narrow the road that leads to life, and only a few find it"?[84]

Why are there so few John Bunyans today? Reflect on his life for a moment. He found that small gate. He treasured God above all other blessings. He lived the New Way.

During his twelve years in prison, away from his wife and four children (the eldest, Mary, was blind), he walked through the small gate onto the narrow road. He could have left confinement any day he chose had he promised to never again preach Jesus Christ. Listen to the words of a man stepping onto the New Way, words that reveal the *second* attitude, the better energy in every Christian's soul that too often lies unnoticed and unstirred:

> I have determined, the Almighty God being my help and my
> shield, yet to suffer, if frail life might continue so long, even
> until the moss shall grow on my eyebrows, rather than to
> violate my faith and my principles.[85]

What vision of God released that consuming passion for God? More than mere will power was involved.

The first step in our drawing near to God, to tasting any passion and vision for Him, is to identify where we are. If we draw near to Him, He *will* draw near to us. It's a promise. What more could we want?

Especially in suffering we can see the two paths before us and the two energies within us. We're drawn both to the blessings of a better life and to the joy of a better hope, communion with God.

Look for the red dot. If you find it, you'll feel the tug of war within you, the battle between the two energies.

Can you feel your desire for blessings and your willingness to do whatever it takes to get them? Can you recognize it as idolatry, as preferring the god of blessings over the God who is? *I'll get it right, just bless me. That's what I most want!*

That's half the dot. Can you feel the other half, an energy moving you toward God, not to use Him, but to become absorbed with Him, to honor Him, at any cost? Is there an appeal to the prospect of simply presenting yourself, with all your disappointments, demands, and discouragements, to the Father, then remaining steadfast and faithful while you wait for Him to draw near to you? *God, I come to You. Let me know You. That's what I most want.*

ALWAYS BROKENNESS

The choice before us isn't easy. It wasn't for Bunyan.

> The parting with my wife and poor children hath often been
> to me in this place as the pulling of the flesh from my
> bones.... O the thoughts of the hardship I thought my blind
> one might go under, would break my heart to pieces.[86]

Choosing the New Way is costly. If we don't regard God as our chief joy, we won't have the capital to pay the price. It's by faith we see Him as the source of supreme pleasure; it's a faith that keeps us coming to Him until He gives us a taste of the pleasure we believe is available, and then coming to Him again.

If we do regard God as our chief treasure and live accordingly, we'll seem inhuman to some; we'll appear as radical freaks who take God too seriously and end up leading an unbalanced life.

Listen once more to Bunyan as he expresses two beliefs that empowered him to choose the New Way. The first he drew from 2 Corinthians 1:9—"But we had the sentence of death in ourselves, that we should not trust in ourselves, but in God which raiseth the dead" (KJV).

"By this Scripture," Bunyan said,

> I was made to see that if ever I would suffer rightly, I must
> *first* pass a sentence of death upon everything that can prop-
> erly be called a thing of this life, even to reckon myself, my
> wife, my children, my health, my enjoyment, and all, as dead
> to me, and myself dead to them. The *second* way was to live
> upon God that is invisible, as Paul said in another place; the
> way not to faint is to "look not at the things which are seen
> but at the things which are not seen; for the things which are

seen are temporal, but the things which are not seen are eternal" (II Cor. 4:18).[87]

Consider what Bunyan did. He listed all the blessings of a better life, all that were available to him and all that he wished for, and declared himself dead to them all. Of course he still longed to enjoy them, but his resolve was to draw near to God; as he put it, "to live upon God that is invisible."

Is that even attractive to us? To a church upon whom the glory of God sits lightly, to people who believe a life of blessings in this world is necessary and is their due, Bunyan's attitude seems reckless, at least a bit overdone. We prefer a vending-machine God to a sovereign, personal one. No one cuddles up to a vending machine. We insert the proper change, pull the appropriate lever, reach for our treat, then enjoy it as we walk away.

Isn't that the abundant life Jesus came to give, a buffet table lavishly spread with blessings?

Or is it an abundance of Him?

Make every effort, Jesus said, to find the narrow door leading to life because "many, I tell you, will try to enter and will not be able to."[88]

Remember the proud Pharisee who came into the temple, stood up tall, and *prayed about himself?* "God, I thank you that I am not like other men—robbers, evildoers, adulterers—or even like this tax collector. I fast twice a week and give a tenth of all I get."[89]

In other words, I got it right. Now bless me!

Notice the difference between the proud Pharisee and the humble tax collector. Neither had any right to claim God's blessings. One knew it. The other didn't. The Pharisee still believed in the modified Law of Linearity: If we get the law mostly right, then everything we do will prosper. The tax collector pinned all his hopes on the Law of Liberty—come as you are, undeserving, broken, desperate, and trust God will come near to you rather than banish you from His presence—which is all you deserve.

A principle worth remembering emerges from this parable:

Self-discovery that is led by God's Spirit always generates brokenness, deepens humility, and energizes dependence and gratitude.

I tremble when I think of all that has passed for self-discovery in therapy offices during the past several decades. We've seen our pain, felt our longings, faced our abuse, embraced ourselves as victims, and found the freedom to pursue whatever dreams promise life. The effect has been a deepening of narcissism and a shallowing of humility. We're more proud and less broken than perhaps ever before. *We've discovered in ourselves only those appetites that more blessings can satisfy.* As a culture, modern Christianity is committed to the Old Way.

It could be different.

The Few Who Find

It's time for a revolution, away from the Old Way and toward the New. To help us move forward on our spiritual journey, let me close this chapter by listing *three characteristics* of people who never find their red dot, who never recognize the bad energy within them as bad, and who never gratefully delight in the new energy that is even more deeply lodged in their being. Then I'll mention *three opposing characteristics* of the few who find the red dot, who recognize both energies within them, who discover the small gate, and who, like Bunyan and the tax collector, step through it in brokenness to walk the narrow New Way.

Followers of the Old Way organize life into a System.

They hate mystery, they do all they can to resolve tension, they work to find some way to bring into their lives whatever blessings they believe will make them happy. They love the idea of linearity; it sustains the illusion of control. Find the system that makes life work—find the *A* that leads to *B*. It prolongs the hope of a better life now.

Followers of the Old Way deny whatever reality they come across that contradicts their System.

When a tither goes broke, he finds a way to fault his tithing. As a child, I could never figure out why I sometimes aced a math test the day after I was bad. I explained it by assuming I had been good enough to offset the bad I had done.

Followers of the Old Way mistake vulnerability for brokenness.

They're willing to "get real" and "tell it like it is," assuming that their vulnerability is a virtue deserving compassion. They become aware of their longings, perhaps even their thirst to know God better, but remain ignorant of either their thirst for God Himself or their falling short that disqualifies them from receiving any blessing apart from mercy. It is characteristic of the Old Way to become aware of only those longings that some blessing other than God's presence can satisfy. It sustains the pride of independence.

And now the opposing characteristics.

Followers of the New Way accept the unresolvable tension in life.

Mystery remains and always will. They realize no system can be known or harnessed that will make all of life predictable. Behaviorists like B. F. Skinner are wrong. Existentialists like Jean-Paul Sartre come closer to reality. Although sometimes terrified, New Way followers step into the mystery of life with no final hope other than a gracious sovereign God, who moves in a mysterious way.

They're not existentialists. They believe in objective meaning. It's just hidden for now. Their willingness to live in tension permits a kind of dialogue that those who demand a system can never tolerate. Their hope is in the invisible God.

Followers of the New Way struggle to be truly authentic.

When life confuses or enrages them, they admit it. When God disappoints and frustrates them, they talk it over with Him—and others. They enter dark nights with trembling confidence that somewhere there is light and someday they'll see it. Their rest is in the present God.

Followers of the New Way are cautious about vulnerability but vulnerable to brokenness.

They recognize that what we call vulnerability is often a narcissistic parade intended to draw support. These folks prefer to face in themselves only what draws them closer to God. Sharing pain is secondary. Sharing hunger for God and facing what impedes their search for Him is primary. Their excitement is in the relational God.

Where are you? Have you found the red dot? If you're a lover of systems, preferring predictability and control to mystery and trust, if you tend to deny whatever doesn't fit neatly into your system, if you're quite willing to share your hurts but determined to hide your failings, then you haven't found the red dot. Where you think you are, what you know about yourself, will only encourage Old Way living.

But if you accept tension, knowing mystery is the opportunity to trust rather than plan, if you face whatever you see with integrity because you value authenticity, and if brokenness over weakness and sin is more important to you than vulnerability about the wounds others have inflicted on you, then likely you have found the red dot. What you've discovered in yourself creates a momentum—it's a miracle of the Spirit—to move toward God. You've found the small gate and are ready to make the effort to step onto the narrow path of the New Way.

If we've become small enough to squeeze through the gate, perhaps now we can see what makes the New Way narrow—and be drawn to it.

CHAPTER EIGHTEEN

YOUR CHOICE
OF CYCLES

I think I'm beginning to understand why Jesus told us to "make every effort" to get on the New Way. It sometimes can be hard work to remember and believe that God is good and that He's present with His goodness in every circumstance of life.

A front-page headline today read, "Pursuing a cure, living a nightmare."[90] The disturbing article tells the story of two families, each with a child suffering from a rare disease called neurofibromatosis. Bob Terrill stands before his twenty-four-year-old daughter's swollen face and, with his fingers, spells out D-A-D I-S H-E-R-E. A-R-E Y-O-U H-A-V-I-N-G A-N-Y P-A-I-N?

There's no response. Denise can no longer dip her right eyeball, her former way of saying "Yes." Her father tells the interviewer, "We don't know if she's hurting. We don't know how she's feeling. We just don't know."

There's no mention of God in the article. There's no evidence of His presence in the story. If that story were my only data, I would not believe in God. How could I?

The Old Way urge within me wants to quickly turn to the sports section. Tiger Woods is set to mount a third-round challenge. Then to the comics. *Peanuts* reruns are still great.

Nothing's wrong with following a golf tournament or chuckling over cartoons. Diversions provide welcome relief from life's hardships. But my near frantic urge to move toward them reminds me why I'm writing this book.

IF TOMORROW FELL APART

Is there really a way to know God that keeps hope alive, not hope for this life improving, but hope that we'll be able to taste joy no matter what goes wrong?

Or is what we call faith something that works only with certain blessings in place? Is Old Way living inevitable for even the most sincere Christian? When life turns sour, are my only options distraction or despair, suck it up or give up?

Sometimes I think so. Sometimes joy seems so dependent on my wife remaining healthy, my kids and grandkids doing well, my health and ministry and bank account keeping on a good course, my friends staying friendly. Sure, things go wrong. As the bumper sticker says, "Life happens!" My father is in a wheelchair and failing fast. Mother never leaves the Alzheimer's unit. When I visit, she greets me as she would a stranger.

I used to like the hymn "Count Your Blessings." Now it seems to fit too easily into Old Way thinking: It's tough, but I've still got some wonderful blessings to count.

Could I praise God without them? For what? Does His presence mean anything in my life? Would I revel in the Better Hope if my Better Life crumbled, if my wife were dead, if one of my sons were away from God, and the other lay motionless with neurofibromatosis, if no publisher wanted my next manuscript, if my grandkids got sick or seriously rebelled?

What would it take for me to agree with Job's wife that it's time to curse God and die? Might I get there? Have I ever really *tasted* God? Is the taste good enough and strong enough to abandon myself with joy to His invisible presence?

This is no morbid speculation. I am not preoccupied with all the bad things that could happen. The Lord told us not to. "Do not worry about tomorrow, for tomorrow will worry about itself. Each day has enough trouble of its own."[91] Good advice. Of course! It comes from God.

But bad things happen today. And I wonder. Would my faith in God's goodness survive what has happened to others? Do I enjoy God's presence today with a reality that would continue if tomorrow fell apart? If all other food were taken away, could I still hear God's Spirit invite me to the banqueting table to feast on Christ? Would I come? Would I even want to?

Am I coming now? Or am I still trying to get it right so life will work? Am I living the Old Way or the New? How about you?

Perhaps one way to know is to look at three cycles of life, three approaches to living, and to ask which one best describes how we're moving through our lives. The first two draw from Old Way energy and aim toward the Old Way goal of a better life now. The third requires supernatural energy, the kind that moves us along the New Way and sets its sights on the Better Hope of knowing God well.

In the last chapter I discussed the first of five core ideas for entering and living the New Way: *Reflect on where you are.* In this chapter, I consider the second: *Recognize the fork in the road that is always before you.*

How do parents of a suffering daughter cope? Every day they're faced with her condition, knowing it will not change. There's no cure. Nothing would be more cruel than to suggest that if they only believed, she would be healed. That is linear thinking at its most evil. To believe she *could* be healed and to pray for it, fervently, is Christian; to believe she *would* be healed if enough people with enough faith prayed is anti-Christian. It is the Old Way. It is demonic. It elevates our blessings above God's glory.

But if our foundation for thinking about life is the Old Way, if we believe that doing something right will make our lives work better, if we aim no higher than toward a better life, then we're likely to see only two paths open before us. I call the first the Adjustment Cycle. Here's how it works.

Old Way Plan 1—The Adjustment Cycle

Start by *denying* whatever you cannot handle. If it takes a martini every evening—or morning—drink up. If it aids denial to watch Tiger charge the flag or laugh as Snoopy takes on the Red Baron, wonderful. Or perhaps an hour of prayer works better. Or memorizing Psalm 23. Do whatever it takes to stay distant from difficult realities that might overwhelm your coping skills, whether that reality is inside your heart or outside in your circumstances.

Then find your bootstraps, grab them, and pull up hard. *Strategize.* Life is hard. You admit that. But you can handle it. Let's see. How? Strip clubs? No, at least for now, they remain over your moral line. Get out more. Exercise. Join a small group at church. Remodel your kitchen. Read good books. Throw a dinner party. Date someone. No, you're still married. Well, just think about it.

Now that you've experimented with several coping strategies, *evaluate.* See which ones seem to work best. Perhaps you'll realize that making moral choices, following spiritual counsel, attending Bible conferences, and praying a lot seems to help. Good. Christianity does work. The Bible study you've been involved with, however, is boring. You leave lonelier than when you arrived. Drop it. It's not working. Consider a few alternatives. Maybe you would enjoy gardening. You have the money. Hire a gardener to work with you.

You are now ready to *refine* your approach to recovering your life. Quit the Bible study. Stay moral. Plant roses. Keep reading. And maybe change jobs. At least keep your options open. You never know how God might lead.

There! You've got it now. You still have bad days, and nights are especially difficult, but you're getting through pretty well. Sometimes you feel really good. It's true you're eating too much, but food is such a reliable source of pleasure. And you're not fat. You just look prosperous. The important thing is you feel restored. You like yourself. You like most of life.

And you're able to keep your distance from the ache in your soul that tells you something is dreadfully wrong. The need to keep denying, strategizing, evaluating, and refining your methods continues. But for now you're pretty *stable*. The Old Way is working. Praise God! Or whomever.

The Adjustment Cycle

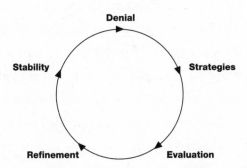

Denial

Stability

Strategies

Refinement

Evaluation

OLD WAY PLAN 2—THE THERAPEUTIC CYCLE

Sometimes the Adjustment Cycle fails. You can't cope. When you're unable to develop a stable strategy for handling your life, the therapeutic culture offers its services. Consider the Therapeutic Cycle.

Therapy that *is* Christian encourages New Way living. Much therapy that *claims* to be Christian amounts to little more than smoothing out some bumps on the Old Way. Remember the core energy that keeps us moving toward the Better Life of Blessings: It's the determination to find a way that will make this life work coupled with the belief that such a way exists. It must. How could it be otherwise in a world created and controlled by a loving God?

That same energy determines the direction taken in many therapy hours. Here's how the Therapeutic Cycle works.

Start by lifting denial. *Openness* about how you "really feel" begins the cycle. Therapy creates a safe place for emotional vulnerability. Someone actually listens to you without disdain or judgment. And it helps. When you share your secret emotions and face the ones you've buried, you do feel better. The burden seems lighter. There! You're off to a good start. You feel hope.

Next comes *insight*. If your therapist is directive, the insight might be carefully presented. Otherwise, under the influence of probing questions, clarifying comments, and well-timed silence, you may come to new realizations on your own. Yes, you're angry. About what? What needs lie deep within you that remain unmet? How good to know God loves you and wants you to feel the joy of needs well met. You're thankful that you're seeing a *Christian* counselor. Now you can see that your husband's affair stirred up your hidden fear of abandonment. Your father was never there for you, not at the critical moments. Now you clearly see the relationship between earlier disappointments and current hurts.

With insight comes *direction*. What course of action does your new awareness suggest? Well, how did you handle your dad's neglect? You became a bottled-up good girl, always trying to please, desperate for even a morsel of attention. *That's what you've done with your husband!* There, that's another insight. Now you know what to do. It's time to let him know what you're feeling, to stop being a neurotic little girl and become an assertive, self-respecting grown woman. As you think of becoming that woman, you can feel yourself coming alive. The energy of, well, *self* courses through your being. You feel strong, together, whole for the first time in your life. You have needs, too, and he's going to know about them. You love your newly developing freedom.

But it's scary. What will he do? More rejection would be hard to handle. But you must take the risk. You must become your own person; hang the fear. *Support* helps, from your therapist, from friends who love you and believe in you and take your side. You've been stuck so long at a childish developmental level. With help you can break out. You can do it!

Now comes the tough part. It's time to *align* your behavior with your insight, to move in the directions that now seem so right, and to do it with support. Remember Jesus loves you. He's *for* you. He wants you to love yourself and to feel the freedom to be who you are. Visualize Him cheering you on. Let Him, along with the Spirit, be your primary support group as you follow the Old Way to a better life.

The Therapeutic Cycle

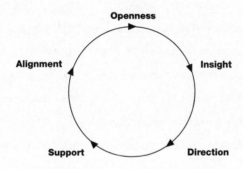

Cope with life. Get help if you need it. Be conformed to this world. Let your mind remain fixed on the idea that life is all about you and that God is here to help. It's the Old Way.

But there's a new way to live, and it's radically different. Be still. Reflect on where you are. You've been *using* God to make your life work. That puts you above Him. You're insisting that blessings come your way, at least certain ones. You're not *wanting* blessings; you're *requiring* them. You're depending on them for your joy. God is not your supreme treasure. Christ is not preeminent in your life. The Spirit lies quenched within you; His invitation to feast on God goes unheeded.

As you see what's been going on inside you, as you identify the red dot, you feel more than a little sheepish. In your humility, you hear the Spirit whisper, "There's a new way to live. There's another path to follow."

THE NEW WAY'S ONLY PLAN— THE SPIRITUAL CYCLE

New Life begins at the Cross. It's there you realize how arrogant you are. You don't welcome trials. You've lived for no greater purpose than to avoid them or reverse them if they come. Your ambition has risen no higher than a life that works pretty well. Perhaps you've disguised your narcissism by dressing it up in Christian clothing. Find fulfillment in ministry. Clean up your life. Overcome your sexual addiction. Live by the Book. But now you see that none of it had God at the center. God's glory has mattered little to you. A quality life is what you're after. And Christianity, or the Christian culture, provides you with the meaning, the sense of community, and the respect you desire. The Spiritual Cycle begins with *brokenness*. It hurts. The two Old Way cycles are much more seeker friendly.

From brokenness the Spirit leads you to *repentance*. You've assumed you deserved satisfaction. You thought, with God's help, you could arrange for it. You believed you were living the Christian life. How could you have been so deceived? You thought God was here to cooperate with your agenda. But only He can say, "I AM." You can say only, "I serve at Your pleasure."

Yes, this is a new way to think. Your mind has changed. Repentance has begun. And it feels clean, right, strangely good.

The Spirit then moves you from brokenness through repentance to *abandonment*. When blessings filled your life, you lived for them. You didn't trust God. You negotiated with Him to keep life working. But now, standing over your daughter's swollen face, leaving the divorce court by yourself, praying for your son who lives with his boyfriend in a homosexual relationship, you resist the urge to run to cartoons or watch television or drink a martini. You also resist the very real temptation to curse God and drown your sorrows any way you can. Even harder, you resist the desire to nobly persevere and present yourself to others as a courageous martyr. Instead, you listen to the Spirit speak through the Bible. This world is fallen. Things happen that make no visible sense. But somehow, through it all, God is telling a good story. Without the ending, the story is not good. But nothing happens, nothing can happen, nothing ever will happen that God cannot redeem to move the story along to its glorious climax. You believe that. You therefore abandon yourself to the invisible God, the One who for a moment became fully visible as He hung on the cross.

Abandonment, surprisingly perhaps, arouses *confidence*. The Spirit witnesses to your spirit that you do belong to God, that He is working all things together for good, that eternity will vindicate your choice to abandon the well-being of your soul to this mysterious, mostly invisible, seemingly fickle, certainly unpredictable God. When you lived the Old Way, you had no real confidence that He was present with you, cooperating with your purposes. *Because He wasn't.* But now that you're living for His glory and drawing near to Him to enjoy His nature, you experience a developing confidence that He actually is present, even during your darkest night. You know, because the Spirit tells you, that He is present as you walk the New Way toward the Better Hope of knowing, glorifying, enjoying, and revealing to others the wonderful, spectacular God who is really there.

Spirit-given confidence that God is there and worthy of absolute trust breeds the freedom to *release* what is most alive within you. You begin to feel something stirring in your innermost being. It may take awhile, but at some point you realize, *These are the springs of living water!* When you stumble badly, you can still hear God sing over you; you have a *new purity*. When you remember your sexual abuse, you can walk with dignity; you have a *new identity*. The urge toward sexual sin, though strong, isn't what you really want; you have a *new inclination*. The grief that formerly overwhelmed you is no longer in control; you have a *new power*. You find yourself released to be the person you've longed to be—loving, joyful, peaceful, patient, kind, gentle. Never perfectly, but sometimes at least genuinely. And now you praise God and no one else.

The two Old Way cycles keep us dependent on life working, at least

The Spiritual Cycle

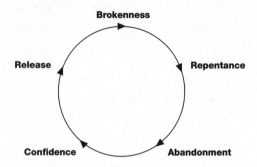

reasonably well, and on our resources to make sure it does. By encouraging movement toward the Better Life of Blessings, they keep the pressure on. We've got to get it right. And both of those cycles leave us vulnerable to pride when life works and angry despair when it doesn't.

The New Way cycle, the way of the Spirit, draws us toward the Better Hope of enjoying God. It provides everything we need to come to Him, and to keep coming, no matter what life brings.

Because the Spirit supplies the needed resources to reach our goal, the pressure's off. The New Way sharpens our focus on what life is all about.

And that's the third of the five core ideas for how to live the New Way, and the one we'll examine next: *Refocus your goals.*

CHAPTER NINETEEN

First Thing Focus

The change has been gradual, imperceptible except in hindsight. Like frogs in slowly boiling water, we haven't realized that the warmth we're now enjoying is about to kill us. The surface is already bubbling.

As a culture, present-day Christianity has redefined spiritual maturity. The reformers knew we were saved to glorify God. We moderns live to be blessed. The mature among us are now thought to be the successful, the happy, the effective people on top of things and doing well. We're so committed to discovering and applying God's principles for making life work that we no longer value intimacy with God as our greatest blessing. We're more attracted to sermons, books, and conferences that reveal the secrets to fulfillment in everything we do than to spiritual direction that leads us through affliction into the presence of the Father.

It seems that our highest ambition has been lowered to producing people whose circumstances are pleasant enough to make it easy for them to praise God. We no longer identify ourselves as a community of visibly broken saints, men and women profoundly grateful for grace, knowing we're dead without it; existentially dependent on the Spirit, knowing we won't keep on without Him; and stubbornly hopeful in the sometimes dim light of eternity, knowing that blessings in this life come and go.

We seem more interested in managing life into a comfortable existence than in letting God spiritually transform us through life's hardships. Divine *encounter,* spiritual *community,* and soul *transformation,* the three primary goals of a pilgrim, are not what we're after. We've settled down in this world and are doing our best to make it a comfortable home, claiming healing, fulfillment, and success as the point of knowing Christ now.

We haven't seen the danger. As the blessings of good circumstances and success and personal fulfillment warm our lives, we don't realize they're burning our souls to cinders with heat from hell.

Pascal anticipated the parable of the boiling frogs four hundred years ago when he wrote, "When everything is moving at once, nothing appears to be moving, as on board ship. When everyone is moving toward depravity, no one appears to be moving. But when someone stops, he shows up the others by acting as a fixed point."[92]

Listen to two fixed points from long ago who, by standing still and looking up to a vision of a satisfying God, may help us see our movement away from God. This from Cardinal Nicholas of Cusa, a fifteenth-century Tyrolian bishop:

> And what, Lord, is my life, save that embrace wherein Thy
> delightsome sweetness doth so lovingly enfold me? I love my
> life supremely because Thou art my life's sweetness.... Now I
> behold...that blessed regard wherewith Thou never ceasest
> most lovingly to behold me, yea, even the secret places of my
> soul.... There is the source of all delights that can be desired;
> not only can naught better be thought out by man or angels,
> but naught better can exist in any mode of being! For it is
> the absolute maximum of every desire, than which a greater
> cannot be.[93]

Don't let the archaic language cause you to miss the force of his radical way of thinking. What he is saying is this: "I love life because I know God and I know He loves me, not because things are going well." That's the New Way.

Go back further, to the third century. Listen to Clement of Alexandra:

> Jesus Christ, by coming into this world, has changed the
> sunsets of time into the sunrises of eternity.[94]

It isn't just the church fathers who thought the New Way. Thomas Dubay, Roman Catholic spiritual director, is a fixed point in our generation. In his excellent book *Seeking Spiritual Direction,* he wrote, "Everything in the divine plan is aimed at the eternal ecstasy of heaven begun on earth."[95] In this, he echoed Jean Pierre de Caussade, who believed that everything that happened to him, both blessings and trials, led him to God.

Heaven's ecstasy will flow from the literal presence of Christ. The beginning of that ecstasy, in this world, depends upon the *appreciated* presence of Christ. The Old Way, by its focus on tangible blessings now, severely limits the depths of that appreciation. In the New Way, appreciating Christ's presence as the "sunrise of eternity" is possible. Not automatic. Never complete. But possible. And the possibilities are staggering.

WANT IT AND WAIT

Whether we realize the possibilities depends in part on which goals we pursue. Let me illustrate the point.

I spent an hour last night, from 1 A.M. till 2, weeping in prayer. The phone jangled me awake at 12:45. I've heard worse news before, and I've responded with less emotion to more disturbing crises.

For reasons I can't fully sort out, this one struck a deep nerve. The difficulty was real but vague, the issues making things difficult were cloudy, and a panel of wise men could not have agreed on the right thing for me to do.

Occasionally, a not visibly severe event gathers into it all the pain and terror of existence, and our souls are undone. Agony rolls down into our deepest heart, crowding out any experience of gladness or hope. All is dark, with darkness too thick to see even a pinpoint of light. All we can do is wail.

James wrote to followers of Jesus and said, "Is any one of you in trouble? He should pray."[96] For what? He earlier told us to come to God *so that God would come to us*.

Plenty of Scripture supports our praying for tangible blessings, relieved suffering, and a sense of well-being. It's okay to hurt, and it's okay to pray for blessings, and it's okay to be happy when blessings come. But it's not okay to ground our anchoring joy in the Better Life of Blessings.

When trouble comes, our first thing focus must be on entering God's presence (encounter), participating with others on the journey to God (community), and cooperating with the Spirit in forming Christ in us (transformation). Because of the New Covenant and its place in the Immanuel Agenda, the focus that must *be* is the desire that already *is*. We simply need to get in touch with it. Our most fervent desire will aim us toward the New Way goal.

It begins with encounter. According to the apostle John, fellowship with the Father, the Son, and the Holy Spirit is the central point of the Christian message,[97] and that fellowship is the absolute maximum of every desire. It changes earth's sunsets into heaven's sunrises and moves us along toward heaven's ecstasy.

It was now one in the morning. The phone call had just ended. The Better Life was not in sight. Neither was the Better Hope. Had the choice been given, I would have moved toward blessings.

I could feel both energies within me. The urge to straighten out life felt more compelling. Probably because I was in the middle of writing this book, I knew the other urge should be stronger, but I had no power to make it so.

I came as I was, wailing over the lack of what I wanted in my life. I thought of John Bunyan and St. John of the Cross and Paul—and Jesus—and I could sense a wish rising within me for the Better Hope to mean more than it did. At that moment, something became clear: Whether my passion for God became compelling in this or any moment is up to the Spirit. It's a sovereign work of grace. All I can do is want it and wait.

That realization shrunk my swollen head enough to let me fit through the small gate. Our progress on the New Way is all about humility and dependence.

And then, from inside the gate, the fork in the road became clear. I could see two paths, the one I had already stepped onto and the other one still available if I backed up. Both the Adjustment Cycle and the Therapeutic Cycle, the two tracks on the Old Way, had their appeal.

But having entered through the narrow gate, the Spiritual Cycle was also in sight, the New Way, the narrow way. The hope of meeting God, of joining community, and of growing spiritually stirred deep within me.

Strange as it sounds, *brokenness* became attractive—whatever it takes to encounter Him! I could see that *repentance* offered freedom and that *abandonment* aroused excitement. And I could sense a developing *confidence* in what He's doing—and not doing. And I felt an internal momentum toward *release*. I saw myself jumping off a cliff into a dark abyss supported only by the rope of God's love. It seemed a privilege.

Then the image changed. The rope broke, and I plunged downward. Terror seized me. But rather than crashing on rocks or falling endlessly into darkness, I found myself landing gently in the ocean of God's love. The water was warm enough to soothe and cool enough to refresh. The frog didn't boil. Rather, a saint, calmed and strengthened, began to swim. I could see myself entering the world of trouble with new purpose.

And that carried me into the third of the five core ideas: *Refocusing goals*. It's an important one, perhaps the most vital of all five.

A Pilgrim's Goals

Let me now draw together what I've already said into a discussion of a pilgrim's goals.

With cut-to-the-chase candor, Teresa of Avila once wrote,

> All that the beginner [in New Way living] has to do...is to
> be resolute and prepare himself with all possible diligence to
> bring his will into conformity with the will of God.... The
> more perfectly a person practices it, the more he will receive
> of the Lord.[98]

That will not happen, it *cannot* happen, until we believe that all things in life, including early morning phone calls, are part of a grand design. They're intended by an uncontrollable, mysterious, and relentlessly single-minded deity to immerse us in His relational life. That, God knows, is the very best blessing He can give us. And that, God also knows, is the deepest desire in every heart His Spirit indwells.

Permit me to revisit my early morning story. After the phone call, I immediately went downstairs. I wanted solitude and the freedom to come exactly as I was into His presence. Coming to God is sometimes best done alone. Other times it's best done with fellow pilgrims. This was a time to come alone.

The first words to escape my mouth were these: "This shouldn't be happening to me. What have I done to deserve this?" The red dot began to appear.

Then the dam burst. Indignation covered sorrow. And I couldn't access the sorrow till the indignation was expressed. I had to come as I was, drippy nose, smudged face, and torn clothes. It wasn't a pretty sight.

Strong tears burst from my very being. Some flowed from legitimate hurt over blessings denied; some from proud indignation that insisted, for a few minutes, on screaming *"Unfair!"* Some, from the center, came out of a desire to meet God in a difficult moment.

The red dot was now clear: I could feel the two energies within my soul competing for dominance. Seeing those energies focused my eyes on the small gate that opened onto the New Way. I had a choice to make. And I was broken by the realization that a very real part of me wanted to use God, just as the prodigal son used his father.

At that point, the fork in the road was obvious. One path promised a Better Life, the other a Better Hope. "God," I cried, almost reflexively, "I want a Better Life, but I want to know You more. Please! Don't let these tears and this awful moment in my life be wasted. I present myself to You. I know You're there. I abandon myself to Your Spirit with the confidence that He'll release me to live in Your presence—and to find gladness of heart and the power to follow Your will."

The veil lifted. It was now about a quarter to two in the morning. I could see the finish line. I could see the victor's wreath that was to be placed on my brow in this life. It was *not* an increasingly blessed marriage. It was *not* the exhilaration of realized manhood. It was *not* continued freedom from cancer.

I wanted to know God, to experience the revolution within achieved through the New Covenant. I wanted to…

> *encounter God,* to fellowship with each member of the Trinity, to join Their party.
>
> *participate in community* with other broken, desperate, grateful saints who, stunned by grace, were journeying toward God, unwilling to settle for lesser joy.
>
> *experience transformation,* to be spiritually formed until others, but especially the Father, could see in me an actual resemblance to Jesus.

By two in the morning, I could taste the prospect ahead of me. I was "destined to be enthralled without end by gazing on the Father, the Son, and the Spirit and thus transfigured into divine beauty."[99] Laodiceans were not my people. They seemed to me like frogs enjoying the lukewarm water, not knowing it was about to boil. I didn't want to be merely "decent and respectable...to enjoy moderately the pleasures of life...and to take care that religion" did not engross me.[100]

With all my heart, I did *not* want to settle for the happiness that comes from an easier life. For a few supernatural moments early one Tuesday morning, I wanted nothing less, nothing else, only God. As miracles go, that one rivals the Red Sea. All praise to God! I wanted *encounter* with God more than I wanted blessings from God.

And I wanted to bless others, to give them a taste of the kind of relating that goes on among the Trinity all the time. I still longed to be known, explored, discovered, and touched, but for just a moment, I wanted more to bless another, to participate in *community* by offering community. Another miracle, not permanent, not even long-lasting—by breakfast I was grumpy again—but it was real.

Still looking down the narrow path, I could see the sunrise of my transformation. I knew that by the Spirit's power, someday, in this life, I could be
> *still loving, though discouraged,*
> *still giving, though spent,*
> *still patient, though exasperated,*
> *still sensitive, though offended,*
> *still hopeful, though worn down by life.*

Me. Like Jesus! Could Stalin have loved like Mother Teresa? Could Hitler have preached like Billy Graham? What can God do?

For a moment, sunlight blazed. Heaven's ecstasy began. And it all started with a tough phone call.

The best hope survives the worst tragedy. And it surfaces because of it: We can come into the presence of God to *encounter* Him, to join a *community* of broken, troubled seekers who want more of Him, and to be *transformed* by the Spirit till we actually resemble Jesus. No longer dying in the boiling water of demanded blessings, now swimming in the refreshing ocean of God's presence—that's life in the New Way.

Refocus your goals: That's the third of the five core ideas for how to live this New Way. Movement toward these goals is the work of God's Spirit. We must learn to depend on Him. And that's the fourth idea.

CHAPTER TWENTY

GOD IS IN
CONTROL—OF WHAT?

In A.D. 410 the unthinkable happened. Rome was sacked. Ambrose, a prominent religious leader of that day, asked, "If Rome can perish, what then is safe?"

In September 2001, the economic and military centers of the mightiest nation on earth were attacked. Airplanes hijacked by terrorists crashed into New York's World Trade Center and into the Pentagon, sitting proudly near the nation's capitol. It was unthinkable, unimaginable—and yet it happened. Religious leaders, as if in chorus, tried to reassure an unnerved citizenry by saying, "God is in control."

I kept asking myself—*of what?* The intent of the words was to help us feel safe—*from what?* Do we really think that if buildings were destroyed on God's watch, something more—and worse—couldn't happen?

NOTHING THWARTS HIS PLAN

By affirming God's ultimate control over all things, no one was assigning responsibility to Him for the wicked deeds of others. The holocaust, Stalin's atrocities, and terrorism are properly blamed on sheer evil and on those who yield to it.

So, too, is every instance of drunk driving, sexual abuse, gossip, parental indifference, overeating, lying, sexual immorality, and cowardice, though arguably at a lesser level. God is not to be blamed for any of these things. For reasons we can't quite understand, He *allows* evil. He never *causes* it. "Natural" disasters may be His doing, but not the sinful choices of His depraved creatures.

On that point most agree. And yet we continue to insist God is in control. What do we mean? What should we mean? And what comfort are we to draw from whatever we mean?

I cannot even approach an answer to these age-old questions without first fixing two thoughts firmly in my mind. First, *this life is only an introduction to another life, for followers of Jesus a better one.* If that's not true, I would embrace no higher goal than personal relief now, for me first, then for you. If this life is all there is, then I cannot reconcile my belief in an all-good, all-powerful God with my experience and observation of suffering.

If this life is all there is, if life ends with death with no conscious existence in another world, the only reasonable and compassionate response to pain is to do all that we can, perhaps anything we can, to relieve it. Everyone, including whatever God exists, should devote their resources to that end. Those who do otherwise cannot be trusted. They're not good. Which leaves us in a bind. If God does exist and if He really is in control, it's patently clear that He isn't doing all He could to relieve suffering.

But if this life is but the shadow of an age to come, then conceivably suffering could have a future point that justifies letting it continue in order to do its work. *If* the future point is eternally good *and if* that good can be reached in no other way, *then* I can still believe in a good and mighty God even when people hurt.

That's the first thought. The second is this: *God is devoting His power to an agenda I don't properly value.* Ask people what their greatest need is. In the aftermath of terrorism, many would speak of safety within our national borders.

Let time pass. After thousands of planes again take off and land without incident, after workers subway into the city, elevator to their offices in tall buildings, and subway home later that afternoon, people regain a more personal understanding of their greatest need. Once our need for *physical* well-being is satisfied, we attend more to *personal* longings for happy families, short lines, productive and well-compensated work, close friendships, inexpensive gas, deep fulfillment, healthy grandkids, inner peace, hot coffee, and material prosperity.

We want the Better Life and we trust God to provide it. After all, He is in control. He *can* give it all to us. The only question is—*will* He? So we set about to persuade Him to use His power on our behalf. We try to get it right so life will work well.

Somehow we've missed the arrogance in this thinking. Believing that our greatest need is to be happy, safe, and fulfilled is all about us. And we believe, deep down, that we're *entitled* to whatever we think we need.

We need it. God should provide it. That's His job. We can't fathom a good God entertaining any agenda other than satisfying our needs, just as my one-year-old grandson is offended when his mother won't let him play with a knife. He wants it. He should have it. That's how he thinks. So do we.

Nothing is wrong with desiring safe airplane flights and warm marriages and a decent, even a very decent, income. But none of these things, none of our hopes for a Better Life of Blessings, represents God's priority agenda. We don't *need* to be protected from physical suffering or personal pain. And we don't *need* to be affluent or even healthy. We need *only* to be safe from any power that opposes God's agenda for our lives. And we are!

God is in control. Of what? *Of seeing to it that nothing thwarts His plan for His people.* What is that plan? To give us a Better Life now, as we define it? No. It's to reveal Himself as the greatest treasure the human heart could ever imagine, to draw people into a relationship with Him that utterly delights their souls. It's the Immanuel Agenda.

What then is our greatest need? We need...

radical forgiveness that makes it possible for unholy people to come near to a holy God and live;

supernatural love that empowers naturally selfish people to care more about someone else other than themselves, thus revealing God;

spiritual might that actually changes bad people into good people, not good merely by society's standards—we have plenty of folks like that—but good like God, good enough to value ultimate goodness.

When Rome was proven vulnerable, Augustine wrote the *City of God*. He spoke of two cities, one made by man, the other by God. His central point was that God is in control of building His city, His kingdom, and that He is doing whatever it takes to populate that city with citizens who love Him above all else. The plain fact that we moderns have trouble grasping is that God is not cooperating with our agenda to make this world a safe and wonderful place to live. Building the City of Man is our purpose, not His. We cannot say "God is in control" and by that mean that God will help us build our city.

But God is in control of what He wants to accomplish. He's moving through all of history—through earthquakes and picnics, through terrorism and church dinners, through divorces and anniversary celebrations—toward one thing: the Immanuel Agenda. And He'll reach it. He'll have a people who think He is the greatest, who value knowing Him and worshiping Him and serving Him above all other blessings.

That's His purpose. He's in control. His purpose will be reached. Neither Osama bin Laden nor Hugh Hefner will stand in His way.

I feel a great burden to be unmistakably clear: *We cannot count on God to protect us from suffering of any kind or measure. The worst evil can happen to the best Christian. But we can count on God to enable us to draw near to Him whatever happens and, eventually, to experience deep joy when we do.*

If we're living for any other goal, if we supremely value the Better Life, we are not His disciples. We're quenching, not following, the Holy Spirit. We're cooperating with the world, the flesh, and the devil in opposing the Immanuel Agenda, and Immanuel's power will either change us or destroy us.

But if we're His disciples, if we pant after God like deer after water, if we seek only one thing—to gaze upon the beauty of the Lord because we believe that unmatchable pleasure is available in communion with Him[101]— then we're on the spiritual journey. We'll learn to radically depend on the Holy Spirit. And as we do, we'll experience miracles; we'll witness in our own lives the supernatural power of the God who is in control of all things.

COUNT ON GOD

In the rest of this chapter, I develop two points: *One,* we can count on God to perform three miracles in our lives. He wants to perform them, He can perform them, and He will perform them in the lives of New Way followers. *Two,* there's nothing we can do to make these miracles happen. By following the New Way, we create space for Him to work in a certain way. But we remain utterly dependent on His sovereign grace to bless us as He chooses and when He chooses. Dependence is a good thing, because God has sent His Spirit to do a sevenfold work that makes it possible for us to live the New Way.

Whatever else may happen, followers of the New Way can expect to participate in three miracles of grace. They *will* happen. They will not happen in the lives of those who follow the Old Way.

Miracle 1: We'll Encounter God

We can come into God's presence as we are—lustful, envious, discouraged, ugly enough to be reviled, selfish enough to deserve rejection, arrogant enough to be stomped on—and be welcomed and enjoyed.

As we sense God's welcome and feel His delight, as grace stirs us, we discover that beneath all the stain and smell, we're actually beautiful, even desirable. We share in Christ's loveliness. We're pure, we belong at the Father's table, we like to be good, and the power to do good is in us.

When God's grace surprises us, and not until, we will worship. Until then, we negotiate. Even when the tumor grows and is declared inoperable, even when our best efforts at reconciliation with spouse or children fail, even when terrorist evil kills thousands, we'll still worship. We will hurt, sometimes badly, but we will worship. *The miracle of encounter will be properly esteemed.*

Miracle 2: We'll Experience Community

With at least one other person, sometimes a handful, we'll enter into levels of closeness that surface enough conflict to sink any relationship—and spiritual intimacy will emerge. After feeling the impact of failure and hurt and reeling with defensiveness, recrimination, and withdrawal, we can expect, if we live the New Way, to discover a power within us sufficient to face every relationship-destroying force and to carry us into true community.

Non-Christians often "get along." Only Christians are capable of loving in the truest meaning of that word. When we recognize that we're ruled by ugly self-interest, when we see no escape, and when the way we relate crushes us into hopelessness, and not until then, we will love supernaturally. We'll still occasionally fuss and demand and sulk, but we will love. *The miracle of community will be gratefully celebrated.*

Miracle 3: We'll Be Transformed

An encounter with God and an experience in community will open our eyes to see how unlike Jesus we really are. We'll be appalled. Like Job when he finally heard God speak, we'll acknowledge, "I am unworthy."[102] And then, when we *see* God, we will, again like Job, exclaim, "My ears had heard of you but now my eyes have seen you. Therefore I despise myself and repent in dust and ashes."[103]

Brokenness and repentance will lead to abandonment. We'll never abandon ourselves to the Spirit as long as we think we can change without Him. But when we sense our desire not merely to feel good about ourselves and to enjoy life but to *resemble Jesus*, and when we realize how utterly incapable we are of moving even one step in that direction without supernatural help, we'll then abandon ourselves more fully to the Holy Spirit.

And then, at unplanned moments, we'll know living water is springing up within us. Something wonderful will come out of us, and we'll tremble with joy. When we stare into the chasm separating who we are from who we long to be and realize we have no means in our flesh to cross from one side to the other, and not until then, we will change. *The miracle of transformation will be humbly enjoyed.*

Three miracles will take place in every follower of the New Way:

encounter with God,

community that survives honesty, and

surprising *transformation* into the likeness of Christ.

But hear a caution. We must not define these miracles as the Better Life we desire and then try to arrange for them to happen. That would represent a shift from the New Way back to the Old.

And we must not expect miracles that cannot take place until heaven. Three come to mind.

First, we'll never in this life enjoy God consistently and fully enough to worship perfectly. There will always be reason for brokenness over our failure to esteem God as our greatest treasure.

Second, we'll never in this world experience the impact of grace deeply enough to relate perfectly with anyone. Superior feelings, insecure neediness, and unfair criticism will cloud every effort to love. There will always be reason for repentance over our failure to offer spiritual community.

Third, we'll never depend on God's Spirit enough to fully reveal who we already are in Christ. Until heaven, our transformation will always be incomplete. There will always be reason for further abandonment to God, stronger confidence in God, and freer release through God.

The simple truth is we'll be a mess until heaven. We'll never get it fully together. We'll never completely depend on the Holy Spirit—until we see Christ.

ALL THE SPIRIT DOES

But the Spirit continues to do His work. And the more we see all that He is doing, the more the pressure falls off. Dependence deepens. We rest in the sevenfold work of God's Spirit.[104] That rest, that dependence, is the fourth core idea in learning to live the New Way.

Let me now describe that sevenfold work and suggest how we can depend on all that the Spirit does as we seek to draw near to God.

The Spirit's First Work: Reminding

Just before He promised them peace, Jesus told His disciples that "the Counselor, the Holy Spirit, whom the Father will send in my name, will teach you all things and will remind you of everything I have said to you."[105]

When dreams shatter, when terrorists win and marriages fail, the Spirit is not silent. He reminds us that what matters most is unthreatened. The Father's agenda is on track. Christ did all that was needed for us to draw near to God and for Him to draw near to us. And the Spirit will tell us that the Trinity can conceive no greater blessing.

If we live the New Way, we'll spend time in Scripture, not to master content, but to hear the Spirit. And we'll sense a weighty anchor holding our ship steady in the worst storm. Like a seasoned nurse coming to our bedside and saying, "I've just checked with the doctor. Your disease has been cured. You'll be fine," the Spirit reminds us what Jesus has said: "In this world you will have trouble. But take heart! I have overcome the world."[106]

The Spirit's Second Work: Glorifying

When the Spirit comes, Jesus said, "He will bring glory to me by taking from what is mine and making it known to you."[107]

Coming to God can seem so pointless. The technician just drew blood from my arm. She frowned as she felt the vein she was about to stick. Reflexively, I shot up a quick prayer for painless and effective entry. Then the thought occurred: "What I really want is an experienced, skilled technician." God may answer that kind of prayer, but it seems more important to manage life by insisting on a seasoned sticker than to pray.

What will the Spirit make known to me while I wait for the needle or while I endure a far more significant trial? Sometimes I'm afraid to pray. Coming to God may rouse hopes that might be dashed and often are.

When I do come, I must come centrally to know Him, not to improve my life, not to have a painless blood draw on the first try. And when I do, the Spirit glorifies Christ by taking what belongs to Him—the eternal value of His life, death, and resurrection—and whispering to me, "The way is open. Whatever happens, God is in control of what matters most. Come boldly. Come close enough to hear the Father singing over you with delight."

In whatever shape I find myself, in the midst of whatever I'm facing, I'll be accepted into God's presence, listened to, understood, and given whatever my loving Father knows is best. Christ made that possible. To Him be the glory. That's what the Spirit is saying. It's His second work.

The Spirit's Third Work: Pouring

The Spirit inspired the apostle Paul to say this: "God has poured out his love into our hearts by the Holy Spirit, whom he has given us."[108]

It's so hard to believe we're loved. Not only do circumstances turn sour and God does nothing, but also we have never fully experienced from family or friends the kind of love we long to know. As in everything that matters most to our souls, we're utterly dependent on the Spirit to convince us that indeed we are fully loved and *can* rest in the love of God for us. He persuades us by pouring the Father's love into our hearts, which is a mystical process.

Without this third work of the Spirit, we'll continue at our core to feel unloved, to hide from love in fear it will not prove genuine, to work hard to manage our lives without being fully loved, to get along on whatever kind of love is given to us.

I have a difficult time receiving love. I find it's safer to give, never to be in the vulnerable position of truly needing anything. It's difficult to meaningfully ask the Holy Spirit to penetrate to the exact center of my heart, find the empty hole, and fill it with God's love. It seems so needy, so weak.

Others seem to revel in that prayer, believing that they're free from responsibility to follow God until that hole is filled. They turn the gracious provision of the Spirit into a self-absorbed demand that their needs be met.

But when I meditate on the Cross, when I open myself to others' touching me with Christ's love by being broken before them, then I may experience the wholeness of being divinely loved. I am indestructible, no suffering can undo me, I thrill at the prospect of strongly marching into my world under the banner of Christian love. That's what happens in me when the Spirit pours God's love into my heart. I wish it happened more often.

The Spirit's Fourth Work: Assuring

Are there more wonderful words for moral failures, lonely people, and abused victims to hear than "The Spirit himself testifies with our spirit that we are God's children"?[109]

Court is in session. All rise. Will the defendant please stand. You are accused of hypocrisy and deception. You claim to be God's child. Are you? That is the matter this court has convened to decide.

The evidence against us is overwhelming. And none of it is hidden. Every secret sin is accurately reported. We cringe. The accuser accuses, the world scoffs, the flesh doubts.

And then into the courtroom convened in our souls strides the Spirit, the mighty God, the Final Truth Teller. He speaks quietly, with the authority of a five-star general commanding his troops or the top medical expert delivering his opinion. "This one belongs to God." Who can argue? The matter is settled. The Immanuel Agenda is progressing in this person's life. This person is me. I *will* encounter God. I *will* participate in true community. I *will* resemble Christ. The Spirit has spoken. I have heard Him. Case closed.

The devil once stood next to a child of God and said, "Look at him. His clothes reek. How can he pretend to be related to royalty?"

Satan had a point. Joshua the high priest's clothes were filthy, covered with excrement.[110] Joshua dropped his head. The charge was true.

Then the Lord stepped forward. "Take those filthy clothes off that man," He ordered His servants. To Joshua He said, "See, I have taken away your sin, and I will put rich garments on you." Then He turned back to His servants: "Put a clean turban on his head." The turban worn by Israel's high priest was inscribed on the front plate with the words "Holiness to the Lord."

If we look only at our lives, we'll wonder if we're His. If we evaluate our progress along the spiritual journey, doubts will rise. But if we learn to listen to the Spirit, we'll *know* we are Christ's. And we'll delight in holy fellowship with God. We'll walk out of the courtroom and into the judge's home. We *are* His children.

The Spirit's Fifth Work: Sealing

When we came to Christ, not only were we included in Christ, but also, having believed, we were "marked in him with a seal, the promised Holy Spirit."[111]

Sealing means safety. The Spirit Himself is the seal. Sealed people are set apart from unsealed people. Think of it! You and I have been given into the keeping of the Spirit to guarantee our encounter with the Father and the Son. We're safe, not from bombs, cancer, or family heartache, but from even an inch of separation from the God who is in control of the Immanuel Agenda. We can come boldly into His presence.

In my father's last month of life, facing increasing weakness, continued sorrow over his wife's deteriorating Alzheimer's, and piercing loneliness, he often said to me, "I have omnipotence on my side. I am safe. To think of that brings a strange quietness beneath all the pain."

My father was sealed by God's Spirit, and because the Spirit revealed it to him, he knew the peace of God.

The Spirit's Sixth Work: Anticipation

"Now it is God who makes both us and you stand firm in Christ. He anointed us, set his seal of ownership on us, and put his Spirit in our hearts as a deposit, guaranteeing what is to come."[112]

The Spirit is the *earnest* of our inheritance, the *deposit* of what's ahead, and the *guarantee* that it's coming. He is a part of the whole, a taste of the meal, a sample of what we can anticipate.

Augustine understood grace (correctly, I believe) as an experience of joy that so far exceeds the pleasures of sin that we gladly give them up. The Spirit deposits within our souls a rush of joy that we occasionally experience, an unshakeable hope that's there when we need it, an overwhelming vision of beauty that we sometimes see. We glimpse what's coming and eagerly persevere through whatever is now.

When I talk openly with believers, I encounter what I see so often in myself, a cynicism about whether anyone truly experiences that kind of joy in God. Winning the lottery? Yes, that stirs deep excitement. Time with God? Frankly, a little boring; passion-filled for only a few mystics and contemplatives.

But God is essentially a community of passionate persons who profoundly like each other. When He created people, He built into them a capacity for that same kind of passion and enjoyment. And when He redeemed us, He put within us one member of the Trinity as a deposit, we might say a teaser, of what's coming. Given how vividly the Bible speaks of the pleasure and satisfaction and joy that God provides, we can only assume that the deposit within us is an experienceable taste, a felt pleasure, a palpable emotion, a little sample of what's in store for all of us.

There's more to knowing God than we dare imagine. It's time to put aside our cynicism and come to God, waiting consciously, deliberately, and with discipline for the Spirit to delight our souls with the rich fare of God.

The Spirit's Seventh Work: Anointing

"But you have an anointing from the Holy One, and all of you know the truth.... The anointing you received from him remains in you, and you do not need anyone to teach you."[113]

For years I have struggled off and on with depression. My interior world is often the scene of a battle against self-hatred, obsessive worry, discouraged inactivity, and hypersensitivity. What should I do? One physician and more than one friend have recommended antidepressants. Practical therapy like cognitive restructuring or dynamic therapy that explores hidden emotions and issues of existential angst might help.

Here's my view. The first step in dealing with any difficulty in our lives—rebellious kids, tense marriages, indecisiveness, gluttony, or depression—is *not* to set the goal of making things better and then coming up with an action plan. That's the Old Way.

The first step is to come to God.

Admit where you are; find the red dot.

Identify the two paths before you, the Old Way and the New Way.

Make it your highest ambition to encounter God, to participate in community, and to become like Jesus.

Learn dependence on the Holy Spirit and expect those three ambitions to be granted as miracles.

Pray as a pilgrim on a journey (I'll discuss how in the next chapter).

Coming to God for the Better Hope of enjoyed intimacy with Him (which brings glory to His Name) releases something from us. Loving passion and discerning wisdom are given to us by the Spirit. We sense His leading on what to do. That's the anointing we have received from Him. It's a divinely directed game plan for dealing with whatever is going on in our lives.

I am sensing a clear release to eat more responsibly, exercise more faithfully, and confess a spirit of fear and self-pity. More faithful time in the Word, praying more often as a pilgrim, and setting aside time to move slowly to better enjoy family, friends, recreation, and leisure seem to me an anointing from the Spirit. If after moving in these directions, there's no lifting of my occasional heaviness, I may conclude that I struggle with a chemically induced depression and consider antidepressants. Or I may, with Spurgeon, receive my depression as a tool ordained by God to help me live more dependently and minister more powerfully.

I take this seventh work of the Holy Spirit, this spiritual anointing, to mean that followers of the New Way will be given the passion and wisdom of Christ to respond to every challenge they meet in life. When the Spirit came on the incarnate Christ, He was granted wisdom, power, and delight-producing fear.[114] And now in Christ are hidden all the treasures of wisdom and knowledge.[115] If we learn what it means to come to Him, we'll receive an anointing that enlightens us about what to do and empowers us to do it in any circumstance of life.

If we believed that, it would change the face of Christian counseling. We would cease to think of counseling or therapy as an expert offering specialized knowledge to a patient. It would become a focused opportunity for a seasoned fellow pilgrim to join another on the journey into God's presence. Counseling as we know it would be swallowed up by spiritual direction and spiritual friendship, by two folks together coming to God to wait on Him for His direction and to be filled with His energy.

WE HAVE WHAT WE NEED

That's the fourth core idea for what it means to live the New Way: *Depend on the Spirit* and His sevenfold work.

We can depend on Him to…

- let us know the bottom line is okay. The plan the Father thinks is best for us is on track no matter what may be happening in our lives.
- show us the way into God's presence opened up by Christ. We have a new purity, a new identity, a new disposition, and a new power that make it possible at any time, in any condition, to come to God.[116]
- pour God's love into our hearts until we're amazed that the unlovable is really loved.
- persuade us that we do belong to God even when the evidence is woefully inadequate.
- keep us safe from any power that can get us off track in our cooperation with the Immanuel Agenda.
- provide enough of a taste of God's presence and reality to keep us eager to know Him better.
- grant us the motivation and method, the passion and the wisdom, to deal with all of our decisions and responsibilities in a way that glorifies Him and gives us joy, even when life's problems don't get better.

God is in control—of what? Of the Immanuel Agenda. Through the rubble of destroyed buildings and messed-up lives, He is moving powerfully toward His end. Followers of the New Way share His excitement for that end and, through dependence on the Holy Spirit, journey toward the day when Christ is all in all and God is our supreme treasure at every moment.

In the Spirit we have what we need to journey on. The pressure's off. We don't have to make this life work. There's a new way to live.

And much of the fuel for the journey is provided through prayer, a certain kind of prayer, the prayer of the child on a journey home. I call it the Papa Prayer. It's the fifth (and final) core idea for entering and living the New Way.

CHAPTER TWENTY-ONE

THE PAPA PRAYER

Someone I love very much is hurting. I hurt for her and I'm scared. What will happen? I don't know. So I pray.

But as I pray, the pressure increases. I feel more scared, almost hopeless, and a little angry. These emotions are unacceptable, so I choke them off and pray for a few more minutes, but now without passion, indifferent, cynical. Do I really expect Him to change what disturbs me and troubles the person I love because I pray?

For years I've assumed that the biblical command to "believe and not doubt"[117] when we pray has to do with petitionary prayer, with our requests that God make our lives better. Laboring under that assumption, I've tried to work up confidence that He would do whatever I ask, as long as I ask only for good things. Despite my best efforts, unbelief and doubt continue to nag in the back of my mind as I pray. And, I think, for good reason.

Before James tells us to believe and not doubt when we pray, he talks about suffering, about hardships that no one would include in their definition of a Better Life. And he instructs us to welcome them as friends, to let them do their work of maturing us. Nothing whatever in that passage is said about using prayer to get rid of trials.

That makes me think that James assumes we're praying the New Way, not focusing on our desires for a Better Life but yearning for the Better Hope of knowing God and becoming like Him.

In his last year of life, my father more than once told me, "I know God could cure Mother's Alzheimer's in a moment. I believe that. And I pray for it. But I don't believe He will. Or at least I'm not sure. If He doesn't, then somehow this suffering is useful for a good purpose I can't see. And when I pray that *those purposes* will be accomplished in her life and mine, I'm confident He'll answer that prayer. Of that I have no doubt."

THE ESSENCE OF NEW WAY PRAYER

It has recently dawned on me that there's an Old Way to pray and a New Way to pray. Christians who treasure a Better Life of Blessings from God above the Better Hope of Intimacy with God pray the Old Way. Petition takes precedence over surrender. Requests nudge aside worship. Gratitude depends on blessings.

Old Way prayers come in at least three varieties:

Change that.

> Whatever in my life is causing pain, I ask you to change it. Straighten out my daughter, give me a spouse, restore my health, provide an income.

Use this.

> Show me what principles I'm to follow to make it happen. Direct me to the person or resources I need to help make it happen.

Satisfy me.

> I long to feel alive, content, fulfilled, and happy. Do whatever it takes to make me feel satisfied with me, with life, and with You.

Nothing is wrong with these prayers *unless they represent the deepest passion of our hearts.* Then they're Old Way prayers with more demands than petitions.

New Way prayers include petition, but they never start there. The beginning, the primary content, and the ending of New Way prayers are all the same: *I come.* "Lord, I come to You, just as I am. One thing I ask—let me see Your beauty. And seeing Your beauty, let me love like You and live like You."

Petition may follow that prayer, but it never becomes priority. "Let me draw near to You, whether through blessing or trial, and draw near to me so I can be an instrument of Your love in all the particulars of my life. As Your child, I ask on behalf of my daughter—give her a heart for You. I ask for a spouse—give me a companion for life. I ask for health—may the cancer not come back. And I ask for an income—let me pay my bills and enjoy a few things only money can buy. But not my will, rather Thine be done. Believing and without doubting, I ask that You let me come to You and live in Your presence."

This morning I prayed for the loved one who is hurting. I'm not wrong for wishing and then asking that God would change what is difficult. I'm not wrong for asking God to show me what to do or who to ask that might make things better. And I'm not wrong for asking God that both I and the one I love will experience deep contentment and rest.

But I am wrong for wanting the trouble to go away more than I want to draw near to God, more than I want to enjoy Him and reflect Him in this situation. Desiring my blessing more than His glory should occasion brokenness, not petition for more blessings. Paul spoke strongly against "not *acting* in line with the truth of the gospel";[118] the Spirit has spoken strongly to me against not *praying* in line with the truth of the gospel.

Change that! Use this! Satisfy me! I pray like that all the time. Make me a wise parent so I can help my sons walk more closely with You. Give me the wisdom I need to relate well to my wife so we grow even closer. Bless my doctor with medical wisdom so she'll properly diagnose the back pain I've been feeling.

Are those prayers wrong? Yes, when they express the deepest passion of my heart. No, not when they express desires that are subordinate to my passion for God Himself, for His glory to be revealed through my valuing Him above all else.

We can pray a New Way. We can stop insisting that God *change that,* *use this,* and *satisfy us.* When someone we love is hurting, when we're scared and feeling inadequate, when pain in our souls seems unbearable, when our cynicism about answered prayer reduces us to rote praying, we can pray, not to change that, use this, or satisfy me, but rather *Lord, I come.* That's the essence of the New Way prayer.

EXPRESSING YOURSELF TO GOD

I call it the Papa Prayer:

> *P*resent yourselves to God as you are.
>
> *A*ttend to where you notice God's presence or absence.
>
> *P*urge yourselves of whatever, at that moment, might be keeping you from noticing more of God.
>
> *A*pproach God with abandonment and confidence, dedicating yourselves anew to coming to Him to know and enjoy and reveal Him, not to using Him to make your life better.

I suggest you set aside at least twenty minutes to pray the Papa Prayer. Spend five minutes on each of the four parts. Do it in this deliberate way several times per week. Write a letter to God expressing yourself in each category, five minutes presenting yourself to God, then five minutes attending to Him, five more minutes purging yourself as the Spirit leads, and a final five minutes approaching Him.

The same rhythm of prayer can easily be followed anytime day or night in only a few moments by simply speaking to God as you lie in bed or drive your car or watch a boring movie. "God, *here's* where I am. I sense You *here* but not *there.* I'm aware that *this* keeps me from hearing Your voice. But I declare again, right now, *my desire to come to You* whether You bless me or not in other ways I want."

Let me describe the Papa Prayer. It represents how followers of the New

Way can come to God to glorify Him rather than feeling the pressure to get something right so life works better.

Present Yourself to God

Reflect on your life. Be brutally honest, knowing by God's grace revealed in the New Covenant you'll discover nothing that will make God reject you and believing, because of that same grace, that beneath the dirtiest dirt lies radiant beauty.

What passions within you seem deepest? Ask a few (only a few) trusted friends for feedback: What are you like to be with? What's your "pull," that is, what do people sense you're wanting from them, what's your effect on them, in the moment?

Make the incredibly difficult decision to face yourself, to feel your rage, lust, and terror as well as your compassion, kindness, and joy. Pretend about nothing. But as you honor that commitment, avoid the twin errors of *denial* ("I'll face only what I can handle, what doesn't make me feel too threatened") and *obsession* ("I'll face everything all the time").

I remember one recent morning when I couldn't get my mind off my struggles. I recited Scripture, I asked for peace, I set an action plan for the day. Nothing helped. And then it occurred to me, I'm telling myself all about my troubles. I could be presenting myself to God.

Here's part of what I wrote that morning in my Papa journal under presenting prayer:

> Dear Accepting One,
>
> I am so distraught right now. My conversation last night with my father was hard. I felt dismissed, lectured to, not believed in. He's such a good man. How could I feel that way? I think my rage has more to do with questions I can't answer— is what I'm doing really important? Have I heard from You,

or am I coming up with stuff out of my own prejudice and craziness? I am a mixture of such pressure and joy. And I'm weird. As I dressed this morning, I see a belt to put on, shirt buttons to connect, socks to slide on my feet—and I feel I must do everything at once. What on earth is that all about?

For me that was the red dot marking where I was that morning. That began my Papa Prayer.

Attend to God

Where have you noticed God's *presence* in the past hour or day? Where have you been aware of a longing to sense that He was with you but felt only His *absence?*

The spiritual journey is centered in the experience of God. But it's rooted in the revealed truth of God. Attend to what you experience of God, but during this part of the prayer, focus also on what you know is true, whether you experience it or not. Remember the sevenfold work of the Spirit as you ponder whatever biblical text you read.

Listen to the Spirit remind you of all that Jesus said, especially that everything is under control. Nothing ever takes God by surprise. The Immanuel Agenda is on course.

Hear Him glorify Christ. Everything you need to experience the life of true abundance is in Christ and in the New Covenant made in His blood.

Notice when He pours love into your heart. Be still, tune your ear to the music of heaven, hear the Father sing over you with delight.

Depend on the Spirit's witness that you are a child of God, even when the evidence you see makes you wonder.

Relax in the safety of His seal on your life. No act of terrorism, no stock market slide, no medical scare, no rejection, no broken family has the power to thwart God's work in your life. Everything can be redeemed by the Spirit for good purposes.

Taste whatever sample He gives you of the meal that's coming. It might be a moment of overwhelming joy or a deep release of built-up pressure to get it right so God will bless.

Trust the Spirit's anointing. Anticipate that He'll grant you the passion and wisdom to handle every situation you face in a way that honors Christ and advances His agenda.

Here's a brief excerpt from my Papa journal expressing an attending prayer:

> Dear Anchor Who Lets Me Drift Only So Far,
> You spoke to me last night through Bilbo Baggins in *The Hobbit*. He fought the battle that counted in the tunnel alone. The issue is courage. I heard you say, "Be of good courage!" And waiting, with faith and courage. Yes, I'm down but not out. You are with me in the tunnel. Remarkable. Tolkien wrote that book years ago. And you spoke to me through it yesterday. The bottom line's okay. I'm safe, not alone, and alive.

Don't expect your sense of God's presence to directly relate to what you presented to Him. It may. It may not.

Purge Yourself Before God

Start by reciting David's prayer:

> Search me, O God, and know my heart;
> test me and know my anxious thoughts.
> See if there is any offensive way in me,
> and lead me in the way everlasting.[119]

Reflect on what is in you—attitude, motive, determination—and on what you're doing that makes it difficult for you to hear the Spirit, to believe His Word, to trust God.

Assume whatever it is has roots in a preoccupation with yourself. A focus on *your* desire, *your* dreams, *your* hopes, *your* disappointments, *your* pain can drive you to Old Way living. The effect of a focus on self, though encouraged by the therapeutic culture and sanctioned by much Christian teaching, is to accept another gospel, the gospel that God is here for us more than we're here for Him.

For me, purging often includes brokenness and repentance as I confess how committed I am to never looking foolish and how much I think I should be noticed and appreciated for what I do. I reflect on my experiences of great shame and great satisfaction to understand what I live to avoid and gain. *That* caused terrible pain. It must never happen again. But *this* brought deep pleasure. I want to see it repeated.

For me, to live is avoiding what hurt and gaining what I enjoyed. God, arrange my life accordingly. How awful! For Paul, to live was Christ.

This from my Papa journal:

> Dear Gentle One,
>   I so badly want to improve my life in ways that feel good.
> It's so much easier and more predictable to enjoy an obvious
> blessing than to enjoy coming to You. I walk right by Your
> Living Water to go dig another leaky well.

Approach God Because You Want Him

As you present yourself to God—with all of who you are, with all you know God to be, with all your ongoing struggle against the flesh—respond in faith to God's invitations:

Come, all you who are weary.

Come, all you who can't get it right.

Come, all you who are struggling to make life work.

You're aware of the burdensome pressure of Old Way living and the heinous arrogance beneath it, but you're also aware of a spiritual hunger, of a longing to come to God to…

glorify and enjoy Him in an *encounter* with Him,

join the *community* of His people,

be *transformed* by His Spirit till you actually resemble Jesus.

Expect to experience a sovereign joy that will displace every affection other than God from the center of your heart. Anticipate that, by the Spirit, the Father and Son will show themselves to you. Trust the Spirit to provide the loving passion and the spiritual wisdom you need to handle every situation in life in a way that furthers the Immanuel Agenda.

Tell God, with tears if they're there, with whatever genuineness is alive within you, that you want Him more than any other blessing—to know Him, adore Him, enjoy Him, serve Him, reveal Him, become like Him. As you pray, you'll find petition flowing from your heart for others, especially for their salvation and growth, and for yourself, that you'll be an instrument of grace. You'll come with confidence, making known all your burdens without a spirit of anxiety or demand, but with trust in a Father whose love can be trusted.

I wrote these words as part of an approaching prayer:

> Dear Waiting Father,
>
> At this moment, 10:30 A.M. on June 22, 2001, somewhat unfelt but still true, I surrender my heart to the ONE GOAL of knowing You. I resolve:
>
> —to distrust all joys coming from all other sources yet to celebrate them as gifts from you,
>
> —to write my next book in a spirit of self-aware dependence on You,

—to live in the freedom You provide, with all
that feels like a risk to me.
Even as I write, I am stirred. I really do want You, to glorify You in my life.
AMEN!

BELIEVE, DON'T DOUBT

Thrill to the miracle taking place in your soul. The pressure's off! You actually want to come to God more than you want to use Him. You're living
the New Way!

Then tomorrow will come. Life will continue messy and perhaps get
messier. You'll feel tied up in knots again. It's time for the Spiritual Cycle to
continue—brokenness, repentance, abandonment, confidence, and release.

Find the dot. Recognize the two paths. Reset your goals. Listen to the
Spirit. Pray the Papa Prayer again and again and again.

Let me end by paraphrasing the apostle James:

"Dear friends, when difficulties come, don't try to figure out what you
can do to make things better. Welcome whatever is going wrong as a
chance to more deeply encounter God, to enter community, and to experience transformation.

"If you're not sure how to actually do that, ask God, not for improved
circumstances or happier experiences, but for the wisdom to let your suffering draw out your desire for God. When you ask for that, know that He
gives generously and never criticizes you for where you are. Believe, don't
doubt. If you waiver between wanting the New Way and still clinging to
the Old, you'll receive nothing from the Lord.

"It's time, brothers and sisters, to abandon ourselves fully to God.
There's a New Way to live. Draw near to God, and He'll draw near to you.

He'll meet you, fill you, delight you, and use you to further the great plan of the ages, the Immanuel Agenda. Then we'll all go home."[120]

Are you weary?

Having trouble getting it right?

Struggling to make your life work?

The pressure's off.

There *is* a New Way to live.

WITH GOD IN THE BATHROOM

"Adam," God said, "it isn't good for you to be without a human companion. I am your chief delight, but I intend for you to enjoy many other pleasures as well, and I'll provide them all."

A little while later, Adam's second most wonderful blessing became, in his mind, his first. He chose to move toward Eve when treasuring God required him to move away. Each of his descendants, ever since, has made the same choice—to value someone or something more than God.

"We now have one objective." The Father was speaking. "We must change people's hearts so that they value Us above everything else. Until that happens, We cannot provide all the good things We would love—and are able—to give them. To do so would encourage their natural bent toward finding joy in lesser things and thus keep them from experiencing true joy."

"All humans are guilty of the greatest evil imaginable, Father," said the Son. "They don't see in You all the beauty their hearts could ever want. That one sin will lead to all others. Justice requires that You give them over to their wrong understanding of pleasure. But that would mean leaving them in an eternal world where every pleasure is available but You, which is no pleasure at all. That would be hell.

"Father, I will satisfy justice to reveal Your grace. I will become one of them, but unlike them, of course, I will always love You more than all. How could I do otherwise? I will assume responsibility for their wicked foolishness in loving anything more than You. Then, Father, punish Me instead of them. Let Me experience the horror of absolute separation from You. Then justice will be satisfied. You can forgive for their evil all who accept the punishment You inflict on Me as the punishment they deserve."

The Father declared, "That is My plan."

Many years passed. After the Son experienced the Father's withdrawal and was then welcomed back into heaven with great celebration, the Spirit spoke. "Now I can enter the very souls of each one You forgive. I'll plant within them a yearning to know You, Father, and I'll nourish that desire until You become their supreme treasure.

"I'll use every bit of suffering You allow to stir their hearts toward You, until they want You more than every other pleasure. And then, when You decide, We'll bring them here to see the Son and, through Him, to see You. From that moment on, You will forever be their chief value, their highest pleasure, their greatest joy. How could it be otherwise? How could it ever have been otherwise? And then—oh, what a day—We will lavish on them every blessing Our infinite love can conceive, with no possibility that anyone will become more attached to Your blessings than to You."

TWO FOUNDATIONS

We now live between Calvary and the Coming, between Pentecost and the Parousia (the appearing of our great God and Savior). We live in this world. We stay busy in this world. We deal with what happens in this world. And we should. But we have a choice. We live our lives on one of two foundations.

Most of us accept the challenge to effectively, wisely, and morally engage with life in this world with the expectation, at least the hope, that blessings will follow. A few accept the invitation to come to God to find in Him everything their hearts desire, and then to live their lives in this world as He directs and enables, with no stronger wish than to hold His Name high.

If we build on the first foundation, the flesh, our core passion will be for blessings, whichever ones we value most. And our core experience, beneath whatever else we feel, will be pressure, the pressure to live a certain way to get the life we want.

If we build on the second foundation, the Spirit, our core passion will be for God, to know Him and honor Him in any circumstance. And our core experience will be freedom, the freedom to draw near to God across a bridge we neither constructed nor maintain. And in that freedom we'll discover both the passion to live well and the wisdom to know what that means.

Living on the foundation of the flesh looks like this:

Core Attitude: My will be done

↑

Core Hope: I expect good things to follow

↑

Core Strategy: I will figure out what to do and do it

↑

Core Experience: I must get it right so blessings come

↑

Core Passion: I live to be blessed

The New Way to live, the way of the Spirit, looks very different:

```
Core Attitude:   Thy will be done
        ↑
Core Hope:   I expect to become like Jesus
        ↑
Core Strategy:   I will trust His provision
        ↑
Core Experience:   I come to Him to celebrate His glory
        ↑
Core Passion:   I live to know Christ
```

JUST LET ME KNOW YOU

Permit a final illustration.

When I was three years old, our family lived for a while in my grandparents' big, old-fashioned house. The only bathroom was on the second floor.

One Saturday afternoon (I know it was Saturday—Dad was home), I decided I was a big boy and could use the bathroom without anyone's help. So I climbed the stairs, closed and locked the door behind me, and for the next few minutes felt very self-sufficient.

Then it was time to leave. I couldn't unlock the door. I tried with every ounce of my three-year-old strength, but I couldn't do it. I panicked. I felt again like a very little boy as the thought went through my head, "I might spend the rest of my life in this bathroom."

My parents—and likely the neighbors—heard my desperate scream. "Are you okay?" Mother shouted through the door she couldn't open from the outside. "Did you fall? Have you hit your head?"

222

"I can't unlock the door," I yelled. "Get me out of here!"

I wasn't aware of it right then, but Dad raced down the stairs, ran to the garage to find the ladder, hauled it off the hooks, and leaned it against the side of the house just beneath the bathroom window. With adult strength, he pried it open, then climbed into my prison, walked past me, and with that same strength, turned the lock and opened the door.

"Thanks, Dad," I said—and ran out to play.

That's how I thought the Christian life was supposed to work. When I get stuck in a tight place, I should do all I can to free myself. When I can't, I should pray. Then God shows up. He hears my cry—"Get me out of here. I want to play!"—and unlocks the door to the blessings I desire.

Sometimes He does. But now, no longer three years old and approaching sixty, I'm realizing the Christian life doesn't work that way. And I wonder, are any of us content with God? Do we even like Him when He doesn't open the door we most want opened—when a marriage doesn't heal, when rebellious kids still rebel, when friends betray, when financial reverses threaten our comfortable way of life, when the prospect of terrorism looms, when health worsens despite much prayer, when loneliness intensifies and depression deepens, when ministries die?

God has climbed through the small window into my dark room. But He doesn't walk by me to turn the lock that I couldn't budge. Instead, He sits down on the bathroom floor and says, "Come sit with me!" He seems to think that climbing into the room to be with me matters more than letting me out to play.

I don't always see it that way. "Get me out of here," I scream. "If You love me, *unlock the door!*"

Dear friend, the choice is ours. *Either* we can keep asking Him to give us what we think will make us happy—to escape our dark room and run to the playground of blessings—*or* we can accept His invitation to sit with Him, for now perhaps in darkness, and to seize the opportunity to know Him better and represent Him well in this difficult world.

Will we choose the Old Way, the way of pressure? "I'll do whatever You say; just get me out of here!"

Or will we discover both God's heart and ours and choose the New Way, the way of freedom and joy? "I'll sit with You anywhere, in darkness or light; just let me know You and serve You!"

It's time to choose the New Way of the Spirit and follow it until we play forever in the fields of heaven, always looking to Jesus as our greatest blessing.

It's time to be with God in the bathroom until He opens the door to eternity. *It's what we want.*

A TEN-YEAR-AFTER
AFTERWORD

In 2001, one year before *The Pressure's Off* was released, I wrote these words:

> At the time of this writing, I'm pushing toward the sixth
> decade of my life. My hair is white, two little kids call me
> Pop-Pop, twenty-five minutes on the treadmill is my equiva-
> lent to climbing Mount Everest, and I can look back on
> nearly half a century of living life as a Christian.

Those two sentences, one brief, the second one too long, open chapter
2 of my book. And now, ten years later, I begin a new "introductory after-
word" with these two sentences.

> As I write these words, I'm looking back on my sixty-seventh
> birthday. My hair is still white, not yet thinning; five kids
> now call me Pop-Pop, the oldest thirteen and the youngest
> two (to my delight, Kenzie can now say my name); an unex-
> plained ache in my right leg makes time on the treadmill
> more difficult; more than a half century, now almost six
> decades, has passed since I declared myself a Jesus follower;

and I'm less than a month away from a second round of
surgery for cancer that was removed fourteen years ago
from near my pancreas and now has returned to my liver.

Still two sentences, one short, the second much too long—but made
possible with commas and semicolons. And both sentences are true as I
push my way through the seventh decade of my life, now with some uncertainty. Less is now clear, but more is now certain.

Age, I think, either hardens or humbles its victim. Hardness is easier. A
crust of cynical denial can keep unpleasant reality at bay. Humility pokes
holes in whatever crust has formed and leaves you no choice but to become
authentic. The process is not always comfortable.

Ten years ago I wrote this near the end of *The Pressure's Off* (page
196): "We can count on God to perform three miracles in our lives." The
first miracle I labeled an *encounter with God*. The second I described as an
experience of community. The third, I wrote, involved *spiritual transformation,* the felt knowledge that "living water is springing up within us.
Something wonderful will come out of us, and we'll tremble with joy"
(page 198).

I've asked myself: *Does humility require me to recant, maybe to soft-pedal
those three miracles, perhaps dilute them into more realistic, less supernatural
happenings, no longer miracles we can count on God to perform?*

My answer is no. I understand the three miracles a little differently
now, but in ways that more amazingly highlight their miraculous nature.
Let me explain.

Try to make life work, be good so God does you good, what I called the
Old Way to live, and you will not encounter God as God. You will be treating God as a manipulable uncle, perhaps as a leniently doting grandfather.
And community (the second miracle), the kind of intimate community
that defines the Trinity that we are now capable of genuinely but not fully
enjoying, becomes impossible. We are out for ourselves, using God and

spouses and children and pastors and friends to get what we want out of life. Self-centeredness eliminates true relational connection.

And real transformation, being formed by Christ, never happens. In the Old Way, self-centeredness, socialized and disguised to look Christian, is seen as a virtue. The kind of transformation that God's Spirit produces requires brokenness over self-centeredness and a hungry vision of what it would mean to become radically other-centered.

What (following Paul) I called the New Way to live—demanding nothing now, sacrificing everything now for the glory of God in anticipation of knowing Him then by actually meeting Jesus, of enjoying community with the three divine Persons and their huge family, of living forever as a completely changed, holy, loving person—frees us from looking out for ourselves and frees us to live now to advance God's kingdom by becoming like Jesus through dependence on the Spirit's indwelling reality.

Read this book again. You'll find nothing different from what I just said. But you might hear the following more clearly.

MIRACLE 1

You most consistently and truly encounter God by expressing God. Contemplating God in solitude may lead to divine encounters, but relating to others in a way that reveals God and releases His life into others provides the assurance that you know God.

MIRACLE 2

You meet others in true spiritual community most deeply in shared brokenness over sin and in shared celebration of grace. Working together with shared missional energy is good, and it bonds servants together. But looking personally bad in the presence of another's grace-filled love brings souls together in worship. There is no richer bonding with fellow Christians.

MIRACLE 3

You change most thoroughly by feeling your emptiness and facing your brokenness, then waiting on God's Spirit to transform your emptiness into thirst and your brokenness into gratitude. Waiting well means immersion in Scripture, corporate worship, relational prayer, and sacrificial service. Transformation does not centrally mean to feel what you want to feel and to behave as you want to behave. Rather, it means to feel painful thirst that will not be fully satisfied until the next life and to express the deepest gratitude for the forgiveness you enjoy. Thirsty people who trust God wait for His Son to return, demanding no satisfaction now. And grateful people live not for their own interests but for the interests of others. They relate with other-centered passion. And that's a new way to live.

More letters than I can count encourage me to appreciatively believe that God has used *The Pressure's Off* to introduce scores of people to a paradigm for following Jesus, to abandon the Old Way and embrace the New Way. And that is literally life changing. Keep the above three thoughts in mind as you read or reread this book, and its message will reach deeper and provide greater freedom to demand nothing now and to joyfully anticipate everything then.

WORKBOOK

QUESTIONS YOU MAY HAVE
ABOUT THIS WORKBOOK

What will *The Pressure's Off Workbook* do for me?

This workbook will help you discover and understand what the Bible calls "the new way of the Spirit." As Dr. Larry Crabb writes in *The Pressure's Off,* "This new way leads through a life that doesn't work very well into a mysterious certitude that anchors us in storms of doubt, into moments of ecstasy that keep bigger hopes alive when good dreams die, into the terrifying experience of death to self that allows our true selves to walk out of the tomb into the light of day."

Should I read the book first?

Your best approach is to read *The Pressure's Off* as you go through this workbook. However, many key portions from the text are included here to give you a sufficiently broad and accurate indication of the content.

To help as you go through this workbook, you'll find the appropriate chapters to read listed at the beginning of each weekly lesson.

The lessons look long. Do I need to work completely through each one?

This eight-lesson workbook is designed to promote your thorough exploration of each week's material, but you may find it best to focus your time and discussion on some sections and questions more than others.

Also, you may decide to follow a slower pace than one lesson per week. This could be true whether you're going through the workbook individually or in a group. In a group that meets weekly, for example, you may decide to spend two weeks of discussion time on each lesson. (In your first meeting, decide together on what you believe to be the best pacing and schedule.) If you're going through the workbook on your own, you may simply want to try completing two or three questions each day.

Above all, keep in mind that the purpose of the workbook is to help guide you in specific life application of the biblical truths taught in *The Pressure's Off*. The wide assortment of questions included in each weekly lesson is meant to help you approach this practical application from different angles and with expansive reflection and self-examination.

Allowing adequate time to prayerfully reflect on each question will be much more valuable for you than rushing through this workbook.

Fellow seeker, will you dare to imagine
what for so long you've feared may not be available?
Will you join me, a trembling pilgrim,
in putting aside the cynicism that skillfully avoids the risk of hoping?
Will you embrace your desire for the one thing
you would give all else to gain—
an actual encounter with Jesus Christ, now, before heaven?

—from the opening pages
of *The Pressure's Off* by Dr. Larry Crabb

OLD WAY OR
NEW WAY?

*This week's lesson is based on
the introductory content
("A Parable: Night Question"
and "Introduction: Two Paths")
plus Part I: "There's a New Way to Live."*

As you begin each week's study, remember to ask for the Holy Spirit's help in hearing and obeying His words for you at this time.

Included in each weekly study you'll find a number of excerpts from *The Pressure's Off*, each one marked at the beginning and end by this symbol: 📖. These excerpts serve not only to convey Dr. Crabb's message from the book, but also to stimulate your reflection and discussion and to guide your exploration of Scripture. The excerpts are usually brief, so you may want to frequently refer back to *The Pressure's Off* and review their fuller context.

1. At the beginning of *The Pressure's Off* is a section entitled "A Parable: Night Question" (see pages 3–9). Read this short section now.

Think about the beginning mind-set of the woman in this parable. What appears to be her view of God and her overall view of life?

How would you summarize what happens to the woman in this parable?

In your own words, how would you express the message or "point" of this parable?

TWO PATHS

In his introduction to *The Pressure's Off,* Dr. Crabb describes two paths and what it's like to walk each one. He writes that all of us are always walking one or the other of these two paths—and that we're doing so "right now, at this very moment."

2. Below are several lines of description that Dr. Crabb gives for what it's like to walk one or the other of these two paths. How closely does each statement match the path you seem to be on at this moment? Rate each statement from 0 to 5—the higher the number, the more closely the description matches your life at present.

____ You've decided that what you most want out of life is within your reach, and you're doing whatever you believe it takes to get it.

____ Your life is filled with pressure. Inside, where no one sees, your soul is weary. You see no way to step off the treadmill.

___ Life is going well, and you're satisfied. But you sense something's wrong, something's missing. The pressure is still there.

___ You've realized that what you most want is beyond your reach, and you're trusting God for the satisfaction you seek. You want Him. Nothing less, not even His blessings, will do.

___ You have hope. Your soul may be weary, your interior world may be filled with struggles no one sees, but you have hope. At times you rest.

___ Something is alive in you; the desire of your heart is not smothered. You can taste freedom. And the taste brings joy.

3. In the preceding question, the first three descriptive statements have to do with the Old Way, an approach to living that Dr. Crabb describes and exposes in many ways throughout *The Pressure's Off.* In the book's introduction, he says that "most people live the Old Way all of their lives" and that "most people who go to church live a religious version of the Old Way." He also writes this:

📖 The Old Way involves a quid-pro-quo arrangement with God or, if not with God, then with the order in the universe, with the rules that make life work. If you do what you should, then you get what you want, either from a moral God who rewards good behavior or from an orderly world that you effectively use. It leaves you in control of how things turn out in your life. The Old Way promises a better life filled with good things that make you happy.

But it never delivers, though it may seem to for a long time. The Old Way doesn't work for one reason: You never keep your end of the bargain, not completely. No one does. 📖

At this point, how strongly do you agree with Dr. Crabb's conclusion that the Old Way "never delivers"?

What questions do his comments raise in your mind?

4. At this point in his discussion, Dr. Crabb introduces the phrase *Law of Linearity*—"a law that states there is an *A* that leads to the *B* you want. Figure out what *A* is, do it, and you'll have the life you most desire. The pressure's on." This Law of Linearity, he says, is a belief held by people who follow the Old Way.

   To what degree have you believed in this Law of Linearity in your own life?

   Dr. Crabb states that belief in this law brings pressure to our lives. What pressure does it bring? And is this pressure good or bad, according to your understanding of it?

5. The New Way is in stark contrast to the Old Way, and those who live the New Way follow a different law:

   📖 People who live the New Way believe the *Law of Liberty*. They come as they are. They do not bathe before they approach God. They come to God for the bath. They feel no pressure to change either their inner life or their outer life, but they *desire* change in both spheres. And they are eager to do whatever will create the opportunity for change, even if it

means dipping themselves seven times in a muddy river or
marching around an enemy's wall for seven days and blowing
trumpets. They live for the truest desire of their hearts: to
know God and to enjoy Him. They do not live for a better
life in this world. And when their life here is hard, when
things fall apart, they most clearly reveal who they are.
They're citizens of another world who most want what this
world can never provide. So they wisely indulge their deepest
desire and trust God to reveal Himself to them. That's the
Law of Liberty. 📖

Describe here the ways in which this description matches your own
spiritual desires and longings.

RULES TO LIVE BY

📖 I have no strategies in mind to give you a better marriage,
better kids, a more complete recovery from sexual abuse, or
quicker healing after your divorce. Nor, I believe, does God.

I want all these things for you. So does God. And I want a
better life for myself. So does God. *But He wants something
more for both of us.* And only when we pursue the more will
He grant the less. Or He might not. 📖

6. As you consider carefully the preceding quotation, what questions
come to your mind? In what respects do you agree with what these
paragraphs have to say about God?

If you agree with the central message in those paragraphs, what do you think is the "something more" God wants for us?

What Scripture passages and teachings can you think of to support your conclusion about this "something more" that God wants for us?

> I'm troubled by how unquestioningly we live out our determination to make this life work. All our hopes for happiness are bound up in it. It's as if we believe this is the only world we ever plan to inhabit.

7. Ask yourself to what extent your hopes and expectations for happiness are bound up in this life rather than in your eternal life. As you honestly face this issue, what kind of observations come to mind?

8. Dr. Crabb affirms that the Old Way's Law of Linearity "sometimes works." How have you seen it working in your own life?

9. "We all want our lives to work well," writes Dr. Crabb, "to become better than they are or to remain as good as they are." But the problem comes, he says, "when that desire becomes our goal, the objective we most value.... Our lives then become a sustained effort to discover and follow whatever principles will provide a life that lets us feel pretty good."

Here's the result:

📖 You might end up farther from God. And you *will* end up farther from God if you think of these principles as methods to produce the better life you want. 📖

How would you explain in your own words the point Dr. Crabb is making here, as it relates to your own life?

📖 When we live to make this life work, whether we follow natural wisdom or biblical principles, we become either proud or discouraged, self-congratulating or self-hating. 📖

10. Think back to some moment when you experienced either self-congratulating pride or self-hating discouragement. To what extent can you recognize that this may have been caused simply by your commitment "to make this life work"?

OUR SET PATTERNS

📖 I lead a linear life. I want this life to work, and I'm willing to do whatever it takes to make it happen. No wonder I feel so much pressure and struggle with so much disillusionment and doubt. When things work well, I publicly say, "Praise God," and privately whisper, "Of course. I did what I was told. I got it right." When things go poorly, I publicly declare, "God is working for my good. I will trust Him"; privately I wonder, "What did I do wrong?" 📖

11. In what ways, if any, does the description in the preceding quotation reflect your own experiences, past or present?

12. Think carefully about the following words from the author.

> 📖 Let me propose a radical thought: *Maybe we have it all wrong!* Maybe the Christian life is not about "doing right" to "get blessed." Maybe the Christian life is not about the blessings of life we so badly want and doggedly pursue. Maybe our obedience and faithfulness are to be energized by a very different motive than receiving the good and legitimate blessings we long to experience in this life....
>
> The spiritual journey is *not* about living as we should so life works as we want. It's *not* a linear path.
>
> It's *not* about growing up into the maturity of a good self-image and developing the energy to do good things; it *is* about growing down into the brokenness of self-despair and deepening our awareness of how poorly we love compared to Trinitarian standards. It's *not* about working hard to get it right so we can present ourselves before God to receive the blessings we desire; it *is* about coming before Him as we are, honestly, pretending about nothing, becoming increasingly convinced that we can't get it right though we try as hard as we can, then listening for the whisper of the Spirit, "Welcome! You're home. You're loved. You'll be empowered to speak with your unique voice as you hear the Voice of God singing over you with great love." 📖

How fully convinced are you of the accuracy and biblical soundness of the assertions made in these paragraphs? Explain your response here:

THREE PASSAGES TELL THE STORY

Dr. Crabb cites three passages that he says are "representative, I believe, of the entire message of Scripture."

13. The first of these representative passages "establishes the Law of Linearity as the basis of a Better Life of Blessings from God, as it summarizes the conditions of an arrangement God put into effect with His Old Testament children."

    Here's the passage:

    > "Carefully follow the terms of this covenant,
    > so that you may prosper in everything you do."
    > (Deuteronomy 29:9)

    How would you state in your own words the core message of this verse?

    📖 But notice something easily overlooked. Once we accept this linear arrangement—*A* then *B*; you do this, God will do that—not only is the pressure on, but failure is guaranteed. We find ourselves in the same pickle as Israel: We can't keep our part of the bargain. When God instructed His people to "carefully follow the terms of the covenant," He was not setting a *fairly* high standard. He was not prepared to provide blessings to people who followed His rules *reasonably* well.

The standard was perfection—perfect love for God and for others at every moment, in every interchange. 📖

14. Why do you think this aspect of the biblical Law of Linearity—that the standard is always nothing less than perfection—is "something easily overlooked," as the author explains? Why do we resist the notion that "failure is guaranteed"?

15. Now consider afresh what God did to rescue us from that guaranteed failure:

> 📖 Life under the harsh Law of Linearity would be unlivable. But if someone delivered you from that arrangement (not because the law was unfair but because you weren't good enough to keep it), if someone found a way to let you live as a beloved son or daughter of the king with a royal position established not by performance but by relationship, you would be profoundly grateful. Your one thought would be to get to know that person, to draw near to him.
>
> That story is true. It isn't a fairy tale. It happened. The Deliverer has come. 📖

This deliverance is the theme of the second representative passage Dr. Crabb highlights, a passage in which "the writer tells us that God has annulled that Law of Linearity":

> "The former regulation is set aside
> because it was weak and useless

(for the law made nothing perfect),
and a *better hope* is introduced,
by which we draw near to God."
(Hebrews 7:18-19)

As fully as you can, how would you explain the ways in which your own life is affected by the truth in this passage?

16. Dr. Crabb explains the incredible effects of our "new arrangement" with God in these words:

📖 Under the new arrangement, the reason for right living has changed. We no longer depend on a linear relationship between performance and blessing to arrange for the life we want. That arrangement has mercifully been declared obsolete and has been replaced by something new, something better. 📖

Why do you think this truth is so important for believers to fully and deeply understand?

Do You Wish to Be Enslaved?

"But there are two difficulties with this new arrangement," notes Dr. Crabb.

📖 One, it requires us to yield control over what happens in our lives and to trust God to do whatever He thinks best.

Regular quiet times and fervent prayer do not guarantee the cancer won't come back; neither do they ensure expanded and effective ministry. We prefer to claim influence, if not control, over which blessings come our way.

Two, it's harder to enjoy God than His blessings. Offer a young child the choice of having Daddy present Christmas morning with no gifts *or* having Daddy absent and a stack of gifts piled high beneath the tree, and the child might choose the gifts. Only the mature value the blessing of *presence* over the blessing of *presents*. 📖

17. Assess those two "difficulties" as they relate to your own life. When is it hardest for you "to trust God to do whatever He thinks best"?

To what extent do you find yourself more willing and able to enjoy God's blessings than to enjoy God?

18. "It's the situation," writes Dr. Crabb, "reflected in our third representative passage" in which "the apostle Paul expresses bewildered amazement that people who had the chance to draw near to God would value the Better Life of Blessings over the Better Hope of Intimacy and would again put themselves under pressure to 'get it right' to 'make life work.'"

Here's the passage:

"We were in slavery
under the basic principles of the world....

> But now that you know God—
> or rather are known by God—
> how is it that you are turning back
> to those weak and miserable principles?
> Do you wish to be enslaved by them all over again?"
> (Galatians 4:3,9)

Dr. Crabb adds the following commentary on this passage:

📖 The word translated "principles" literally means "sequence." It's a word used by the Greeks to refer to elements in sequence like letters in the alphabet. The basic sequence that could be observed by watching how things work was not the rigid sequence of holy linearity established by God. By "basic principles of the world," Paul meant the natural order by which life could be managed, principles for effective living common to all religions and ethical systems. And their aim was always the same—to make life better. 📖

In his teaching to the Galatians, Paul called these common principles "weak and miserable." Is this how you would describe the "principles for effective living common to all religions and ethical systems"? Why or why not?

19. Dr. Crabb concludes Part I of *The Pressure's Off* with these words:

📖 I devote the rest of this book to presenting the New Way of the Spirit in a manner that I pray will arouse an appetite for the Better Hope of drawing near to God. But I have no power to make that happen. *Holy Spirit, reveal to our hearts that, because of Christ,*

the pressure's off,

there's a new way to live,

and it's better than the old way. 📖

With those words in mind, how would you express your personal goals or expectations for the time you'll spend going through this workbook?

20. In quietness, review what you've written and learned in this week's lesson. If further thoughts or questions come to your mind and heart, you may want to write them here.

21. What for you was the most meaningful concept or truth in this week's lesson?

How would you talk this over with God? Write your response here as a prayer to Him.

A WORM IN
THE APPLE

*This week's lesson is based on
chapter 4, "A Worm in the Apple,"
chapter 5, "What Dark Forces?"
and chapter 6, "The Left-Out Dragon."*

"Ever since Eden," writes Dr. Crabb, "people have had the unique capacity to believe they're heading north while their feet take them south. Our moral compass, the internal sense that approves or disapproves of what we're doing and where we're going, is seriously out of whack."

In this week's study we continue to explore what exactly is "out of whack" in our typical approach to the Christian life.

COME A LITTLE CLOSER

With our almost limitless capacity to deceive ourselves, it's possible (and the possibility has been realized to epidemic proportions) for people to sincerely believe that they're living the Christian life when in fact they're following a highly Christianized version of the Old Way.

1. As you consider what you've learned so far in this workbook, what do you think are some common ways in which Christians might deceive themselves in the manner mentioned in the preceding quotation?

2. "For years," Dr. Crabb writes, "I've held to an image of myself that made me want to go deep, but not too deep, and to be personally vulnerable, but only to a point." Listen as he further explains.

📖 Since graduate school days, and probably before, I've viewed myself as a shiny red apple sitting in a fruit bowl positioned on the center of a dining-room table. Look at me from a distance and you'll be drawn. The apple is big, there are no visible bruises, and it's well shaped.

Come a little closer...and your impression that the apple is good fruit might be strengthened. You may want to pick it up and take a bite.

If you do, you'll likely enjoy the taste. Have a conversation with me, come to me for spiritual direction, join a small group with me, combine your gifts with mine to develop a ministry— and you might conclude that indeed I'm the juicy, substantial, sweet-tasting apple I appear to be.

But I know. I know what you don't know and what I'm determined to never let you discover. There's a worm in the center. A few more bites, and you'll spit me out. I must keep you from moving too close. To know me much is to like me. To know me fully will reveal how disgusting I really am. 📖

To what extent does this image of the worm in the apple also fit any image you've had of yourself?

3. The author continues his self-revelation with these observations:

> 📖 You see, there really is a worm in the apple. It's foolish to try to convince me it's a nice worm. There's no such thing. God sees it and hates it. So I should too. I know myself well enough to know I'm often self-absorbed. I hold grudges against people who harm me. I'm capable of hating others. My insecurities have less to do with a lack of needed affirmation, whether during childhood or now, and more to do with a demand that I be honored above another.
>
> Of course I have intrinsic value as a bearer of God's image. Of course I can revel in the wonder and fullness of God's love for me. Of course I'm privileged to live as someone unique, as a masterpiece-in-the-making of God's creative genius who has something of eternal significance to give to this world.
>
> But my self-hatred doesn't come from a failure to appreciate these truths. It comes from a God-denying demand that I be more special than you, that my efforts be recognized and effective, that I never be slighted or demeaned, that I have the resources to get what I want from life.
>
> My self-hatred is rooted in pride. I insist that someone see value in me, that I see value in myself. And when one or the other doesn't happen, I spin down into the abyss of wailing about life and loathing everything in it, including myself. 📖

4. How well can you relate to these personal disclosures from Dr. Crabb? In what ways—and how strongly—can you identify with what's portrayed in these words?

5. Dr. Crabb also explores another side of himself:

> 📖 Sometimes, like you, I stand on rock. Goodness actually comes out of me. I give for the right reasons. I love another with no pre-occupying concern for myself....
>
> I'm a mystery to myself. Sometimes the Spirit flows freely within me, and I'm full of joy and spiritual power. Other times, another source of energy takes over, and I'm out of sorts....
>
> Sometimes I can feel the rock beneath my feet, and I stand tall in the storm. Other times I know I'm losing my balance as the sand beneath me begins to shift. 📖

Again, how well can you relate to this? In what ways, if any, does this description reflect your own experiences?

6. Then comes this confession from Dr. Crabb:

> 📖 Sometimes I'm just too weary to worry which path I'm walking.
>
> But then I feel the pressure. I realize God has become a distant relative and I'm handling life on my own. Christ is my ticket to heaven but not my best friend. What I think represents the Spirit's nudgings only increases the pressure—

"Why aren't you reading your Bible more?" "Why did you refuse to meet your friend for coffee?" "Do you think you're too important for him?"

And then I long to live the New Way. I want to know the pressure's off. 📖

Once more, put into words your thoughts on how closely you can identify with this portrait.

At this time in your life, how strong is your desire for wanting "to know the pressure's off"?

OUR GREATEST NEED

Dr. Crabb states that "meaningful change in our culture, enduring change rooted in improved character rather than legislated cosmetic change, can come only after revival hits the church." He also says, "Revival in the church must begin with revolution in the soul."

"The order," he says, "is important."

📖 First, *spiritual revolution* that moves us from Old Way living to the New Way; then *true revival* of safe community in our churches; and finally, a much-prayed-for *cultural reformation* where salty believers make unbelievers thirsty for Christ. 📖

Let's explore further these three things.

📖 First, *spiritual revolution* in our interior worlds, a shift from the Old Way to the New....

Our greatest need is for a fresh encounter with God that exposes sin as repulsive and reveals as repulsive sin our determination to make this life work, no matter how spiritually we may go about it.

Our greatest challenge is to recognize the Old Way of the written code, to realize how often we live it, to see the New Way of the Spirit open before us, and to discover our consuming desire to follow that path into the presence of God....

Are we longing with relentless passion to draw near to God, are we desperately hungry to know Christ, are we listening intently for the Spirit's voice in our noise-filled lives? 📖

7. How strongly do you agree with what the author describes in the previous quotation as our "greatest need" and our "greatest challenge"?

How would you answer for yourself the questions in the final paragraph in the preceding quotation?

📖 Second, *true revival* in our church worlds, where the Spirit works through self-effacing leadership to release congregations to become safe communities, communities that exalt the Father, not the pastor; that center on Christ, not visible success; that listen to the Spirit, not people's expectations....

We tilt at windmills when we thrust our swords at pornography, abortion, fatherlessness, and teen violence without first

weeping over shallow community in our churches. When the
Holy Spirit moves, He draws us together before He sends us
into battle....

Are we embracing the Law of Liberty by coming boldly,
exactly as we are, into the divine community? 📖

8. In what ways do you either agree or disagree with the author's asser-
tion that the Holy Spirit "draws us together before He sends us into
battle"?

How would you answer for yourself the question in the final paragraph in the previous quotation?

📖 And third, *cultural reformation* in our everyday worlds
that lifts the satisfaction of virtue and humility above the
thrill of achievement and power, and values right relationship with God over improved self-esteem....

Our greatest challenge is *not* to Christianize secular culture into accepting family values and biblical morals....

As we pray, "Thy kingdom come, Thy will be done, on
earth as it is in heaven," we must not too quickly rise from
our knees to get busy with kingdom work. We must for a
season remain on our knees, humbled and dependent, begging the Spirit's help to realize which way we're taking. 📖

9. What is your response to the author's various statements in this quotation? Which of them do you agree most strongly with and why?

Which statements bring questions to your mind, and what are those
questions?

WHAT DARK FORCES?

After setting forth our supreme need for spiritual revolution, true revival,
and cultural reformation (in that order), Dr. Crabb states, "As long as my
soul is ruled by a spirit that allows jealousy, judgmentalism, and general
jerkiness to so easily be aroused and then to dominate, I won't be capable of
worshiping God, of relating well to my brothers and sisters, or of attracting
unbelievers to Christ. I will soil the Name of God by the way I live."

He then asks this:

> 📖 What dark forces sometimes rule in my interior world?
> What allows ugly emotions that I don't like and don't choose
> to develop so easily and rule so completely? 📖

10. To the best of your scriptural understanding, how would you summa-
    rize the Bible's overall answer to those questions?

11. As you read carefully the following excerpt, think in an honest way
    about your own personal ambitions and desires.

> 📖 It's a hard pill to swallow, but we must get the medicine
> into our souls.
> When any ambition other than drawing near to God
> assumes first-place significance in our hearts, whether

the ambition is blatantly self-serving or clearly kingdom-advancing, we're living the Old Way. 📖

In your own life, what would you say are the "ambitions other than drawing near to God" that are most likely to take on "first-place significance" in your heart?

📖 When our first-place privilege of nearness to God remains in first place, we abide in the vine; second-place desires become sought-after blessings. Then fruit grows on the branch. That's New Way living.

But the moment we let our desires for blessings become demands, the moment we expect blessings to come because we've met the requirements for God to grant them, the moment we think any blessing other than nearness to God is essential to life and is therefore promised now, we've chosen to live the Old Way.... We end up leading natural lives, lives energized by the flesh no matter how religiously disguised. 📖

12. Consider your own deepest motives and longings and your usual way of thinking about these. In your life, what is it that can cause a desire to become a demand?

When this happens—when our "desires for blessings become demands"—then according to Dr. Crabb it means that "we've forfeited the opportunity to experience supernatural reality and must now depend on our own resources to arrange for the blessings we want." Record here your response to this statement. In what ways do you agree or disagree with it?

    📖 Listen to Paul speak strongly to Christians who were being influenced to measure up to certain standards in order to gain full favor with God: "Mark my words! I, Paul, tell you that if you let yourselves be circumcised, Christ will be of no value to you at all.... You...have been alienated from Christ; you have fallen away from grace" (Galatians 5:2,4).

       Paul's point is this: *Christ promises no help when you make it your ultimate goal to secure certain blessings by doing good things.* You can pray and fast and attend seminars and buy books and double-tithe and refuse cable service on your television and practice contemplative prayer and never miss an anniversary or your son's ball games—the resources of the Spirit will have no value to you at all. God will not help us live the Old Way. 📖

13. Describe your response to the preceding biblical commentary from Dr. Crabb. You may want to include any additional scriptural content that supports your response.

14. In regard to these "resources of the Spirit" that are worthless when we're living the Old Way, Dr. Crabb points to "four distinct resources within us that make supernatural living possible," placed there by the Spirit:

    📖 A *New Purity* that makes us clean in God's sight even when we roll in mud;

a *New Identity* that permits no labels other than ones like saint, child of God, beloved, and heaven-bound pilgrim to be accurately pinned on us;

a *New Disposition* that actually prefers holiness to sin;

a *New Power* to draw near to God as a forgiven heir who longs to behold the beauty of the Lord. 📖

Take a moment to evaluate your life with respect to your appropriation of these resources. Which of them are you using most fully? Which of them do you need to draw upon more faithfully?

MODERN JUDAIZERS

"The modern church has been infiltrated by an updated version of Judaizers," states Dr. Crabb. They correspond to the Judaizers of the New Testament era:

> 📖 In Paul's time, particularly in the Galatian church, certain teachers were acknowledging that Jesus was indeed the Messiah, but then they added the idea that Christians had to conform to the law to gain full standing with God. They were encouraging Old Way living....
>
> Paul called the Judaizers "dogs, those men who do evil" (Philippians 3:2).... They put "confidence in the flesh" (3:3); they taught from a settled persuasion that merit brought blessing in this life....
>
> The Galatian Christians were drawn to this teaching. It returned control into their hands and restored pride in their own value....

Rather than depending on New Covenant resources that were gifted to them so they could draw near to God in perfect liberty, the Galatians were thinking it might be a good idea to get "religious" so they could enjoy superior blessings. 📖

15. In what ways do you recognize that the Old Way appeals to us by putting control into our hands and restoring pride in our own value?

📖 Listen to Paul scold the Galatians for buying into this different view of spiritual growth:

"You foolish Galatians! Who has bewitched you? Before your very eyes Jesus Christ was clearly portrayed as crucified. I would like to learn just one thing from you: Did you receive the Spirit by observing the law, or by believing what you heard? Are you so foolish? After beginning with the Spirit, are you now trying to attain your goal by human effort? Have you suffered so much for nothing—if it really was for nothing? Does God give you his Spirit and work miracles among you because you observe the law, or because you believe what you heard?" (Galatians 3:1-5). 📖

16. Record here the main points you recognize in Paul's response to the Galatians on this issue.

17. With that helpful background on New Testament Judaizers, we can better understand those who are like them today. Listen carefully to this critique from Dr. Crabb:

📖 Modern Judaizers assume the same law but give it a different spin in their message to today's Christian: Now that we
know God by faith in Christ's atoning work (justification), *He's
now available to bless us,* to give us what we so badly want and
what we think will give us a sense of personal wholeness....

God is the *means* of blessing, the modern Judaizers say.
Implied, but never stated, is that God Himself is not the
blessing we seek. It's therefore right, and actually His plan,
that we use Him to get a better life....

The error is subtle and terribly appealing....

Modern Judaizers cheapen God's eternal word by twisting
it, like the serpent did in Eden. Rather than insisting that the
blessings of life were indeed made available to any who kept
God's law perfectly from the heart, and then teaching that
Christ kept the law as a man and then was cursed in our
place because we broke the law, they teach that it's possible to
keep the law well enough to win the blessings we desire....

Modern Judaizers appeal to our lower nature, to our
wrong-headed idea (first suggested by Satan) that blessings
are to be valued above relationship with the Blesser. 📖

In what ways have you seen for yourself the influence of these modern
Judaizers?

18. Dr. Crabb notes one of Paul's methods for resisting the Old Way's
appeal:

📖 *Paul spoke openly about his pain,* not in complaint, but as
a reminder that the abundant life of following Jesus means

abundant opportunities to draw near to Him in hard times, not an abundance of pleasant circumstances and good feelings.

Listen to his words to the Corinthians, Christians who were more intent on feeling now what God promised they would feel only in heaven. "We are hard pressed on every side, but not crushed; perplexed, but not in despair; persecuted, but not abandoned; struck down, but not destroyed" (2 Corinthians 4:8-9).

Paul's life was not a pleasant experience. By *admitting* it and by abandoning all hope that it ever would be pleasant, the pressure was off to figure out some way to make life work. Paul lived to know God, not to use Him. He lived to draw near to God, to become like Jesus, to follow the Spirit, not to live a certain way that would please God enough to get Him to pour out the blessings of a better life. 📖

In what ways do you agree or disagree with the definition of "the abundant life" as given in the first paragraph of this quotation?

To what extent would you say that you, like Paul, are living "to know God, not to use Him"?

19. Think about the most meaningful concept or truth you've explored in this week's lesson. How would you talk this over with God? Write your response here as a prayer to Him.

What's So Wrong with the Old Way?

This week's lesson is based on
chapter 7, "What's So Wrong with What We Want?"
and chapter 8, "Blinding Deception."

"What makes the Old Way wrong?" Dr. Crabb asks.

📖 Is it really *evil* to live for blessings available in this world?
Or, for some unfortunate people, is it merely frustrating?

How can anyone seriously maintain that trying hard to
make this world a better place for us to live is immoral, especially if we do so "Christianly," if we take no unfair advantage of others and resist the lure of illegitimate pleasures?
And suppose we aim for spiritual meaning, and fill our days
with ministry activities, and carefully and seriously follow
biblical principles as best we can. We might corrupt the
search for satisfaction into a selfish pursuit—and that would
be wrong—but if we trust Christ to fill our lives with adventure and fulfillment and community, are we not walking a
good path? Are we not then His disciples? 📖

1. From what you've learned and reflected upon so far in this workbook, how would you answer the questions in the preceding quotation?

SOMEWHERE ELSE THAN GOD

2. "The only consistent message coming from the world, the flesh, and the devil," writes Dr. Crabb, "is this: *Seek your deepest enjoyment somewhere else than in God.*"

   How have you seen this to be true in your own temptations to sin?

3. Think about the overall fundamental message that you've understood from the life and death of Jesus Christ. Then read these words:

   📖 Jesus came to earth to tell us He is the way, the truth, and the life. His death opened the *way* into God's presence, the greatest blessing of all. His teaching made clear the *truth* that life does not consist in a return to Eden's comforts; it doesn't even consist in graduation to heaven's bliss. True life is knowing God. Jesus said so (see John 17:1-3). And the *life* is Christ Himself, not the bread He could multiply or the corpse He could resurrect, but Him. Being in Him, having Him in us, living with His energy, chasing after His purposes, loving what He loves, seeing Him form in us until we're actually like Him—that's life. And it can be enjoyed in bankruptcy or affluence, from a hospital bed or a deck chair on a cruise ship, or when you walk out of a divorce court you never thought you'd see or into a surprise party celebrating fifty years of your wonderful marriage. 📖

How consistent is Dr. Crabb's view with your own understanding of what true life is, according to the teachings of Jesus?

4. "The Old Way sees things differently," Dr. Crabb asserts:

> 📖 "Yes, you do want Jesus. He's the one who can restore your marriage, provide great ideas on raising kids that really work, and prosper your ministry. Jesus teaches principles to live by, He offers methods to follow that will give you the life you want. What must you do to be saved from an unfulfilling life and strained relationships? What must you do to be saved from persecution and trouble? He'll tell you. Go to Him to find out what you must do to make life work!" 📖

In what ways, if any, do you recognize that these thoughts are actually opposed to the true life that Christ offers and provides?

In contrast, Dr. Crabb cites the words of Anne Graham Lotz, who after telling of hardships in her life then added, "Don't give me sympathy. Don't give me advice. Don't even give me a miracle. *Just give me Jesus!*"

Do you think it's wrong to pray for sympathy, advice, or a miracle when we're undergoing genuine hardship? Why or why not?

5. How strongly can you identify with the following feelings and experiences?

📖 But…I want my life to work. I enjoy it when it does.
I hate it when it doesn't.

Only when my dreams shatter, and then only for a
moment, do I sometimes feel a desire to draw near to God
that I know is stronger than my desire for restored blessings.
Only during specially intense times with God—rare in frequency and short in duration—do I pant after Him more
than His blessings.…

I say that the pressure's off.… Do I have any idea what
that means? Maybe I really do value what Christ can do for
me in this life more than I value the opportunity to get better acquainted with Him. Have I ever actually derived more
pleasure from spending time with Him than from vacationing with my wife or watching my sons do well or holding
my grandchildren? Is there really more joy in knowing Christ
than in standing before large crowds and watching good
things happen and making good money to boot? 📖

Record your response here:

It Can Be Done

"It helps to know it *can* be done," Dr. Crabb writes, "that the way to God
has been cleared, that the resources needed for the trip have been provided,
and that the Spirit can stir up the waters that will carry us, like a fountain
carries a leaf, into the presence of God."

He points to the experience of John, as we see it in the opening chapter
of Revelation, as an example of how "supernatural reality can break into
our lives and gush out of our souls."

📖 As John wrote about what happened, he tells us he was "in the Spirit" (Revelation 1:10)—indicating, I think, that a sense of expectancy seized him, likely after many desperate days of waiting on God to meet him on the rock he called home. 📖

6. What does being "in the Spirit" truly mean for you in your relationship with God?

📖 The apostle was an old man, living in the prison of a barren island, exiled there for the crime of preaching Jesus, eating poorly, sleeping uncomfortably, performing hard labor that not even a twenty-year-old should be forced to do, aware that the band of disciples was gone (most of them martyred), and discouraged by the spiritual condition of several local churches.

If he had followed Christ in hopes of enjoying a better life, he would by now have been sorely disillusioned. But then Christ appeared to him. Notice, however, what *didn't* happen when He appeared. Christ did not bring John a mattress. He did not spread a table with good food. He did not magically lift John off Patmos and set him on the mainland to hold seminars in Sardis and Laodicea.

What did happen was far better. The Spirit revealed Jesus Christ. I can hear John saying, "My life is miserable, but I ask not for sympathy, not for help, and not for a miracle. Just give me Jesus!" And that's what the Spirit did. It's a prayer God always, eventually, answers. 📖

7. Describe what it means for you, at this time in your life, to pray the
prayer "Just give me Jesus."

AN INSULT TO GOD

📖 More is available to us in Jesus Christ than we dare imagine. There's more to Jesus Christ than we've ever dreamed.
We experience so little of Him when we approach Him only
with requests. We taste so little of the mouth-stopping,
complaint-ending, desire-deepening awe that His presence
creates when we think more about our problems and how
to solve them than about *meeting Him.* We experience so
little of the joy that sustains us in suffering and the hope
that anchors us amid shattered dreams when we come to
Him looking for the pathway out of hardships instead of
the pathway *into His presence.*

In his unpredictable expressions of mercy, the Spirit gives
us glimpses of Christ that fill us with supernatural reality and
shine a spotlight on the entrance to the New Way. 📖

8. Are you convinced that "more is available to us in Jesus Christ than
we dare imagine"? Why or why not?

9. Dr. Crabb states again, "More is available to us in Jesus Christ than
we dare imagine. We settle for so much less. We taste Him so little.
Why?"

He begins answering that question with these words:

📖 The central obstacle to His life flowing in us and pouring from us is this: *We want something else more.* And that's evil. We want the blessings of a better life more than we desire to draw near to Jesus. 📖

He illustrates that point in this way:

📖 We're like the prodigal son telling his father, "I could care less about being with you. I just want your wealth. You can die as far as I'm concerned. *Just give me my inheritance.*"

That's the Old Way. It's not only foolish, it's evil....

Living for a better life in this world with more energy than we pursue a deeper relationship with Christ is evil....

It's an insult to God. He gives us the best heaven can offer, and we ask for something else. 📖

Why is it actually *evil* to want something else more than God?

DIFFERENT PEACE

📖 There's a peace the world gives. It's the tranquillity of a life that works reasonably well—decent relationships, adequate health, enough resources to enjoy life, meaningful work....

Jesus offers a different kind of peace. "*My* peace I give you. I do not give to you as the world gives" (John 14:27). The peace Jesus gives isn't dependent on deserved blessings. It depends entirely on the one supreme blessing He guarantees to all His followers: the opportunity to draw near to Him, to put every egg in the basket of His presence with us even when His absence is all we feel, to depend on Him to be doing a good work in us even when everything that happens seems bad. 📖

10. How would you evaluate the degree and quality of peace that you've already experienced in this world?

What kind of peace are you actually looking for? How would you describe the degree and quality of peace you most deeply long for in this world?

11. When you hear Jesus saying, "Come to me, all you who are weary and burdened, and I will give you rest" (Matthew 11:28)—what kind of "rest" do you expect to experience in coming to Him?

What does it essentially mean to you to "come" to Him?

Sowing to the Flesh

📖 Although it brings me to deeper levels of brokenness to say it, it must be said: *Whenever we focus on the blessings we want, even if they're worthy blessings, and study Christianity to understand how to get those blessings, we're sowing to the flesh. We're living the Old Way.* 📖

12. In regard to the legitimate blessings you want in life, do you agree that it's wrong to "study Christianity to understand how to get those blessings," in the way that Dr. Crabb means? Why or why not?

13. Consider your own observations of contemporary Christianity as you read these words:

> 📖 Perhaps the greatest mistake in the modern church is its unrecognized tendency to encourage Old Way living. Books, sermons, and seminars present an appealing blessing, then tell us how to get it. "God longs to bless you," we hear. "Live in such a way that His blessings are released into your lives." 📖

Have you seen this tendency for yourself in contemporary Christianity? If so, what examples can you cite?

> 📖 We're living under deception. The supreme blessing He longs to give us is Himself. No other blessing is guaranteed until heaven. The blessings we now claim are so often something less than an empowering, enlivening, pride-destroying, self-effacing, joy-giving encounter with God. 📖

14. How do you respond to Dr. Crabb's statement in the preceding quotation?

15. "This widespread deception," Dr. Crabb notes, "has consequences."

   📖 1. *It breeds confusion and pressure.* Wasn't I a good enough husband? Is that why she left me? I tried so hard to be a good parent. What did I do wrong? Was I too firm? Not firm enough? What do I do to make things better? God, why won't You tell me what I can do that will work?…

   2. *It weakens our view of God.* If the Christian life is all about blessings, then when trials come instead, we conclude either that we aren't living right or that God isn't really in control. In *this* situation, at least, Satan must enjoy the upper hand.…

   3. In the Old Way, *humility becomes a technique.* We humble ourselves and draw near to God in hopes that He'll draw near to us, not to let us *encounter* Him, but with *blessings* in hand. Humility becomes a maneuver. We come with empty hands but with a finger pointing: Give us that! Dependence gives way to methodology. 📖

In what ways, if any, have you experienced any of these consequences?

16. Another consequence, says Dr. Crabb is this one: *"We develop a wrong view of psychological problems."*

   📖 I've been wondering: Could Old Way living have more to do with our troubles than we suspect? Does our insistence that this life provide more satisfaction than it can, and our determination to figure out some way to get it, lie beneath what we call psychological disorder? 📖

In pursuing this issue further, Dr. Crabb explores the first chapter of Paul's letter to the Romans:

    📖 "Although they knew God," Paul said, people "neither glorified him as God nor gave thanks to him, but their thinking became futile.... Although they claimed to be wise, they became fools and exchanged the glory of the immortal God" for something else. "Therefore God *gave them over* in the sinful desires of their hearts to sexual impurity...to shameful lusts...to a depraved mind, to do what ought not to be done. They have become filled with every kind of wickedness, evil, greed and depravity" (Romans 1:21-29).

    People pursue a source of primary satisfaction other than God. They do not value Him above all other treasures. That's the Old Way. Their thinking becomes futile. Their lives revolve around the false gods of better kids, good health, fulfilling relationships, effective ministries—anything other than God. And that devotion to a lesser god turns loose all manner of trouble. Selfishness rules. The springs of human nature are polluted. Vile water gushes out.

    Like a shopper who mistakenly purchases the wrong size garment, we've exchanged the glory of God for an outfit we think might fit our soul a little better. We turn away from God and chase after other blessings. 📖

Summarize your understanding of the connection Dr. Crabb is making here between Paul's teaching in Romans 1 and the Old Way approach to living as described in this workbook.

17. Dr. Crabb notes three possible outcomes to our pursuing any primary satisfaction other than God:

📖 1. *We may experience enough blessings to persuade us we're on the right track.* Old Way thinking is confirmed as good. We're getting it right, and life is working. We become successful law keepers, modern Judaizers, happy Pharisees.

   2. *A mixture of blessings and trials may keep us in the game and open us to any method to make life better.* We become pragmatists. Biblical principles are bent if we see personal advantage in compromise. Or we become legalists, more rigidly resolved than ever to do it right so life will work. We may decline into neuroticism, getting caught up in strange behaviors that protect us from internal pain.

   3. *Life may become so hard, and our efforts to improve things may seem so futile, that we give up.* Now we slide into major depression, conscienceless living, or insanity—serious neurosis, character disorder, or psychosis. 📖

In what ways have you observed any of these outcomes either in your life or in the lives of other Christians you know well?

18. Dr. Crabb continues exploring this issue in Scripture.

📖 With these thoughts in mind, I read another verse from Paul—and I tremble:

   "The god of this world has blinded the minds of the unbelieving so that they might not see the light of the gospel of the glory of Christ, who is the image of God" (2 Corinthians 4:4, NASB).

Unbelievers do not see Christ as their greatest treasure. *Neither do most believers.* We live as blind people, chasing after the light we can see—the satisfaction that blessings bring—and not valuing the light we cannot see—the glory of Christ.

It could be different. We could live a new way. "For God, who said, 'Let light shine out of darkness,' made his light shine in our hearts to give us the light of the knowledge of the glory of God in the face of Christ" (2 Corinthians 4:6). 📖

What thoughts come to mind as you read these conclusions? In what ways is it easy for you to agree with them? In what ways do you find it difficult to agree?

19. Think about the most meaningful concept or truth you've explored in this week's lesson. How would you talk this over with God? Write your response here as a prayer to Him.

WHAT THE NEW WAY IS

*This week's lesson is based on
chapter 9, "Behind a Door Marked Private,"
chapter 10, "Coming Dirty and Dancing,"
and chapter 11, "Reaping What We Sow."*

At this point in *The Pressure's Off,* Dr. Crabb writes, "I dedicate the rest of this book to the growing number of people whose journey through life has been deeply disillusioning.… Whether through the emptiness of blessings or the anguish of trials, you're disillusioned."

📖 Your life isn't working, and you're losing hope that it ever will. You worry that your faith is weakening, that you're losing confidence in God.…

Even when things go well, when wrongheaded faith and misplaced confidence seem validated, you sense an ache in your soul for something more. Your good marriage, good kids, good friends, good health, good church, good job, and good ministry don't satisfy. You receive whatever blessings come your way as mercies from God, and you're grateful. You do enjoy them—and you should…. But in the midst of enjoyed pleasure, you cannot suppress the question, "Is this all there is?" You're disillusioned by the emptiness of blessings….

The ache won't go away. Something is missing. But whatever it is, it's hard to find. The ache continues and deepens. Pornographic fantasies or expensive travel or rich desserts or frenetic ministry or hardened cynicism provide more relief than prayer. Or they provide no relief, and you're just miserable.

You want a new way to live, but you're not sure what it is, and you're not sure how to live it. 📖

1. In what ways, if any, does that description reflect your own experiences, past or present?

2. Listen with your heart to Dr. Crabb's invitation:

> 📖 I invite you to join me as I journey with you through a profoundly disillusioning life, a life filled with opportunities for shallow and temporary pleasure and fraught with unpredictable experiences of deep and lasting sorrow. Walk with me through the grocery store of existence on this planet, and notice that there are only a few stale donuts on the shelves.
>
> But let's keep our heads up and our eyes forward. I can see that door marked Private. Beneath that forbidding word I can make out the fine print: *Family Only Beyond This Point.*
>
> Let's remember that the blood of Jesus has opened a new way, a *living way*—not into a method for making life work,

but into the presence of God (see Hebrews 10:19-23). Let's not forget that Christ died for sin not to make our existence here pleasant, but rather to bring us to God, and that if we draw near to Him, He will draw near to us (see 1 Peter 3:18; John 14:21,23; James 4:8). 📖

What appeals to you most in this invitation?

TO SEE AND SAVOR JESUS

📖 Christians come in two varieties: those who trust Jesus to get them to heaven while trusting Him now to provide a good life of blessings till they get there, and those who trust Jesus to get them to heaven and discover that what they really want even now is to "see and savor Jesus Christ" [a phrase from author John Piper]. They're actually willing to lose every blessing and suffer any indignity if it will bring them into deeper relationship with Jesus. 📖

3. At this point in your life, how would you describe your desire for a deeper relationship with Jesus?

📖 This second variety of Christians—they're the New Way revolutionaries—have been disillusioned by the Old Way approach to life. Unexpected troubles, ones that cannot be traced to a specific failure on their part, have shattered their dreams of how their Christian lives would turn out. Senseless suffering, the kind they have no guarantee of avoiding in the future, has confronted them with a choice between two responses:

1. *Abandon God.* What good is He when life falls apart? It was His job to see to it that it didn't. He failed. He's a grocery store with empty shelves, holding no appeal to a starving man. If He doesn't stock what we need, or if we lack the money to meet His price for what is available, why bother with Him? To someone whose job was just lost, who cries every night from unrelieved loneliness, whose most important dreams have been shattered, a God who declares His benevolence is worth nothing.

2. *Abandon yourself to God,* humbling yourself enough to stop telling Him what He should be doing in your life, committing yourself to whatever He's doing, and believing it is good. 📖

4. Especially as you recall the most difficult troubles you've experienced in life, how difficult do you find it to follow the second response mentioned in the preceding quotation?

ONE SUPREME PASSION

In the New Way, Dr. Crabb writes, "we come to Him *as we are,* with full self-disclosure."

📖 Although we feel no pressure to be better or different, we intensely desire personal holiness more than we want relief from personal pain, and we're broken by how far short we fall. Tears over our self-centeredness and arrogance burn hotter in our eyes than tears over trials.

We come humbly, gratefully, and boldly, trusting that because of the Cross, God will come near, not to destroy us, but to embrace us, change us (sometimes painfully), and use us for His purposes. We keep coming and trusting, even when we see not a shred of evidence that He's warmly moving toward us or that we're meaningfully increasing in holiness. To keep coming toward the Light when all we can see is darkness is a measure of our absolute dependence. We have no other direction to go. 📖

5. In order to come to God fully in the way described in the preceding quotation, what kind of view of God should we have? What must we believe about Him?

📖 Whether we travel the Old Way or the New, there's a certain passion that fuels our movement along the path. Consider with me what that passion is. If we explore the depths of our hearts, and if we close our eyes to everything else long enough, we'll discover a core motive, a supreme desire, a compelling urge around which our entire lives revolve. Whatever we want *most* becomes the center of our lives. Like tribesmen dancing around a totem pole, our movements are all oriented around the object of our longing.

Call it our *first thing* passion. It isn't the only passion in our lives, but when a choice must be made, we dance around the thing that attracts us most. We're all loyal worshipers of something. 📖

6. As you think back, what have been your "first thing passions" at different seasons in your life?

📖 God asks only one question: "Am I your supreme passion or is it something else?" 📖

7. At this time in your life, is God your supreme passion, or is it something else?

📖 In the Old Way the passion that rules comes in a thousand varieties, but it consistently aims toward its central value—a *better life now!* Something must come to pass—some emotion must be felt, some increase in our sense of personal worth must be experienced, some thrill must delight us, some blessing must be granted—before life is worth living. As one woman put it to me after I preached on this subject, "Why would I come to God if He didn't give me what I wanted?" She hadn't yet realized that what her heart most deeply wanted was actually God Himself—and that's what He longs to give her. 📖

8. How would you answer the woman's question in the preceding quotation?

DANCING TOWARD THE THRONE

📖 We may want God, but experiencing God is not a predictable reality. We can arrange conditions favorable to encountering God, but we aren't in charge of whether He shows up.

Followers of the New Way realize they're mere beginners in the School of Divine Delights.

New Way revolutionaries accept their place in kindergarten; they realize they don't know much, but they're hungry to learn. And they're focused. They know what they're after. 📖

9. What is it that you most want to learn at this time in your life?

📖 It sounds extreme, perhaps unrealistic, but followers of the New Way want to know God more than they want anything else. Delightful children who love them; close friends they can trust; honor for what they do; success in family, job, and ministry; an experience of adventure and wonder as they live their lives—all desires, but all *second thing* passions. No blessing matters more to these people than the Blessing of Encounter. 📖

10. How "extreme" and "unrealistic" does the preceding quotation sound to you?

📖 For followers of the New Way, the Spirit's nudgings become recognizable. His wind fills their sails. They discover their center; they embrace their identity as spiritual, Spirit-ruled people; they cease defining themselves by their reflection in the thousand mirrors of others' expectations.

When they speak, they hear themselves as sheep bleating.
Only then can they make out the Shepherd's voice. 📖

11. What does it mean personally to you to embrace your identity as a
spiritual, Spirit-ruled person? In your own words, express this as fully
as you can.

📖 Followers of the New Way dance with Christ to the
rhythm of the Spirit into the presence of God. But they don't
dance especially well. Sometimes they trip over their own
feet. Sometimes they lose step with the rhythm and trounce
on the Lord's toes....

Over time, after embarrassingly clumsy attempts, they
begin moving to the Spirit's rhythm. They feel His nudge the
way a woman feels her dance partner lead. They fix their eyes
on Christ just as the dancing woman adoringly looks up to
the one she trusts to set the pace. And they find themselves
dancing toward a throne filled by the glory of sheer love. The
Spirit blows them to their knees. The Son walks up the steps
and stands by the throne, on the right-hand side. The Father
speaks, "Welcome into My presence...." Joy! Joy! Joy! Peace!
Love! Inexpressible joy! An encounter with God! A taste of
what's to come. A taste never enjoyed by followers of the Old
Way. 📖

12. What images in the preceding quotation match most closely your own
longings for your relationship with God?

RADICAL GRACE

"The Old Way misses out on the chief blessing of seeing God," writes Dr. Crabb. "It requires that we pretend. We wipe our own noses, wash our faces, and sew the rip in our clothes—we make ourselves presentable. Then we say to God, 'Look what I've done. I got it right. My nose is clean. Now give me the blessings I want.'"

The New Way is in stark contrast:

> 📖 New Way revolutionaries believe in radical grace. They know there's no other way to become holy than first by being declared holy, then by wanting to be holy, and eventually by actually becoming holy.
>
> So they come as they are—insolent, filthy, whimpering, demanding—but they come. How else can they come? That's who they know themselves to be. But they come humbly. They know they're not attractive. They want God— He is their supreme desire, their first thing passion; they depend on grace—it's their only hope. It's our only hope. It's enough. So we come.
>
> And God draws near—in His timing, never in automatic response to our request. But He comes.... We realize that our nose is dripping, our face is dirty, and our clothes are torn. We don't yet see that Christ has already cleaned us up.... The Father looks at us, beaming with delight as if we were the most beautiful children in the universe.
>
> Then we realize: We're as beautiful to the Father as Christ is because we're *in Him!* The Father sings. And we collapse with gratitude at His feet. Filled with joy. The Son touches us on the shoulder. We stand. 📖

13. What does "radical grace" mean to you, how strongly do you believe in it, and how have you demonstrated that belief?

ALWAYS NUDGING

📖 Let me share two lessons I'm learning....

The first is this:

The Spirit of Christ is always nudging us toward the New Way if we're not on it and always nudging us farther along if we are. In every circumstance, at every moment, He's stirring our affection for God until He makes it the strongest passion in our hearts....

The Spirit is constantly nudging us toward the New Way and away from the Old, toward the Better Hope and away from demanding the Better Life. This first lesson I'm learning includes a radical and wonderful truth: *Pursuing my deepest pleasure and moving in rhythm with the Spirit both take me in the same direction—toward Christ!* Self-interest and worship go together if worship comes first. 📖

14. What is your reaction at this time to the concept that "self-interest and worship go together," as mentioned in the above quotation? Do you fully "buy in" to this? Do you have doubts or some other form of resistance to it?

If that concept is true, what difference should it make in your life?

15. Here's the second lesson Dr. Crabb says he's learning:

📖 *My passion to know Christ often seems weaker than my desire for blessings.* And unless this changes, I will not consistently live the New Way. I must therefore give disciplined thought to how my desire for Christ can be nourished.

I tend toward superficial living. If life presents only a few bumps, especially if they're small, I don't particularly care whether I know Christ well or not. I figure He's doing His job of blessing me and I'm doing my job of living responsibly. Rather than a thirsty deer panting after water, I'm more like a hibernating bear with paws resting on my full stomach. 📖

In what ways can you identify with this description?

A LINEARITY STILL IN EFFECT

📖 Earlier…I suggested that the Old Way formula of linearity has been abolished. No longer can we work hard to get it right and claim a guarantee that life therefore will work. The Judaizers were dead wrong. The Law of Linearity, which they depended on, is not in effect.

But another linear relationship still holds. And when we see what it is, we'll be deeply interested in nourishing the appetite that will sustain us in New Way living.

Listen to the apostle Paul: "The one who sows to please his sinful nature, from that nature will reap destruction; the one who sows to please the Spirit, from the Spirit will reap eternal life" (Galatians 6:8).

That linearity is still in effect. We reap what we sow. 📖

16. In practical, everyday terms for your life at this time, what do you think it means to "sow to please the Spirit"?

17. "But notice," Dr. Crabb continues, "it isn't the linearity assumed by the Old Way."

📖 The promise of a cause-effect relationship between *getting it right* and *a life that works* is gone. God has put into effect a new linear arrangement:

If we choose the Old Way, we'll end up miserable. We may feel quite good for a long time, but every follower of the Old Way will end up feeling miserable.

GUARANTEED!

If we choose the New Way, we'll experience joy, perhaps after a long season of suffering and searching. But we'll find ourselves and be full, alive, happy.

GUARANTEED!

Choosing the New Way matters. Once you're saved, there's no more important choice. 📖

How do these "guarantee" statements compare with what you've previously thought about God's promises and the right way to live the Christian life?

18. What have you enjoyed learning and exploring most in this week's lesson?

THE IMMANUEL AGENDA

This week's lesson is based on
chapter 12, "The Immanuel Agenda,"
chapter 13, "The Barn Door's Open,"
and chapter 14, "Story of God."

Dr. Crabb portrays God's "Immanuel Agenda" as "the relentless obsession He has for forming a family to gather at His dinner table, with Himself at the head and each of us thrilled to be there."

Listen to the author's paraphrase and commentary based on John the Apostle's words in Revelation 21:2-4:

📖 "He is here…and He has not disappeared. God has let me see all that's happening from heaven's point of view. It's breathtaking. The Lamb is roaring His way through history to complete the Immanuel Agenda.

"I saw the Holy City, the New Jerusalem, coming down from heaven. It's coming down to us, to you and me. And as I watched, I heard a loud voice declare: 'Now the dwelling of God is with men, and He will live with them. They will be

His people, and God Himself will be with them and be their God.'"

I hear John saying, "That's why God sent Jesus. It's the Immanuel Agenda: *God will be with us!* When that happens, when the Better Hope of drawing near to God is fully realized, we'll want nothing more. And that's when the Better Life will be ours as well. No more shattered dreams. Blessings beyond our wildest imagination. No reason to cry, ever, not even to sigh. And all of that with Jesus at the center.

"Stay the course, weary pilgrims. Don't lose heart. The Immanuel Agenda is about to be completed." 📖

1. What is most encouraging to you in that message from John?

Do you have any objections or doubts or qualms about this message? If so, what are they?

2. The author also imagines these words from John:

   📖 "My little children, if you could see the Better Hope ahead, you would not require the Better Life now. He who was seated on the throne said—with my own ears I heard Him—'I am making everything new.' Then He looked straight at me and told me: 'Write this down, for these words are trustworthy and true. My people need to hear them.' I've written Revelation so you would never, no matter how difficult your life may become, lose confidence in Jesus" (Revelation 21:5, the author's paraphrase). 📖

What is most likely to tempt you to "lose confidence in Jesus"?

 📖 Paul said much the same thing to people who thought
the journey to heaven should include a few more blessings.
"If only for this life we have hope in Christ, we are to be
pitied more than all men" (1 Corinthians 15:19). 📖

3. What's the reason behind that statement of Paul's from 1 Corinthians
15:19? Why would that be true?

THE WIND OF THE SPIRIT

Into each of our lives, Dr. Crabb writes, "the wind of the Spirit is blowing."

 📖 But it isn't moving our ship toward the smooth seas of a
more pleasant life. It's rather carrying us into the eye of the
storm, into the presence of God. And we must adjust our sails
accordingly. If we aim for calm waters, we go alone. We resist
the wind of the Spirit. 📖

4. What convinces you that the wind of the Spirit is blowing in your life?

 📖 The apostle John invites us…not into the satisfaction
and pleasures of improved circumstances, closer relationships, and happier feelings, but into the inexpressible joy of
drawing near to God.
  Listen to him speak about it:

"We have heard! We have seen! Our hands have touched! *Life has appeared!* And we proclaim it to you. We can now have fellowship with God. Our fellowship is with the Eternal Father of Endless Love and with His Magnificent Son, the One who died for us, Jesus Christ. We can draw near to God. I know the joy of coming into His presence. I want you to know that joy as well. Then my joy will be complete" (1 John 1:1-4, author's paraphrase). 📖

5. What does "fellowship with God" mean to you—and what do you most *want* it to mean in your own experience?

6. In the following quotation, Dr. Crabb encapsulates the core messages of John's gospel, of the book of Revelation (the "unveiling" to John), and of John's epistles:

> 📖 In his gospel John tells us, "You can trust Christ. He is who He says He is. Life is knowing Him."
>
> In the unveiling…he says, "You'll stay the course through any storm if you know what's coming. And right now, when everything goes against you, the Lamb of the Cross is the Lion of Heaven moving toward His sure purpose. And it's a *good* one. Hang on!"
>
> In his epistles, John issues an invitation: "In the middle of a difficult life, draw near to Jesus. It's the source of your deepest joy."
>
> In everything he wrote, John is presenting the Immanuel Agenda. From the beginning of time, God has determined to be with us. *He will be our God,* as we value no treasure

more than knowing Him, and *we will be His people*, gladly clinging to Him in worship and absolute dependence no matter what happens in this life. 📖

How do these core messages relate to your own desires to turn from the Old Way and live fully in the New Way of the Spirit?

7. "The agenda," says Dr. Crabb, "is on track."

> 📖 God is with us now. He's here. Not the way He'll be here when the Holy City comes down, but He's here to be enjoyed. Our highest calling, our deepest joy, is to celebrate His availability by drawing near to Him, not to use Him to make our lives better, but to enjoy Him for who He is.
> It's a different understanding of the spiritual journey. John invites his readers to walk a new path, to live a new way. We're asked to experience without complaint the disadvantages of a difficult life in order to more deeply experience the "precious thing" of communion with God. 📖

In what ways for you is this indeed "a different understanding of the spiritual journey"?

RICH TOWARD GOD

> 📖 Someone in the congregation came to me after I preached and said, "Am I hearing you right? Surely you aren't saying that we come to God only to know Him. Unless He

gives me the blessings I need to be happy, I can't see why I'd come to Him at all. Your teaching makes me want to not even bother with God."

I mentioned this woman in an earlier chapter. I think she's related (as all of us are) to a man who once called out to Jesus while He was teaching. 📖

Dr. Crabb unfolds this story from Luke 12:13-21.

> 📖 "Someone in the crowd said to him, 'Teacher, tell my brother to divide the inheritance with me.'"
>
> He wanted a better life of more money. Likely it was his due. Fairness was probably on his side. Notice the Lord doesn't even enter the "who's right" debate, something I often do when I listen to one spouse tell me how wrong the other one is.
>
> "Jesus replied, 'Man, who appointed me a judge or an arbiter between you?'" 📖

8. Why do you think Jesus responded to the man's request in this way? (After all, as Dr. Crabb comments, "I thought Christ *was* the judge. Who could be more qualified? Jesus would know the heart of both brothers, and He would know what was right.")

> 📖 "Then he said to them [to the whole crowd, leaving the bitter man still indignant over his plight], 'Watch out! Be on your guard against all kinds of greed; a man's life does not consist in the abundance of his possessions.'"
>
> He sidestepped the fairness issue completely. It wasn't His concern. It would be difficult to imagine a clearer warning

against living the Old Way: *Don't make it your goal to get out of life what you want.* He called it greed. It's the foundation of Old Way living. 📖

9. How would you define *greed* in its widest biblical meaning and as it relates to your everyday life?

📖 To drive home His point, He did what He often did. He offered a story.

"And he told them this parable: 'The ground of a certain rich man produced a good crop.'"

Some people are blessed. I know godly men and women who are rich. I know godly men and women with effective, far-reaching, and much-honored ministries. Blessings are good. We're to enjoy them and use them well. But blessings are dangerous.

" 'He thought to himself, "What shall I do? I have no place to store my crops." '" He doesn't even mention God. All that's on his mind is to enjoy his good fortune and to keep it coming. When your goal is a better life, you're completely selfish. 📖

10. If blessings are genuinely good, why are they also dangerous?

In what ways do you agree or disagree with Dr. Crabb's conclusion in the preceding quotation—"When your goal is a better life, you're completely selfish"?

11. Jesus continues the parable:

📖 " 'Then he said, "This is what I'll do. I will tear down my barns and build bigger ones, and there I will store all my grain and my goods. And I'll say to myself, 'You have plenty of good things laid up for many years. Take life easy; eat, drink, and be merry!' " ' "

He had worked hard, and it paid off. *A* led to *B*. And he liked it. The Old Way is deeply satisfying—not, however, in the deepest depths and not for long.

" 'But God said to him, "You fool!" ' " Today, we'd expect congratulations. "Way to go" seems more appropriate. We've worked hard, we've been diligent in wealth management, and now we can enjoy the Better Life of Blessings. We honor people, including ourselves, whose priority is achievement and who have succeeded. God called this one a fool, and said, " 'This very night your life will be demanded from you. Then who will get what you have prepared for yourself.' This is how it will be," Jesus promised, "with anyone who stores up things for himself but is not rich toward God." 📖

What do you think it means in your life right now to be "rich toward God"?

📖 Jesus went on to warn us about worrying over our lives down here, what we will eat, how our bodies are doing, whether we'll be able to provide for ourselves what we need. He finished this thought by telling us that our hearts belong to what we treasure most. (Luke 12:34—"For where your treasure is, there your heart will be also.") 📖

12. Where is your "treasure" now? To what "treasure" does your heart belong?

DRAWING NEAR

13. Think about the following words from God's point of view rather than your own:

> 📖 We must realize what God is doing whenever He withholds blessings we legitimately desire: He is pursuing the Immanuel Agenda. *He will be with a people who value Him above every other blessing.* He will create that people at the cost of His Son's death and at the cost of being hurt every day by children who really don't want Him except to use Him. He is allowing good dreams to shatter to arouse the better dream of knowing Him. 📖

What impressions of God's character do you gain from those words?

BELIEVE AND WATER FLOWS

Dr. Crabb says that the New Way begins with this promise: "Water is available, and you may drink it, but life may be tough as you draw near."

📖 The focus of the New Way, however, is not on the trials; it's on the availability of cool water and rich food.

"Whoever believes in me...streams of living water will flow from within him" (John 7:38).

That's New Way linearity: Believe and water flows.

"Come, all you who are thirsty, come to the waters.... Eat what is good, and your soul will delight in the richest of fare" (Isaiah 55:1-2).

More New Way linearity. It's a promise! Come along the path God has opened through Christ into His presence—and you'll be satisfied!

"Give ear and come to me; hear me, that your soul may live. I will make an everlasting covenant with you" (55:3).

That's the arrangement. It's a good one. If we hear what He offers, we'll not want to change a thing. 📖

14. Do you "hear what He offers"? Express here, in the most meaningful way for you, your understanding of what God is offering you.

Now add your prayerful response to this offer.

HOW TO LIVE
THE NEW WAY

This week's lesson is based on
chapter 15, "Enjoying God,"
and chapter 16, "Five Building Blocks
of New Way Living."

"Perhaps the Spirit is stirring you as He is me," writes Dr. Crabb. "I long to live the New Way. If there's a road that leads to whatever enjoyment of God is available in this life, I want to take it.

"My prayer is that you do as well. I trust this book so far has aroused your desire to leave behind the pressure of arranging for your own satisfaction and to live in the freedom of knowing God. If it's possible to actually meet God in joy-producing encounter (and even partial joy in meeting God is inexpressible), then you want to walk whatever path leads into His presence. That's my prayer for you and for me as well....

"Now that we're willing, how do we live in the Spirit's New Way? That's the question I discuss in the remaining chapters of this book.

"The pressure's off!

"It's time to experience our freedom."

ENJOY THE FEAST

📖 If you believe it's possible to enjoy God and if you're becoming aware of your desire to actually meet Him, then you've come to a fork in the road. The Old Way—trying hard to do things right so the good things of life come to you—is still available. The allure is powerful....

But you see another path. The sign marking its entrance is shaped like a cross, and the words on the crossbeam read "The New Way of the Spirit." You have a choice to make. 📖

1. At this point in your life, how strongly do you feel drawn to the Old Way? How powerful for you is its allure?

📖 The phrase *image of God* begins to mean something. You realize that your identity, your joy, and your purpose are completely wrapped up in your relationship to God. He is the source, the only source, the complete source, of everything you were built to enjoy. More money, great marriage, beautiful kids, close friends, good ministry—nothing else does it. Perhaps you've tried a few out-of-bounds pleasures. They worked well, but only for a moment. Then deeper emptiness. More addictions. You began to realize you'd been sold a false bill of goods. Lies, all lies....

Blessings are good, but they're not enough. Not for your soul. And now you know you have a soul. You *are* soul, created by God for God to find yourself in God and then to live your life through God.

You cannot rest until you rest in God. You cannot celebrate as you were meant to celebrate until you celebrate God more than everything else that is good—or bad. 📖

2. As honestly as you can, describe your own journey in encountering any of the observations and experiences presented in the preceding quotation.

3. Consider carefully these points:

> 📖 It's time to shed our cynicism, to move beyond nonsacrificial living, and to abandon everything getting in the way of a deep experience of God. I hope you're desperate for a divine encounter, a genuine, noncontrived, deeply felt meeting with God that *both* exposes sinful pleasures as cheap counterfeits of soul joy *and* reveals to us that our nervousness about whether our lives will turn out well is an insult to the God who gives you Himself and says, "Enjoy the feast!"
>
> Of course we'll continue to hurt when bad things happen. *Hurt* over trials, like pain from a kidney stone, is human, not sinful. But *despair* is sinful. It's subhuman to feel as if your source of real joy has been taken from you when a child rebels or a loved one dies or a business fails or an immoral temptation wins.
>
> God is still present....
>
> A former mentor, now partying in heaven with full enjoyment of God, told me, "The Christian always has reason to celebrate. When we fail, celebrate His grace. When we are blessed, celebrate His mercy. When others reject us, celebrate His love." 📖

At this point in your life—this very day—what does it mean for you to "shed your cynicism"?

What does it mean for you—today—to "abandon everything getting in the way of a deep experience of God"?

Today, what do you have to celebrate, and why?

RELATING WITH OTHERS

> 📖 As you discover your appetite for God, you may also be discovering your secondary appetite for relationship with others. You long for conversations that matter. At some point, you'll realize how strongly you want to bless others even if you're not blessed by others. If you're where I am on the journey, you're more aware of wanting to relate in ways that will lift you to a higher level of spiritual experience.
>
> You long to be involved in a few relationships where you can be *known* in loving safety, *explored* with genuine interest, *discovered* by hopeful wisdom, and *touched* from the source of spiritual power. 📖

4. As you think about the perspectives in the preceding quotation, how would you express your own deepest longings for your relationships with others?

📖 The idea of a New Way sounds faddish, like a well-marketed overstatement. Even biblical discussion of this New Way, what you've read so far in this book, can seem like cotton-candy theology. Although the phrase "the new way of the Spirit" was inspired by the Spirit and written by the apostle Paul, it can come across as a lot of fluff and sweetness that offers nothing to sink your teeth into as you live in this world. 📖

5. Have you had similar thoughts to those Dr. Crabb just described?

📖 The phone rings. Something has gone wrong, and you must deal with it. At that moment, talk of enjoying God sounds like an annoying platitude, a pious irrelevance, something of interest only to monastics, contemplatives, people so right-brained that they're out of touch with real-life challenges, people so mystical that they're more interested in spiritually retreating than facing life.

You've got a problem on your hands, a fire to put out. You're wide open to help from God—but *enjoying* Him?...

Enjoy God? When your son's been arrested? When your marriage isn't working? When your wife comes down with Alzheimer's? When your loneliness reaches new depths you can no longer tolerate? When the sexual struggle you thought was under control comes back with more uncontrollable passion than ever?

Enjoy God? *In the middle of all that?* 📖

6. Again, describe any ways in which your own reactions have been similar to those expressed by Dr. Crabb in the preceding paragraph.

7. Dr. Crabb responds, "Enjoy God? Yes. In the middle of hard times? *Especially* then."

    For your own life, how realistic and practical is this counsel from Dr. Crabb?

    📖 In the New Way, whatever we do comes out of a heart that has already come to God, that is anchored in that relationship, that looks to God for whatever joy and hope is needed to carry on, that demands nothing but celebrates God in everything. In the New Way, truth is personalized. For New Way revolutionaries, to live is Christ—not raising godly kids or making new friends or even living morally. 📖

8. What does it mean for you that "truth is personalized"?

LET ISAAC BE BORN!

Dr. Crabb looks at Abraham's life to show us a meaningful picture of the Old Way versus the New.

    📖 When God appeared to the patriarch and said, "You, my aged friend, and your elderly wife will have a baby in one year," Abraham was not excited. "God," he replied (the story is told in Genesis 17), "I've heard that before. Years ago, You told me that Sarah and I would bear a child. Well, it hasn't happened. And now it's too late. It would take a miracle for us to conceive now. I'm not sure I want to be stretched to that level of faith. I've lived by faith in a lot of situations. I left my home on nothing more than Your word. But now You're pushing it. I'm a little tired of living by faith. Frankly, God, I've about given up hope. I think I'd prefer a manageable life, a natural one." 📖

9. To what extent can you identify in your spiritual life with such a response from Abraham? Are you ever "tired of living by faith"?

📖 Then Abraham looked across the plains toward his tent. There sat his once beautiful wife, now a ninety-year-old woman, sexually uninviting, sexually inadequate, and probably sexually disinterested. Ishmael, his teenage son by another woman, was there too. A fine, healthy young man.

Abraham had an idea. "God, how about if You provide me Your promised blessings through the son I already have? Ishmael was born in the natural way, I grant that. No miracle was required, just a moment of compromise. That would make things so much easier. I already did something that worked. Couldn't you let that be enough? Oh God, *let Ishmael live!* " (See Genesis 17:18.)

That's been my cry for fifty years. I want to know that I can do something that will bring about the blessings I desire. To wait for a miracle puts me out of control. I don't like that. I want to believe that if I get it right, my life will work, that God will bless me with whatever I think I need in order to feel joy. "Please, God. You didn't do it for Abraham, but You had special plans for him. In my life, please, *let Ishmael live!*" 📖

10. In what way has your own heart's cry been, "Let Ishmael live"?

📖 To get started on the New Way, we must change our prayer. "God, I don't know how You can produce the fruit in my heart of a consuming love for You. I seem to find so much more enjoyment in the good things of life, and sometimes in sin, than in knowing You. I like blessings more than I love You. I experience more pleasure in other things than in You. It will take a miracle to change that.

"You tell me the miracle has already happened, that I have a new heart that wants You as my ultimate pleasure. But I don't know how to make that real. I can come to You as I am, like Abraham came to Sarah, as a tired old man. It took a miracle for them to conceive. But You did it. I will trust You for a similar miracle in my life. God, I now cast out Ishmael and his mother (see Galatians 4:21-31). I want no more temptation to return to the old way of making my life work. I want to lead a supernatural life. I come to You as I am. *God, let Isaac be born!*" 📖

11. In what ways does your heart cry out now, "God, let Isaac be born"?

Renewing the Way We Think

📖 The revolution I envision will be fueled by the New Way to think, live, and relate. It begins with thinking. We're transformed by renewing our minds, not our circumstances; we're changed not by rearranging blessings in our lives or strategizing to make life work a little better or overcoming our low self-esteem and troubling emotions, but by renewing the way we think about this life. 📖

12. In what important ways do you see that your thinking has already been renewed through what you've explored and learned in this workbook?

TAKING A
DEEPER LOOK

This week's lesson is based on
chapter 17, "Where Am I? Finding the Red Dot,"
chapter 18, "Your Choice of Cycles,"
and chapter 19, "First Thing Focus."

"I invite you now to join me," writes Dr. Crabb, "in taking a deeper look into our interior worlds. As we do so, keep in mind one vital truth that will sustain us: *Brokenness is the path to freedom.* When we see in ourselves things we wish were not there and realize we can do absolutely nothing to clean up the dirt we find, we enter into the liberating experience of brokenness.

"How long we stay there before we feel freedom is up to the Spirit. It may be days, weeks, years. Sometimes the fruit of our affliction is visible only in our legacy. We simply must trust the Spirit. Comfort is His sovereign work."

BROKENNESS

📖 God ordains afflictions and trouble (see Hebrews 12:5-6), but always for the purpose of setting us free to serve Him in the New Way of the Spirit. That Spirit, on His timetable, shines the spotlight on grace and lets us feel Him pour the Father's love into our hearts no matter how we fail and struggle.

It's the taste of divine love, unlike any love we've known, that draws us to the table for more food. At times we can almost see the Spirit smile as He nudges us toward the table and pulls out our chair for us to sit.

Listen closely and you might hear Him say:

"You can come as you are, right now. No penance, just repentance. Yes, I know—you see the mess. I've helped you see it. But the Father sees only the beauty of Christ. Come! Eat. Drink. Enter His presence under the terms of the New Covenant. You are as pure as Christ. You belong to the Father. You desire Him above all other desires. And now I'll deepen your awareness of all that is true, freeing you to come boldly into a place where many have died. Come in the merits of the Cross." 📖

1. Which words and phrases in the preceding quotation can you indeed sense coming to you now from God's Spirit? What else do you sense the Spirit's saying to you?

📖 Brokenness and freedom go together, in that order; first suffering, then comfort; first trouble, then joy; first felt unworthiness, then felt love; first death to the self, then resurrection of the soul.

It's a cycle. First down, then up, then down again, farther down, then up again, this time higher. When we discover the red dot that marks where we are on our journey, we'll always experience brokenness. It's the continual starting point for every next step toward God. Brokenness helps us turn our eyes, not toward the blessings of a better life—those blessings never heal brokenness; they only cover it—but toward the intimacy promised as our better hope.

It is the failure to discover where we are at any moment that keeps us from realizing where we most want to go. Until we face an inner brokenness that no blessing in this life can mend, we'll be drawn irresistibly to the Old Way. 📖

2. What does *brokenness* mean to you?

📖 Now let's see how this works. The New Way journey begins with a stunning revelation, not about us, but about God. The unapproachably holy, incomparably magnificent God wants us to *enjoy* Him, to actually come close and feel really good. He made us for the pleasure *He* enjoys when *we* enjoy Him.

But He, quite properly, is a jealous God. For Him that's only reasonable. He demands we enjoy Him as our supreme good because that's what He is....

God will never allow us to fully enjoy Him as long as we think of Him as one good among many. For one simple reason: It can't be done....

When God's people declare loyalty to Him but demand pleasure elsewhere—spouse, children, friends, ministry, health, success—God charges them with adultery. That's a capital offense. So, first, God kills His Son in their place. Then, like Hosea with Gomer, He separates Himself from them, *but only* to win them back to enjoyed nearness. The separation is designed to arouse their appetite for what is missing, to heighten awareness that only God's presence can satisfy the depths of human desire. 📖

3. What is your understanding of exactly how and why God wants you to enjoy Him?

> 📖 Consider God's invitation to us....
> As our Father, God welcomes His children to the family table and there spreads a magnificent feast—*Himself.* "Come, take your place secured by My Son. My Spirit has brought you here. Now, look at Christ to see Me. Drink Me. Eat Me. Satisfy yourself with My love that lets you see Me and live. Be awed by My splendor and majesty till you realize there is none brighter, none like Me, that you are fish and I am the ocean. All other water is but a puddle of mud in comparison." 📖

4. Record your response here to the words of invitation in the preceding quotation.

Where You Are

"The first step in our drawing near to God, to tasting any passion and vision for Him," writes Dr. Crabb, "is to identify where we are. If we draw near to Him, He *will* draw near to us. It's a promise. What more could we want?"

📖 Now we're ready to ask the question: *Where am I?*...

On the authority of God's Word, I can tell you where you are. It's where I am. I can tell you what's going on inside you. And if you see it, if you recognize where you are, you'll be drawn to the New Way. You'll abandon your love affair with blessings, and you'll bow low before God, demanding nothing. So will I.

There are two distinct attitudes within us. The first is in everyone, Christian or not. Isaiah looked at the people in his day and saw that all of them, like sheep, had gone a wrong way. Everyone had turned to the way that made natural sense: *Do whatever you think is best, and expect life to work.* Isaiah's diagnosis is severe: "From the sole of your foot to the top of your head there is no soundness—only wounds and welts and open sores" (Isaiah 1:6; see also Isaiah 53:6)....

That is the energy of the Old Way. I feel it moving in me. And I know that it's strong. I know it's so strong that only a direct encounter with God will stir the better energy in me until it rules my life. 📖

5. How have you most recently recognized within yourself the reality of this first attitude, this "energy of the Old Way"?

6. "The *second* attitude," writes Dr. Crabb, is "the better energy in every Christian's soul that too often lies unnoticed and unstirred."

📖 Can you feel...an energy moving you toward God, not to use Him, but to become absorbed with Him, to honor

Him, at any cost? Is there an appeal to the prospect of simply presenting yourself, with all your disappointments,
demands, and discouragements, to the Father, then remaining steadfast and faithful while you wait for Him to draw
near to you? *God, I come to You. Let me know You. That's
what I most want.* 📖

How have you most recently recognized within yourself the reality of
this second attitude, the "energy moving you toward God"?

NARROW ROAD, NARROW DOOR

📖 What did Jesus have in mind when He said there's a way
to the abundant life of knowing and enjoying God, but
"small is the gate and narrow the road that leads to life, and
only a few find it" (Matthew 7:14)?...
   Make every effort, Jesus said, to find the narrow door
leading to life because "many, I tell you, will try to enter and
will not be able to" (Luke 13:24). 📖

7. How would you answer the opening question in the preceding
   quotation?

📖 Choosing the New Way is costly. If we don't regard God as
our chief joy, we won't have the capital to pay the price. It's by
faith we see Him as the source of supreme pleasure; it's a faith
that keeps us coming to Him until He gives us a taste of the

pleasure we believe is available, and then coming to Him again.

If we do regard God as our chief treasure and live accordingly, we'll seem inhuman to some; we'll appear as radical freaks who take God too seriously and end up leading an unbalanced life. 📖

8. To the best of your understanding, what do you see as your personal cost in choosing the New Way?

📖 Remember the proud Pharisee who came into the temple, stood up tall, and *prayed about himself?* "God, I thank you that I am not like other men—robbers, evildoers, adulterers—or even like this tax collector. I fast twice a week and give a tenth of all I get" (Luke 18:11-12).

In other words, I got it right. Now bless me!

Notice the difference between the proud Pharisee and the humble tax collector. Neither had any right to claim God's blessings. One knew it. The other didn't. The Pharisee still believed in the modified Law of Linearity: If we get the law mostly right, then everything we do will prosper. The tax collector pinned all his hopes on the Law of Liberty—come as you are, undeserving, broken, desperate, and trust God will come near to you rather than banish you from His presence— which is all you deserve.

A principle worth remembering emerges from this parable:
Self-discovery that is led by God's Spirit always generates brokenness, deepens humility, and energizes dependence and gratitude. 📖

9. With the words of the preceding quotation in mind, think about the following New Way attributes, and converse with God about them. Record in writing a summary or section of your prayer.

brokenness

humility

dependence

gratitude

Telling Characteristics

Dr. Crabb lists the following three characteristics of those "who never recognize the bad energy within them as bad, and who never gratefully delight in the new energy that is even more deeply lodged in their being."

> Followers of the Old Way organize life into a System.
> They hate mystery, they do all they can to resolve tension, they work to find some way to bring into their lives whatever blessings they believe will make them happy. They love the idea of linearity; it sustains the illusion of control. Find the system that makes life work—find the *A* that leads to *B*. It prolongs the hope of a better life now.

10. To what extent, if any, have you seen in your own life this linear system-organizing tendency as well as a disliking of mystery?

    📖 *Followers of the Old Way deny whatever reality they come across that contradicts their System.*

    When a tither goes broke, he finds a way to fault his tithing. As a child, I could never figure out why I sometimes aced a math test the day after I was bad. I explained it by assuming I had been good enough to offset the bad I had done. 📖

11. In what ways have you found yourself denying the reality of any evidence that contradicts your "system"?

    📖 *Followers of the Old Way mistake vulnerability for brokenness.*

    They're willing to "get real" and "tell it like it is," assuming that their vulnerability is a virtue deserving compassion. They become aware of their longings, perhaps even their thirst to know God better, but remain ignorant of either their thirst for God Himself or their falling short that disqualifies them from receiving any blessing apart from mercy. It is characteristic of the Old Way to become aware of only those longings that some blessing other than God's presence can satisfy. It sustains the pride of independence. 📖

12. In what ways does the description in the preceding quotation reflect your own approach to vulnerability, past or present?

Dr. Crabb then lists the three following characteristics of those "who recognize both energies within them, who discover the small gate, and who… step through it in brokenness to walk the narrow New Way."

📖 *Followers of the New Way accept the unresolvable tension in life.*
Mystery remains and always will. They realize no system can be known or harnessed that will make all of life predictable…. Although sometimes terrified, New Way followers step into the mystery of life with no final hope other than a gracious sovereign God, who moves in a mysterious way. 📖

13. How easy is it for you to accept life's unresolvable tensions?

📖 *Followers of the New Way struggle to be truly authentic.*
When life confuses or enrages them, they admit it. When God disappoints and frustrates them, they talk it over with Him—and others. They enter dark nights with trembling confidence that somewhere there is light and someday they'll see it. Their rest is in the present God. 📖

14. To what extent does the preceding quotation reflect your own attitudes?

📖 *Followers of the New Way are cautious about vulnerability but vulnerable to brokenness.*
They recognize that what we call vulnerability is often a narcissistic parade intended to draw support. These folks

prefer to face in themselves only what draws them closer to
God. Sharing pain is secondary. Sharing hunger for God
and facing what impedes their search for Him is primary.
Their excitement is in the relational God. 📖

15. How would you explain in your own words the approach to vulnera-
    bility mentioned in the preceding quotation?

YOUR CHOICE OF CYCLES

"If our foundation for thinking about life is the Old Way," Dr. Crabb
writes, "if we believe that doing something right will make our lives work
better, if we aim no higher than toward a better life, then we're likely to see
only two paths open before us."

> 📖 I call the first the Adjustment Cycle. Here's how it works.
>
> Start by *denying* whatever you cannot handle.... Do what-
> ever it takes to stay distant from difficult realities that might
> overwhelm your coping skills, whether that reality is inside
> your heart or outside in your circumstances.
>
> Then find your bootstraps, grab them, and pull up hard.
> *Strategize*. Life is hard. You admit that. But you can handle
> it. Let's see. How?...
>
> Now that you've experimented with several coping strate-
> gies, *evaluate*. See which ones seem to work best....
>
> You are now ready to *refine* your approach to recovering
> your life....
>
> There! You've got it now. You still have bad days, and

nights are especially difficult, but you're getting through pretty well. Sometimes you feel really good.... The important thing is you feel restored. You like yourself. You like most of life. And you're able to keep your distance from the ache in your soul that tells you something is dreadfully wrong. The need to keep denying, strategizing, evaluating, and refining your methods continues. But for now you're pretty *stable*. The Old Way is working. Praise God! Or whomever. 📖

16. In what ways have you seen yourself following this Adjustment Cycle?

📖 Sometimes the Adjustment Cycle fails. You can't cope. When you're unable to develop a stable strategy for handling your life, the therapeutic culture offers its services. Consider the Therapeutic Cycle....

Start by lifting denial. *Openness* about how you "really feel" begins the cycle. Therapy creates a safe place for emotional vulnerability. Someone actually listens to you without disdain or judgment. And it helps. When you share your secret emotions and face the ones you've buried, you do feel better. The burden seems lighter. There! You're off to a good start. You feel hope.

Next comes *insight*. If your therapist is directive, the insight might be carefully presented. Otherwise, under the influence of probing questions, clarifying comments, and well-timed silence, you may come to new realizations on your own....

With insight comes *direction*. What course of action does your new awareness suggest?... Now you know what to do…. The energy of, well, *self* courses through your being. You feel strong, together, whole for the first time in your life…. You love your newly developing freedom.

But it's scary…. *Support* helps, from your therapist, from friends who love you and believe in you and take your side…. With help you can break out. You can do it!

Now comes the tough part. It's time to *align* your behavior with your insight, to move in the directions that now seem so right, and to do it with support. Remember Jesus loves you. He's *for* you. He wants you to love yourself and to feel the freedom to be who you are. Visualize Him cheering you on. Let Him, along with the Spirit, be your primary support group as you follow the Old Way to a better life. 📖

17. In what ways have you seen yourself following this Therapeutic Cycle?

📖 But there's a new way to live, and it's radically different. Be still. Reflect on where you are. You've been *using* God to make your life work. That puts you above Him. You're insisting that blessings come your way, at least certain ones. You're not *wanting* blessings; you're *requiring* them. You're depending on them for your joy. God is not your supreme treasure. Christ is not preeminent in your life. The Spirit lies quenched within you; His invitation to feast on God goes unheeded.

As you see what's been going on inside you…you feel more than a little sheepish. In your humility, you hear the Spirit whisper, "There's a new way to live. There's another path to follow." 📖

18. Be still and reflect on where you are. Have you been using God? Have you been requiring blessings instead of merely wanting them? Have you been depending on blessings for your joy? Is something less than God your supreme treasure? Respond to these questions here.

📖 New Life begins at the Cross. It's there you realize how arrogant you are. You don't welcome trials. You've lived for no greater purpose than to avoid them or reverse them if they come. Your ambition has risen no higher than a life that works pretty well.... God's glory has mattered little to you. A quality life is what you're after.... The Spiritual Cycle begins with *brokenness*. It hurts. The two Old Way cycles are much more seeker friendly. 📖

19. What does it mean for you at this time to come to the Cross?

📖 From brokenness the Spirit leads you to *repentance*. You've assumed you deserved satisfaction. You thought, with God's help, you could arrange for it. You believed you were living the Christian life. How could you have been so deceived? You thought God was here to cooperate with your agenda. But only He can say, "I AM." You can say only, "I serve at Your pleasure." 📖

20. What does genuine repentance mean for you at this time?

📖 Yes, this is a new way to think. Your mind has changed. Repentance has begun. And it feels clean, right, strangely good.

The Spirit then moves you from brokenness through repentance to *abandonment....* You listen to the Spirit speak through the Bible. This world is fallen. Things happen that make no visible sense. But somehow, through it all, God is telling a good story. Without the ending, the story is not good. But nothing happens, nothing can happen, nothing ever will happen that God cannot redeem to move the story along to its glorious climax. You believe that. You therefore abandon yourself to the invisible God, the One who for a moment became fully visible as He hung on the cross. 📖

21. What does it mean for you at this time to abandon yourself to God?

📖 Abandonment, surprisingly perhaps, arouses *confidence.* The Spirit witnesses to your spirit that you do belong to God, that He is working all things together for good, that eternity will vindicate your choice to abandon the well-being of your soul to this mysterious, mostly invisible, seemingly fickle, certainly unpredictable God.... You know, because the Spirit tells you, that He is present as you walk the New Way toward the Better Hope of knowing, glorifying, enjoying, and revealing to others the wonderful, spectacular God who is really there. 📖

22. How confident are you in God at this time? How would you express
   in your own words the reason for this confidence?

       📖 Spirit-given confidence that God is there and worthy of
   absolute trust breeds the freedom to *release* what is most alive
   within you. You begin to feel something stirring in your
   innermost being. It may take awhile, but at some point you
   realize, *These are the springs of living water!...* You find yourself released to be the person you've longed to be—loving,
   joyful, peaceful, patient, kind, gentle. Never perfectly, but
   sometimes at least genuinely. And now you praise God and
   no one else. 📖

23. Record here your prayer, in your own words, for God "to release what
   is most alive within you."

24. Think about the most meaningful concept or truth you've explored in
   this week's lesson. How would you talk this over with God? Write your
   response here as a prayer to Him.

COUNTING ON GOD

This week's lesson is based on
chapter 20, "God Is in Control—of What?"
and chapter 21, "The Papa Prayer,"
plus the Epilogue, "With God in the Bathroom."

"We live our lives on one of two foundations," writes Dr. Crabb.

"If we build on the first foundation, the flesh, our core passion will be for blessings, whichever ones we value most. And our core experience, beneath whatever else we feel, will be pressure, the pressure to live a certain way to get the life we want.

"If we build on the second foundation, the Spirit, our core passion will be for God, to know Him and honor Him in any circumstance. And our core experience will be freedom, the freedom to draw near to God across a bridge we neither constructed nor maintain. And in that freedom we'll discover both the passion to live well and the wisdom to know what that means."

GOD IS IN CONTROL—OF WHAT?

📖 God is in control. Of what? *Of seeing to it that nothing thwarts His plan for His people.* What is that plan? To give us a Better Life now, as we define it? No. It's to reveal Himself as the greatest treasure the human heart could ever imagine, to draw people into a relationship with Him that utterly delights their souls....

God is in control of what He wants to accomplish. He's moving through all of history—through earthquakes and picnics, through terrorism and church dinners, through divorces and anniversary celebrations—toward one thing: the Immanuel Agenda. And He'll reach it. He'll have a people who think He is the greatest, who value knowing Him and worshiping Him and serving Him above all other blessings....

I feel a great burden to be unmistakably clear: *We cannot count on God to protect us from suffering of any kind or measure. The worst evil can happen to the best Christian. But we can count on God to enable us to draw near to Him whatever happens and, eventually, to experience deep joy when we do.* 📖

1. At this moment in your life, what does it mean to "count on God" in this way?

THREE MIRACLES

"We can count on God," Dr. Crabb writes, "to perform three miracles in our lives."

📖 He wants to perform them, He can perform them, and He will perform them in the lives of New Way followers....

There's nothing we can do to make these miracles happen. By following the New Way, we create space for Him to work in a certain way. But we remain utterly dependent on His sovereign grace to bless us as He chooses and when He chooses. 📖

📖 Miracle 1: We'll encounter God.

We can come into God's presence as we are—lustful, envious, discouraged, ugly enough to be reviled, selfish enough to deserve rejection, arrogant enough to be stomped on—and be welcomed and enjoyed.

As we sense God's welcome and feel His delight, as grace stirs us, we discover that beneath all the stain and smell, we're actually beautiful, even desirable. We share in Christ's loveliness. We're pure, we belong at the Father's table, we like to be good, and the power to do good is in us. 📖

2. Express here, in honest words addressed to God, your trust and confidence that He will perform this first miracle in your life. Express also what this means to you.

📖 Miracle 2: We'll experience community.

With at least one other person, sometimes a handful, we'll enter into levels of closeness that surface enough conflict to sink any relationship—and spiritual intimacy will emerge. After feeling the impact of failure and hurt and reeling with defensiveness, recrimination, and withdrawal, we can expect, if we live the New Way, to discover a power within us sufficient to face every relationship- destroying force and to carry us into true community. 📖

3. Again, in honest words addressed to God, express your trust and confidence that He will perform this second miracle in your life and what it means to you.

📖 Miracle 3: We'll be transformed.

An encounter with God and an experience in community will open our eyes to see how unlike Jesus we really are. We'll be appalled. Like Job when he finally heard God speak, we'll acknowledge, "I am unworthy" (Job 40:4). And then, when we *see* God, we will, again like Job, exclaim, "My ears had heard of you but now my eyes have seen you. Therefore I despise myself and repent in dust and ashes" (42:5-6).

Brokenness and repentance will lead to abandonment. We'll never abandon ourselves to the Spirit as long as we think we can change without Him. But when we sense our desire not merely to feel good about ourselves and to enjoy life but to *resemble Jesus,* and when we realize how utterly incapable we are of moving even one step in that direction without supernatural help, we'll then abandon ourselves more fully to the Holy Spirit.

And then, at unplanned moments, we'll know living water is springing up within us. Something wonderful will come out of us, and we'll tremble with joy. When we stare into the chasm separating who we are from who we long to be and realize we have no means in our flesh to cross from

one side to the other, and not until then, we will change.
The miracle of transformation will be humbly enjoyed. 📖

4. Once more, express in honest words addressed to God your trust and
confidence that He will perform this third miracle in your life and
what this means to you.

ALL THE SPIRIT DOES

Dr. Crabb writes, "God has sent His Spirit to do a sevenfold work that
makes it possible for us to live the New Way.... And the more we see all
that He is doing, the more the pressure falls off.... Let me now describe
that sevenfold work (I follow the outline provided by John Owens in his
classic work *Communion with God*) and suggest how we can depend on all
that the Spirit does as we seek to draw near to God."

5. The Spirit's first work is *reminding*.

> 📖 Just before He promised them peace, Jesus told His disci-
> ples that "the Counselor, the Holy Spirit, whom the Father
> will send in my name, will teach you all things and will
> remind you of everything I have said to you" (John 14:26).
> When dreams shatter, when terrorists win and marriages
> fail, the Spirit is not silent. He reminds us that what matters
> most is unthreatened. The Father's agenda is on track. Christ
> did all that was needed for us to draw near to God and for
> Him to draw near to us. And the Spirit will tell us that the
> Trinity can conceive no greater blessing.

If we live the New Way, we'll spend time in Scripture, not to master content, but to hear the Spirit. And we'll sense a weighty anchor holding our ship steady in the worst storm. Like a seasoned nurse coming to our bedside and saying, "I've just checked with the doctor. Your disease has been cured. You'll be fine," the Spirit reminds us what Jesus has said: "In this world you will have trouble. But take heart! I have overcome the world" (John 16:33). 📖

How do you see the Spirit doing this work in your life? Respond here as fully as you can.

6. The Spirit's second work is *glorifying*.

📖 When the Spirit comes, Jesus said, "He will bring glory to me by taking from what is mine and making it known to you" (John 16:14).

Coming to God can seem so pointless....

Coming to God may rouse hopes that might be dashed and often are.

When I do come, I must come centrally to know Him, not to improve my life.... And when I do, the Spirit glorifies Christ by taking what belongs to Him—the eternal value of His life, death, and resurrection—and whispering to me, "The way is open. Whatever happens, God is in control of what matters most. Come boldly. Come close enough to hear the Father singing over you with delight."

In whatever shape I find myself, in the midst of whatever I'm facing, I'll be accepted into God's presence, listened to, understood, and given whatever my loving Father knows is best. Christ made that possible. To Him be the glory. That's what the Spirit is saying. It's His second work. 📖

Again, how do you see the Spirit doing this work in your life? Respond as fully as you can.

7. The Spirit's third work is *pouring*.

📖 The Spirit inspired the apostle Paul to say this: "God has poured out his love into our hearts by the Holy Spirit, whom he has given us" (Romans 5:5).

It's so hard to believe we're loved. Not only do circumstances turn sour and God does nothing, but also we have never fully experienced from family or friends the kind of love we long to know. As in everything that matters most to our souls, we're utterly dependent on the Spirit to convince us that indeed we are fully loved and *can* rest in the love of God for us. He persuades us by pouring the Father's love into our hearts, which is a mystical process....

When I meditate on the Cross, when I open myself to others' touching me with Christ's love by being broken before them, then I may experience the wholeness of being divinely loved. 📖

How is the Spirit pouring God's love into your life? In what ways do you see this?

8. The Spirit's fourth work is *assuring*.

📖 Are there more wonderful words for moral failures, lonely people, and abused victims to hear than "The Spirit himself testifies with our spirit that we are God's children" (Romans 8:16)?...

If we look only at our lives, we'll wonder if we're His. If we evaluate our progress along the spiritual journey, doubts will rise. But if we learn to listen to the Spirit, we'll *know* we are Christ's. And we'll delight in holy fellowship with God.... We *are* His children. 📖

In what ways has the Spirit given you assurance that you are God's child?

9. The Spirit's fifth work is *sealing*.

📖 When we came to Christ, not only were we included in Christ, but also, having believed, we were "marked in him with a seal, the promised Holy Spirit" (Ephesians 1:13).

Sealing means safety. The Spirit Himself is the seal. Sealed people are set apart from unsealed people. Think of it! You and I have been given into the keeping of the Spirit to guarantee our encounter with the Father and the Son. We're safe, not from bombs, cancer, or family heartache, but from even an inch of separation from the God who is in control of the Immanuel Agenda. We can come boldly into His presence. 📖

Express here your understanding of what the Spirit's sealing means to you.

10. The Spirit's sixth work is *anticipation.*

📖 "Now it is God who makes both us and you stand firm in Christ. He anointed us, set his seal of ownership on us, and put his Spirit in our hearts as a deposit, guaranteeing what is to come" (2 Corinthians 1:21-22).

The Spirit is the *earnest* of our inheritance, the *deposit* of what's ahead, and the *guarantee* that it's coming. He is a part of the whole, a taste of the meal, a sample of what we can anticipate....

God is essentially a community of passionate persons who profoundly like each other. When He created people, He built into them a capacity for that same kind of passion and enjoyment. And when He redeemed us, He put within us one member of the Trinity as a deposit, we might say a teaser, of what's coming. Given how vividly the Bible speaks of the pleasure and satisfaction and joy that God provides, we can only assume that the deposit within us is an experienceable taste, a felt pleasure, a palpable emotion, a little sample of what's in store for all of us. 📖

Because of the Spirit's work, what anticipation do you have?

11. The Spirit's seventh work is *anointing.*

📖 "But you have an anointing from the Holy One, and all of you know the truth.... The anointing you received from him remains in you, and you do not need anyone to teach you" (1 John 2:20,27)....

Coming to God for the Better Hope of enjoyed intimacy with Him (which brings glory to His Name) releases something from us. Loving passion and discerning wisdom are given to us by the Spirit. We sense His leading on what to do. That's the anointing we have received from Him. It's a divinely directed game plan for dealing with whatever is going on in our lives....

I take this seventh work of the Holy Spirit, this spiritual anointing, to mean that followers of the New Way will be given the passion and wisdom of Christ to respond to every challenge they meet in life. When the Spirit came on the incarnate Christ, He was granted wisdom, power, and delight-producing fear (see Isaiah 11:1-3). And now in Christ are hidden all the treasures of wisdom and knowledge (see Colossians 2:3). If we learn what it means to come to Him, we'll receive an anointing that enlightens us about what to do and empowers us to do it in any circumstance of life. 📖

What is your understanding and experience of the anointing you've received by God's Spirit?

THE PAPA PRAYER

"It has recently dawned on me," writes Dr. Crabb, "that there's an Old Way to pray and a New Way to pray."

📖 Old Way prayers come in at least three varieties:

Change that. Whatever in my life is causing pain, I ask you to change it. Straighten out my daughter, give me a spouse, restore my health, provide an income.

Use this. Show me what principles I'm to follow to make it happen. Direct me to the person or resources I need to help make it happen.

Satisfy me. I long to feel alive, content, fulfilled, and happy. Do whatever it takes to make me feel satisfied with me, with life, and with You.

Nothing is wrong with these prayers *unless they represent the deepest passion of our hearts.* Then they're Old Way prayers with more demands than petitions. 📖

12. In your own prayer life, how can you discern when those prayers— change that, use this, satisfy me—involve your deepest passions and become demands more than petitions?

Dr. Crabb writes, "We can pray a New Way…*Lord, I come.* That's the essence of the New Way prayer."

📖 I call it the Papa Prayer:

*P*resent yourselves to God as you are.

*A*ttend to where you notice God's presence or absence.

*P*urge yourselves of whatever, at that moment, might be keeping you from noticing more of God.

*A*pproach God with abandonment and confidence, dedicating yourselves anew to coming to Him to know and enjoy and reveal Him, not to using Him to make your life better. 📖

13. The first part of the Papa Prayer is to *present yourself to God.*

📖 Reflect on your life. Be brutally honest, knowing by
God's grace revealed in the New Covenant you'll discover
nothing that will make God reject you and believing, because of that same grace, that beneath the dirtiest dirt lies
radiant beauty.

What passions within you seem deepest? Ask a few (only
a few) trusted friends for feedback: What are you like to be
with? What's your "pull," that is, what do people sense you're
wanting from them, what's your effect on them, in the
moment?

Make the incredibly difficult decision to face yourself, to
feel your rage, lust, and terror as well as your compassion,
kindness, and joy. Pretend about nothing. But as you honor
that commitment, avoid the twin errors of *denial* ("I'll face
only what I can handle, what doesn't make me feel too
threatened") and *obsession* ("I'll face everything all the
time"). 📖

Exercise your soul at this time to present yourself to God as you are.
Write here a record or summary of your prayer words at this time,
in this first aspect of the Papa Prayer.

14. The next part of the Papa Prayer is to *attend to God.*

📖 Where have you noticed God's *presence* in the past hour
or day? Where have you been aware of a longing to sense
that He was with you but felt only His *absence?*

The spiritual journey is centered in the experience of
God. But it's rooted in the revealed truth of God. Attend
to what you experience of God, but during this part of the
prayer, focus also on what you know is true, whether you
experience it or not. Remember the sevenfold work of the
Spirit as you ponder whatever biblical text you read.

Listen to the Spirit remind you of all that Jesus said, especially that everything is under control. Nothing ever takes
God by surprise. The Immanuel Agenda is on course.

Hear Him glorify Christ. Everything you need to experience the life of true abundance is in Christ and in the New
Covenant made in His blood.

Notice when He pours love into your heart. Be still, tune
your ear to the music of heaven, hear the Father sing over
you with delight. 📖

Where have you noticed God's *presence* in the past hour or day?

Where have you been aware of a longing to sense that God was with
you but felt only His *absence*?

Attending to God can continue in these ways:

📖 Depend on the Spirit's witness that you are a child of
God, even when the evidence you see makes you wonder.

Relax in the safety of His seal on your life. No act of terrorism, no stock market slide, no medical scare, no rejection,
no broken family has the power to thwart God's work in

your life. Everything can be redeemed by the Spirit for good purposes.

Taste whatever sample He gives you of the meal that's coming. It might be a moment of overwhelming joy or a deep release of built-up pressure to get it right so God will bless.

Trust the Spirit's anointing. Anticipate that He'll grant you the passion and wisdom to handle every situation you face in a way that honors Christ and advances His agenda. 📖

Record here your further prayer experience at this time of attending to God.

15. The third part is to *purge yourself before God.*

📖 Start by reciting David's prayer: "Search me, O God, and know my heart; test me and know my anxious thoughts. See if there is any offensive way in me, and lead me in the way everlasting" (Psalm 139:23-24).

Reflect on what is in you—attitude, motive, determination—and on what you're doing that makes it difficult for you to hear the Spirit, to believe His Word, to trust God.

Assume whatever it is has roots in a preoccupation with yourself. A focus on *your* desire, *your* dreams, *your* hopes, *your* disappointments, *your* pain can drive you to Old Way living. The effect of a focus on self, though encouraged by the therapeutic culture and sanctioned by much Christian teaching, is to accept another gospel, the gospel that God is here for us more than we're here for Him. 📖

Record here a record or summary of your experience at this time in purging yourself before God.

16. The fourth part of the Papa Prayer is to *approach God because you want Him.*

    📖 As you present yourself to God—with all of who you are, with all you know God to be, with all your ongoing struggle against the flesh—respond in faith to God's invitations:
        Come, all you who are weary.
        Come, all you who can't get it right.
        Come, all you who are struggling to make life work. 📖

What is your response to these invitations?

Approaching God can continue in these ways:

    📖 You're aware of the burdensome pressure of Old Way living and the heinous arrogance beneath it, but you're also aware of a spiritual hunger, of a longing to come to God to...
        glorify and enjoy Him in an *encounter* with Him,
        join the *community* of His people,
        be *transformed* by His Spirit till you actually resemble
            Jesus.
    Expect to experience a sovereign joy that will displace every affection other than God from the center of your heart.
    Anticipate that, by the Spirit, the Father and Son will show

themselves to you. Trust the Spirit to provide the loving passion and the spiritual wisdom you need to handle every situation in life in a way that furthers the Immanuel Agenda. 📖

Express here in prayer your desire for God, your hunger for Him.

📖 Tell God, with tears if they're there, with whatever genuineness is alive within you, that you want Him more than any other blessing—to know Him, adore Him, enjoy Him, serve Him, reveal Him, become like Him. As you pray, you'll find petition flowing from your heart for others, especially for their salvation and growth, and for yourself, that you'll be an instrument of grace. You'll come with confidence, making known all your burdens without a spirit of anxiety or demand, but with trust in a Father whose love can be trusted. 📖

What petitions are flowing from your heart at this time for yourself and for others?

WITH GOD IN THE BATHROOM

📖 Permit a final illustration.

When I was three years old, our family lived for a while in my grandparents' big, old-fashioned house. The only bathroom was on the second floor.

One Saturday afternoon (I know it was Saturday—Dad

was home), I decided I was a big boy and could use the bathroom without anyone's help. So I climbed the stairs, closed
and locked the door behind me, and for the next few minutes
felt very self-sufficient.

Then it was time to leave. I couldn't unlock the door. I
tried with every ounce of my three-year-old strength, but I
couldn't do it. I panicked. I felt again like a very little boy as
the thought went through my head, "I might spend the rest
of my life in this bathroom."

My parents—and likely the neighbors—heard my desperate scream. "Are you okay?" Mother shouted through the
door she couldn't open from the outside. "Did you fall?
Have you hit your head?"

"I can't unlock the door," I yelled. "Get me out of here!"

I wasn't aware of it right then, but Dad raced down the
stairs, ran to the garage to find the ladder, hauled it off the
hooks, and leaned it against the side of the house just beneath
the bathroom window. With adult strength, he pried it open,
then climbed into my prison, walked past me, and with that
same strength, turned the lock and opened the door.

"Thanks, Dad," I said—and ran out to play.

That's how I thought the Christian life was supposed to
work. When I get stuck in a tight place, I should do all I can
to free myself. When I can't, I should pray. Then God shows
up. He hears my cry—"Get me out of here. I want to
play!"—and unlocks the door to the blessings I desire.

Sometimes He does. But now, no longer three years old
and approaching sixty, I'm realizing the Christian life doesn't
work that way. And I wonder, are any of us content with

God? Do we even like Him when He doesn't open the door we most want opened—when a marriage doesn't heal, when rebellious kids still rebel, when friends betray, when financial reverses threaten our comfortable way of life, when the prospect of terrorism looms, when health worsens despite much prayer, when loneliness intensifies and depression deepens, when ministries die?

God has climbed through the small window into my dark room. But He doesn't walk by me to turn the lock that I couldn't budge. Instead, He sits down on the bathroom floor and says, "Come sit with me!" He seems to think that climbing into the room to be with me matters more than letting me out to play.

I don't always see it that way. "Get me out of here," I scream. "If You love me, *unlock the door!*"

Dear friend, the choice is ours. *Either* we can keep asking Him to give us what we think will make us happy—to escape our dark room and run to the playground of bless-ings—*or* we can accept His invitation to sit with Him, for now perhaps in darkness, and to seize the opportunity to know Him better and represent Him well in this difficult world.

Will we choose the Old Way, the way of pressure? "I'll do whatever You say; just get me out of here!"

Or will we discover both God's heart and ours and choose the New Way, the way of freedom and joy? "I'll sit with You anywhere, in darkness or light; just let me know You and serve You!"

It's time to choose the New Way of the Spirit and follow it

until we play forever in the fields of heaven, always looking
to Jesus as our greatest blessing.

It's time to be with God in the bathroom until He opens
the door to eternity. *It's what we want.* 📖

17. To help you remember, summarize here the most valuable truths
you've learned in going through this workbook.

IT'S TIME

📖 Let me end by paraphrasing the apostle James:

"Dear friends, when difficulties come, don't try to figure
out what you can do to make things better. Welcome whatever is going wrong as a chance to more deeply encounter
God, to enter community, and to experience transformation.

"If you're not sure how to actually do that, ask God, not
for improved circumstances or happier experiences, but for
the wisdom to let your suffering draw out your desire for
God. When you ask for that, know that He gives generously and never criticizes you for where you are. Believe,
don't doubt. If you waiver between wanting the New Way
and still clinging to the Old, you'll receive nothing from
the Lord.

"It's time, brothers and sisters, to abandon ourselves fully
to God. There's a New Way to live. Draw near to God, and
He'll draw near to you. He'll meet you, fill you, delight
you, and use you to further the great plan of the ages, the

Immanuel Agenda. Then we'll all go home" (see James 1:2-7; 4:8,10).

Are you weary?

Having trouble getting it right?

Struggling to make your life work?

The pressure's off.

There *is* a New Way to live. 📖

INTRODUCING
NEW WAY MINISTRIES

We have been released from the law so that
we serve in the new way of the Spirit.

—ROMANS 7:6

With the release of my book *Shattered Dreams,* along with the writings of respected colleagues, I launched NewWay Ministries in 2002. It was birthed out of the passionate conviction that there is a new way to live—made possible by the New Covenant—and this new way of living must become better known. NewWay Ministries (NWM) joins with people who are excited about spiritual formation and authentic community to help ignite a revolution in how Christians live, think, and relate.

Let me introduce you to NWM by outlining its theological foundations, the essence of the New Way to live, and the contribution we hope to make to the revolution.

THE THEOLOGICAL FOUNDATIONS

The Reformation was a reforming of the Christian theology of justification. It provided a clear understanding of how we receive life from God. In my years as a psychologist working with people who desperately want to change, I've come to believe that we need a second reformation, this one reforming our theology of sanctification. We know what it takes to receive life from God. But do we understand what is required to live the life we've received?

The good news that Jesus announced is not only that we've been for-given but also that we've been changed. There is new life within us that is stronger and better than the energy that drove us before we were converted. That new life has four basic elements:

First, a new purity. We're now clean even when we roll in mud. The dirt is on us; the purity of God's life is in us.

Second, a new identity. We're no longer defined by our problems or sins or education or talents. No one is an alcoholic who happens to be a Chris-tian. Now the person who compulsively drinks is a Christian who happens to struggle with strong urges to drink too much. The only label we wear is that we are Christ's ones, Christians. That's who we are; everything else is secondary.

Third, a new appetite. Our deepest and potentially strongest desire is for God—to know Him, to enjoy Him, to obey Him, to reveal Him. When a Christian sins, he is not giving in to his deepest appetite. Becoming like Christ has little to do with sheer moral effort and nothing to do with repair-ing psychological damage from traumatic experiences. It has everything to do with identifying, nourishing, and freely indulging our appetite for holi-ness. The route to personal change is release more than it is reform or repair. The latter two are the work of man. The former is the work of God.

Fourth, a new power. The Holy Spirit has moved in. Our hearts have become His home. The power is within us to live out the new life of purity, identity, and appetite that has already been gifted to us and implanted in our souls. We need a good theology about how to access that power. This new life, given to us according to the terms of the New Covenant, empow-ers us to relate to others in a new way. And doing so further stirs up the life within us so that our interior worlds become more like the interior world of

Jesus. The community that's now possible is one in which we're known, with no secrets. We are explored to help us see all that's inside, we're discovered to be alive with Trinitarian life, and we're touched by the Spirit through others.

NWM stands firmly within the borders of evangelical theology, but it highlights New Covenant truth and an understanding of real community as its distinctive foundation. Too often, our relational experiences fail to express and enjoy that foundation, but life can be different.

THE ESSENCE OF THE NEW WAY TO LIVE

Much of how we live is all about us. If we could see deeply into the motives, maneuverings, and messy emotions of our souls, we would admit that our bottom-line agendas are far more concerned with our well-being than with God's glory. And the self-centeredness we do see strikes us as reasonable and necessary.

When God planned the New Covenant, His intention was to recover His reputation that His Old Covenant followers had pretty well ruined. God's priority then, now, and always is His glory. New Covenant resources are provided so we can live lives that are all about God and not all about us.

The point is that God be glorified in us, not that He become useful to us.

The old life energizes a dad to want to straighten out his drug-abusing son, to be a good father who does things right. The new life empowers a dad to want above everything else to enjoy God and be abandoned and responsive and honoring to Him even when his son stumbles in the door at four in the morning, buzzed and defiant. Living the New Way removes pressure from the dad to "do it right" and relieves the power struggle between father and son. And that opens up possibilities for better relating between them and for wisdom in better responding to a troubled child.

The Old Way is all about us, and it draws on resources everyone has, whether Christian or not. The new way is all about God. Living it requires resources from God that are available only to Christians. Living the New Way attracts outsiders to a life they can't have apart from Christ but which they discover they desperately want.

THE CONTRIBUTION OF NEW WAY MINISTRIES

Our intended contribution to the revolution includes the following four distinct ministries.

1. Library

My earlier books reflected my commitment to biblical counseling. I focused on a biblical understanding of various life areas, such as marriage and manhood. Now, drawing on all that I've previously written, I am zeroing in on three topics:

- encounter—what it means to experience God
- transformation—what it takes to become like Christ
- community—what real community is and what its role is in helping us know God and form spiritually

My books *Connecting* and *Becoming a True Spiritual Community* (formerly titled *The Safest Place on Earth*) began the new focus by looking at the practice and power of community. *Shattered Dreams* and *The PAPA Prayer* directly address the most vital of the three topics: encounter. *The Pressure's Off* and *SoulTalk* lay the groundwork for understanding transformation. And *66 Love Letters* identifies the thread that ties together what it means to encounter God by knowing Him, what it means to be transformed by God, and what it means to relate like God in community.

2. Intensive Training

The School of Spiritual Direction (SSD) is a week-long intensive available to thirty students at a time. The school is an opportunity to understand and experience how the Spirit works deep in our souls to spiritually form us, and to learn and practice a way of following the Spirit in others to arouse and direct their hunger for God.

The objective of SSD is not to prepare people professionally for vocational ministry. It is to encourage Christians to consider the enormous value of spiritual direction and to equip a handful of selected people to engage in meaningful, powerful, soul-shaping conversations with folks who long to move through life's challenges into a deeper relationship with God.

I am persuaded that the absence of such conversations in our lives is significantly responsible for the all-too-common distance and shallowness in our experience of God. Paul speaks of a new way to live in Romans 7:6. He calls it the "new way of the Spirit." I understand spiritual direction to involve the supernatural work of relating to others in a way that guides them into the New Way to think, live, and relate. This is what the gospel makes possible.

The NextStep School of Spiritual Direction is a week-long, hands-on intensive for thirty SSD graduates. The NextStep is an opportunity to focus on translating the teaching of SSD into conversations that matter through modeling, critique of videotaped conversations, and supervision. This is more an experiential time than a didactic time, a week of intensive and personal interaction in community.

The NextStep SSD mission is to more clearly understand—by watching, critiquing, and participating in spiritually directing conversations—how the categories of understanding presented at the SSD can inform our thoughts, guide our words, and stir holy passion as we interact with others.

Certificate in Soul Care: The Ministry of Shepherding. The ministry of shepherding through conversational soul care provides relational opportunities for people, over time, to come out of hiding, to be seen as they are, to "look bad" in the presence of love, to live with no secrets and increasingly free from the power of shame, and to walk together with authentic companions into the amazing liberty of grace. The Certificate in Soul Care prepares people to engage in SoulTalk, to relate with

- vision-inspired confidence,
- concern-motivated curiosity,
- willingly sacrificial compassion, and to thus
- help form a community of people who listen to God and hear Him speak.

Certificate in Spiritual Direction: The Ministry of Healing. The ministry of healing through conversational spiritual direction provides relational opportunities for people, over time, to discern their self-obsessed energy, to understand the devil-inspired influence of background events that have shaped their patterns of self-protective relating, and to recognize those patterns in their relationships. As people experience brokenness over their self-centered ways of relating, the hope of the gospel stirs repentance that releases the life of Christ provided under the blessing of God's New Covenant. Brokenness stirs repentance that motivates abandonment to God, which in turn develops confidence in God's goodness. This releases people into a new way to live, the way of Jesus.

The Certificate in Spiritual Direction prepares people to release the passion of Christ into others as they relate to others with His wisdom. This wisdom/passion approach is designed to provide nonprofessional, relationally focused direction in becoming more spiritually formed.

3. Conferences

In addition to many other teaching opportunities, NWM offers a complimentary weekend conference titled "Life on the Narrow Road: No Shortcuts, No Formulas, Just Life." During this conference, we look at the seven most important questions of life: Who is God? What is He up to? Who are we? What has gone wrong? What has God done about our problem? How is God's Spirit moving today? How do we follow the Spirit's movement in one another's lives? These are the seven questions God has answered to guide us on the narrow road and show us how to travel it to new life as we discover how to

- unmask the deception that makes the broad road look good.
- understand how real men and real women walk the narrow road.
- see why life on the narrow road has no shortcuts or formulas as we experience God and live like Jesus in every circumstance of life.

Together we learn how real change from the inside out develops as we discern whether we're on the narrow road to life.

4. Internet Courses

NWM offers an Internet course titled SoulCare Foundations: A Model for Pastors, Counselors, and Friends. In conjunction with ChristianCourses .com, NWM offers this free, four-part online curriculum in soul care. It is designed to introduce people around the world to the basic concepts of soul care that underlie psychotherapy, counseling, lay counseling, pastoring, spiritual direction, and friendship, and to provide training in the essential practice of soul care.

For more information please visit our Web site:
www.newwayministries.org

There *is* a new way to live.

ACKNOWLEDGMENTS

I've often thought, if I had to give up every ministry activity but one, which would survive? Writing books about our journey through life and talking to people as we journey together—that's my answer. (I know; I cheated. Those are two activities.)

But they're really one. The stories of countless people whose lives I've entered form the backdrop for every book I write. Without them, writing would be dry, academic, lifeless. This book reflects the struggles and satisfactions of a dozen folks I've recently been meeting with who are pushing through darkness to light. To each of you, thanks.

My father died three weeks before I finished the last chapter and put my pen down. No one's story of faith has influenced me more than his. With deep gratitude and respect, I dedicate this book to his memory.

When I submit a manuscript to my editor, I always tremble a bit, like a father carrying his newborn into public for the first time. Will chapter 8 become chapter 12? Will my favorite illustration be cut? Will I hear, "Well, there may be a book here. Let's work on it"? It helps when you trust your editor. Thomas Womack grasps my message, honors my idiosyncratic style, and, with a heart that loves both the beauty and hard edge of truth, works to make my writing as useful as it can be for the kingdom's sake.

To Steve Cobb and the entire WaterBrook team, thank you! You're a delight to work with. Your evident commitment to Christ strengthens mine.

Sealy Yates, agent and friend, skillfully guides the publishing process and cheers me on as I write. Thanks, my friend.

I write on yellow pads of paper, longhand, with Flair Hardhead pens, the way Isaiah and Paul wrote their books. Claudia Ingram translates my scribbles, attacks a keyboard with dexterity and energy, then faxes me each chapter for several rounds of nitpicking revisions. Her limitless patience arises from a heart for God that expresses itself in a servant's spirit. To both Claudia and her husband, Bob, the deepest appreciation from a grateful brother.

So many pray for me, faithfully, as I write. To Phoebe, Trip and Judy, Kent and Karla, Jim and Suzi, Dwight and Sandy, Randy and Marcia, Wes and Judy, Tom and Jenny, Frank and Chris, and many more whose names deserve mention, thank you.

Everything I do, I do with inexpressible love and respect for my two sons, Kep and Ken, and with the prayer that each will continue following hard after Jesus. The same love and prayer flow out of my heart toward three wonderful blessings in my life, my daughter-in-law, Kim, and my two grandchildren, Jake and Josie.

Writing is hard work, more, I think, for the author's spouse than for the author. Every time I finish a book, I envision the Lord adding on yet another room to Rachael's already magnificent mansion. No one is more meaningfully supported than I by my life's partner. Thanks are insufficient. My love grows ever deeper. We journey on together.

NOTES

1. Romans 7:6.

2. Proverbs 3:6 (NKJV).

3. Proverbs 22:6.

4. Deuteronomy 30:17-18.

5. Leviticus, 26:14,16,22,36.

6. See Hebrews 8:13.

7. Thomas Merton, *Spiritual Direction and Meditation* (Collegeville, Minn.: Liturgical, 1960), 16.

8. Isaiah 5:20.

9. See Dwight Edwards, *Revolution Within* (Colorado Springs: WaterBrook, 2001) for a rich discussion of these four resources.

10. Galatians 5:2,4.

11. See 2 Peter 2:7.

12. I do not hold to the view that there have ever been two ways of salvation. Faith in God met by His pardoning grace, which He made available through Christ's substitutionary atonement, has always been the means of access to God, both in justification (acceptance by God) and in sanctification (the opportunity to draw near).

13. Philippians 3:2.

14. Philippians 3:3.

15. Kenneth S. Wuest, *Galatians* (Grand Rapids, Mich.: Eerdmans, 1994), 21.

16. Galatians 1:6-7.

17. Galatians 3:1-5.

18. Deuteronomy 28:13.

19. Quoted in Galatians 3:10 from Deuteronomy 27:26.

20. J. R. R. Tolkien, *The Hobbit* (New York: Ballantine Books, 1982), 214-5.

21. 2 Corinthians 4:8-9.

22. 1 Corinthians 15:19, my paraphrase of "If only for this life we have hope in Christ, we are to be pitied more than all men."

23. 2 Corinthians 4:13, quoting from Psalm 116:10.

24. Psalm 116:12.

25. Psalm 116:15-16.

26. 2 Corinthians 4:14.

27. 2 Corinthians 4:15.

28. That thought is also in a different text, Galatians 4:3,8-11. That morning I spent time in that passage as well.

29. See John 17:1-3.

30. Revelation 1:10.

31. Revelation 1:14-16.

32. See John 7:37-39 and Isaiah 55:1-3.

33. Augustine, *City of God*, ed. Vernon J. Bourke (New York: Doubleday, 1958), 300.

34. John 14:27.

35. Augustine, *City of God*, 300.

36. Matthew 11:28.

37. Romans 1:21-29.

38. 2 Corinthians 4:4 (NASB).

39. 2 Corinthians 4:6.

40. John Piper, *Seeing and Savoring Jesus Christ* (Wheaton, Ill.: Crossway, 2001), 16. I am indebted to Piper for the direction of my thinking in this chapter especially. Any wrong directions are mine.

41. Romans 5:2.

42. Piper, *Seeing and Savoring Jesus Christ*, 21.

43. The quotes and information presented here were drawn from "Anorexia Battle Undone Online," *Denver Post*, Tuesday, 17 July 2001, sec. A, 1,13.

44. Piper, *Seeing and Savoring Jesus Christ*, 125.

45. I recommend Piper's book *Seeing and Savoring Jesus Christ* as vital reading in grasping the New Way.

46. See Jeremiah 2:5-13; 15:16-18.

47. See James 4:10; 5:7-11.

48. These stories are true. Only a few details have been doctored—never worsened—to protect identities.

49. The writer refers to *Connecting* (Nashville, Tenn.: Word, 1997), *The Safest Place on*

Earth (Nashville, Tenn.: Word, 1999), and *Shattered Dreams* (Colorado Springs: Water-Brook, 2001).

50. See Hebrews 10:19-23.

51. See 1 Peter 3:18.

52. See John 14:21,23; James 4:8.

53. Exodus 19:5.

54. Jeremiah 31:34, "'No longer will a man teach his neighbor, or a man his brother, saying, "Know the LORD," because they will all know me, from the least of them to the greatest,' declares the LORD."

55. Hebrews 7:18-19.

56. Galatians 6:8.

57. John 20:31.

58. What follows is my paraphrase of Revelation 21:2-4.

59. My paraphrase of Revelation 21:5.

60. 1 Corinthians 15:19.

61. John Owen, *Communion with God*, ed. R. J. K. Law (Carlisle, Pa.: Banner of Truth, 1991), 1.

62. My paraphrase of 1 John 1:1-4.

63. See Luke 12:13-21.

64. Luke 12:34, "For where your treasure is, there your heart will be also."

65. Quoted from the periodical *Closer Walk* 15, no. 8 (August 2000), 13.

66. See my *Shattered Dreams* (Colorado Springs: WaterBrook, 2001) for a full discussion of this point.

67. Quoted in Richard S. Hipps, ed., *When a Child Dies* (Macon, Ga.: Smyth and Helwys, 1996), 38.

68. C. S. Lewis, *The Silver Chair* (New York: Macmillan, 1953), 17.

69. John 7:38.

70. Isaiah 55:1-2.

71. Isaiah 55:3.

72. Only a multivolume book could do justice to the Story of God. It's already been written. We call it the Bible. I offer only the meagerest of outlines. For a fuller treatment, see O. Palmer Robertson, *The Christ of the Covenants* (Phillipsburg, N. J.: Presbyterian and Reformed Press, 1980).

73. See Genesis 8:21; 9:8-17.

74. The word *cut* is the biblical term for making a covenant. It implies that shedding blood was involved.

75. See Genesis 15.

76. All but the thoughts I imagined in Owen's mind are quotations from Owen, *Communion with God*, 2-3.

77. Although the tearing of one's robe was a recognized way of expressing agony over catastrophe, priests in the Old Testament were forbidden to do so. Priests alone had access to God's presence, and in His presence, there is never cause for despair. See Exodus 28:31-32; Leviticus 10:1-6; Matthew 26:62-65.

78. See Genesis 17:18.

79. See Galatians 4:21-31.

80. See Galatians 5:22-23.

81. See James 4:7-10; John 14:21,23.

82. See Hebrews 12:5-6.

83. Isaiah 1:6. See also Isaiah 53:6.

84. Matthew 7:14.

85. Quoted in John Piper, *The Hidden Smile of God* (Wheaton, Ill.: Crossway, 2001), 56.

86. Quoted in Piper, *The Hidden Smile of God*, 56.

87. Quoted in Piper, *The Hidden Smile of God*, 42-3.

88. Luke 13:24.

89. Luke 18:9-14.

90. *Dallas Morning News*, 18 August 2001, sec. A, 1.

91. Matthew 6:34.

92. Quoted in Peter Kreeft, *Christianity for Modern Pagans* (San Francisco: Ignatius Press, 1996), 95.

93. Quoted in Benedict J. Groeschel, *The Journey Toward God* (Ann Arbor, Mich.: Servant, 2000), 19.

94. Quoted in Groeschel, *The Journey Toward God*, 13.

95. Thomas Dubay, *Seeking Spiritual Direction* (Ann Arbor, Mich.: Servant, 1993), 19.

96. James 5:13.

97. See 1 John 1:1-3.

98. Quoted in Dubay, *Seeking Spiritual Direction*, 80.

99. Dubay, *Seeking Spiritual Direction*, 61.

100. John Henry Newman, *Parochial and Plain Sermons* (San Francisco: Ignatius, 1987), 917.

101. See Psalm 27:4.

102. Job 40:3-4.

103. Job 42:5-6.

104. In this section I follow the outline provided in John Owen's classic work, *Communion with God*, 177.

105. John 14:26.

106. John 16:33.

107. John 16:14.

108. Romans 5:5.

109. Romans 8:16.

110. See Zechariah 3:1-5 for the incident. The Hebrew for "filthy" literally means "excrement."

111. Ephesians 1:13.

112. 2 Corinthians 1:21-22.

113. 1 John 2:20,27.

114. See Isaiah 11:1-3.

115. See Colossians 2:3.

116. Let me again urge you to read Dwight Edwards's *Revolution Within*. In it he powerfully and with clear biblical support discusses the four key provisions of the New Covenant. It is an *important* book.

117. See James 1:2-8.

118. Galatians 2:14.

119. Psalm 139:23-24.

120. See James 1:2-7; 4:8,10.

ALSO BY LARRY CRABB

Basic Principles of Biblical Counseling
Effective Biblical Counseling
Encouragement: The Key to Caring
The Marriage Builder
How to Become One with Your Mate
Understanding People
Understanding Who You Are
Men and Women—Enjoying the Difference
Finding God
Inside Out
Silence of Adam
Hope When You're Hurting
God of My Father
Connecting: Healing for Ourselves and Our Relationships
The Safest Place on Earth
Shattered Dreams